ACCESS GUIDES TO YOUTH MINISTRY

Justice

Edited by
Thomas Bright
&
John Roberto

THE WORLD OF

DON BOSCO
MULTIMEDIA

New Rochelle, NY

Access Guide to Justice
is published as a service for adults who love the
young and want to share the Gospel with them.

It is a guide to understanding the young and a resource
book for helping them. As such, it is addressed to
parents, parish youth ministers, clergy who work with
the young, and teachers.

Forthcoming *Access Guides*:
Leadership
Advocacy

Prepared in conjunction with
The Center for Youth Ministry Development

Access Guides to Yoth Ministry: Justice
©1990 Salesian Society, Inc. / Don Bosco Multimedia
475 North Ave., Box T, New Rochelle, NY 10802

Library of Congress Cataloging-in-Publication Data
Justice / edited by Thomas Bright & John Roberto.
p. cm. — (Access guides to youth ministry)
Includes bibliographical references.
   1. Justice.   2. Youth—Religious life.
     I. Roberto, John.   II. Title: Justice.   III. Series.

ISBN 0-89944-149-1 $14.95

Printed in the United States of America

11/92   9 8 7 6 5 4 3 2

Table of Contents

PREFACE TO THE ACCESS GUIDES SERIES

A NEW CONCEPT

Welcome to the *Access Guides to Youth Ministry* series. The Center for Youth Ministry Development and Don Bosco Multimedia have created the *Access Guides to Youth Ministry* series to provide leaders in ministry with youth with both the foundational understandings and the practical tools they need to create youth ministry programming for each component outlined in *A Vision of Youth Ministry*. *Access Guides* are being developed for Pop Culture, Evangelization, Leadership (Enablement), Family Life, Guidance, Justice, Peace, and Service, Liturgy and Worship, Adolescent Spirituality and Prayer, and Retreats. Each *Access Guide* provides foundational essays, processes for developing that component, and approaches and program models to use in your setting. The blend of theory and practice makes each *Access Guide* a unique resource in youth ministry. To help you understand the context for the *Access Guide* series we would like to provide you with a brief overview of the goals and components of a comprehensive approach to ministry with youth.

A RENEWED MINISTRY

Over a decade ago, Catholic youth ministry engaged in a process of self-reflection and analysis that resulted in a re-visioning of youth ministry — establishing the goals, principles, and components of a comprehensive, contemporary ministry with youth. *A Vision of Youth Ministry* outlined this comprehensive approach to ministry with youth and became the foundation for a national vision of Catholic youth ministry. In the years since the publishing of *A Vision of Youth Ministry*, Catholic youth ministry across the United States has experienced tremendous growth.

From the outset, the *Vision* paper made clear its ecclesial focus: "As one among many ministries of the Church, youth ministry must be understood in terms of the mission and ministry of the whole Church." The focus is clearly ministerial. "The Church's mission is threefold: to proclaim the Good News of salvation; offer itself as a group of people transformed by the Spirit into a community of faith, hope, and love; and to bring God's justice and love to others through service in its individual, social, and political dimensions." This threefold mission formed the basis of the framework or components of youth ministry: Word (evangelization and catechesis), Worship, Community, Justice and Service, Guidance and Healing, Enablement, and Advocacy.

This threefold mission also gives youth ministry a dual focus. Youth ministry is a ministry within the community of faith — ministering to believing youth *and* to the wider society — reaching out to serve youth in our society. While the experience of the past decade has emphasized ministry *within* the community, youth ministry must also address the social situation and needs of all youth in society. A comprehensive approach demands a balance between ministry *within* the Christian community and ministry *by* the Christian community *to* young people within our society and world.

The *Vision* paper described a broad concept of ministry with youth using four dimensions. Youth Ministry is...

To youth — responding to youth's varied needs

With youth — working with adults to fulfill their common responsibility for the Church's mission

By youth — exercising their own ministry to others: peers, community, world

For youth — interpreting the needs of youth, especially in areas of injustice and acting on behalf of or with youth for a change in the systems which create injustice.

Two goals were initially developed for the Church's ministry with youth:

Goal #1: Youth ministry works to the total personal and spiritual growth of each young person.

Goal #2: Youth ministry seeks to draw young people to responsible participation in the life, mission, and work of the faith community.

The first goal emphasizes *becoming* — focusing on the personal level of human existence. The second goal emphasizes *belonging* — focusing on the interpersonal or communal dimension of human existence.

In light of the Church's priority upon justice and peace, and the mission of the Church to transform society (for example, *The Challenge of Peace*, NCCB, 1983; and *Economic Justice for All*, NCCB, 1986), it would be appropriate to consider adding a *third* goal. This third goal would challenge youth ministry to empower young people to become aware of the social responsibilities of the Christian faith — the call to live and work for justice and peace. Youth ministry needs to empower young people with the knowledge and skills to transform the unjust structures of society so that these structures promote justice, respect human dignity, promote human rights, and build peace. This third goal emphasizes *transforming* — focusing on the public or social structural level of human existence and giving a greater comprehensiveness to youth ministry.

Goal #3: Youth ministry empowers young people to transform the world as disciples of Jesus Christ by living and working for justice and peace.

An underdeveloped, but increasingly important, section of the *Vision* paper is the contexts of youth ministry. "In all places, youth ministry occurs within a given social, cultural, and religious context which shapes the specific form of the ministry." This contextual approach seeks to view young people as part of a number of social systems which impact on their growth, values, and faith, rather than as isolated individuals. Among these systems are the family, society, the dominant culture, youth culture, ethnic culture, school, and local Church community. In the last several years, youth ministry has become much more aware of the impact of these systems.

A COMPREHENSIVE APPROACH

The framework (or components) describes distinct aspects for developing a comprehensive, integrated ministry with youth. Briefly, these components include:

Evangelization — reaching out to young people who are uninvolved in the life of the community and inviting them into a relationship with Jesus and the Christian community. Evangelization involves proclaiming the Good News of Jesus through programs and relationships.

Catechesis — promoting a young person's growth in Christian faith through the kind of teaching and learning that emphasizes understanding, reflection, and transformation. This is accomplished through systematic, planned, and intentional programming (curriculum). (See *The Challenge of Adolescent Catechesis*).

Prayer and Worship — assisting young people in deepening their relationship with Jesus through the development of a personal prayer life; and providing a variety of prayer and worship experiences with youth to deepen and celebrate their relationship with Jesus in a caring Christian community; involving young people in the sacramental life of the Church.

Community Life — building Christian community with youth through programs and relationships which promote openness, trust, valuing the person, cooperation, honesty, taking responsibility, and willingness to serve; creating a climate where young people can grow and share their struggles, questions, and joys with other youth and adults; helping young people feel like a valued part of the global Church.

Guidance and Healing — providing youth with sources of support and counsel as they face personal problems and pressures (for example, family problems, peer pressure, substance abuse, suicide) and decide on careers and important life decisions; providing appropriate support and guidance for youth during times of stress and crisis; helping young people deal with the problems they face and the pressures people place on them; developing a better understanding of their parents and learning how to communicate with them.

Justice, Peace, and Service — guiding young people in developing a Christian social consciousness and a commitment to a life of justice and peace through educational programs and service/action involvement; infusing the concepts of justice and peace into all youth ministry relationships and programming.

Enablement — developing, supporting, and utilizing the leadership abilities and personal gifts of youth and adults in youth ministry, empowering youth for ministry with their peers; developing a leadership team to organize and coordinate the ministry with youth.

Advocacy — interpreting the needs of youth: personal, family, and social especially in areas of injustices towards or oppression of youth, and acting with or on behalf of youth for a change in the systems which create injustice; giving young people a voice and empowering them to address the social problems that they face.

WORKS CITED

The Challenge of Adolescent Catechesis. Washington, DC: NFCYM Publications, 1986.

A Vision of Youth Ministry. Washington, DC: USCC, Department of Education, 1976.

ABOUT THE AUTHORS

Thomas Bright, D.Min. is a staff member of the Center for Youth Ministry Development where he serves as Coordinator of Global Horizons — a national justice project for youth and young adults. He has worked in the areas of religious education, youth ministry, and adult education, and spent a year in Haiti (1987-88), where he established a permanent mission house for the Diocese of Norwich.

John Coleman, S.J., Ph.D., is Professor of Religion and Society at the Jesuit School of Theology and the Graduate Theological Union at Berkeley. He has authored *An American Strategic Theology* and is sociology of religion editor for the international Catholic journal, *Concilium*.

John Donahue, S.J., Ph.D., is Professor of New Testament at Vanderbilt University and author of several books and an editor for series in biblical theology.

Donal Dorr, a researcher for the Irish Missionary Union, has done pastoral work in Africa and Latin America and taught philosophy and theology in Ireland. He is the author of several books, including the prize-winning *Spirituality and Justice*, *Option for the Poor*, and his latest, *Integral Spirituality*.

J. Frank Henderson is chairperson of the North American Academy of Liturgy working group on liturgy and social justice and is a member of the International Commission on English in the Liturgy.

Stephen Larson is pastor of the Evangelical Lutheran Church of Geneva, Switzerland and a member of the North American Academy of Liturgy working group on liturgy and social justice.

Daniel Maguire, Ph.D., is Professor of Moral Theology at Marquette University. He is the author of *The Moral Choice*, *A New American Justice*, and *The Moral Revolution*.

James McGinnis, Ph.D., is founder and a staff member of the Institute for Peace and Justice in St. Louis. He is a well-known lecturer and workshop leader. He is the author of numerous articles and books. Among them are *Bread and Justice*, *Solidarity with the People of Nicaraqua*, *Journey into Compassion*, *Helping Kids Care*, *Helping Families Care*, and *Parenting for Peace and Justice — Ten Years Later* (with his wife Kathy).

Albert Nolan, O.P., a native South African, works for the Institute for Contextual Theology in Johannesburg, South Africa. He is a former provincial of the Dominicans in South Africa. In September 1983, he was elected master general of the Dominican order but permitted by the General Chapter to refuse the appointment in order to continue his work in South Africa. He is author of *Jesus Before Christianity* and *God in South Africa*.

Kathleen Quinn is an animator for the Canadian Catholic Organization for Development and Peace and a frequent leader of social justice workshops and retreats.

John Roberto, M.A. Rel. Ed., is Director and co-founder of the Center for Youth Ministry Development. He is the managing editor of the DBM-CYMD publishing project. John has authored *The Adolescent Catechesis Resource Manual* and "Principles of Youth Ministry" (*Network Paper #26*), and served as editor for the *Access Guides* on Evangelization, and Liturgy and Worship, and for *Growing in Faith: A Catholic Family Sourcebook.*

David Selby is the Director and **Graham Pike** is a Research Fellow at the Centre for Global Education, University of York, England.

Jim Wallis, founder and pastor of the Sojourners Fellowship in Washington, D.C. and editor of *Sojourners* magazine, is author of *The Call to Conversion, Agenda for Biblical People*, and editor of *Waging Peace* and *Peacemakers.*

ACKNOWLEDGEMENTS

Excerpts from "A Theory of Justice" by Daniel Maguire is reprinted courtesy of Harper & Row from *The Moral Revolution* (1986).

"Four Components of Justice" by James McGinnis is reprinted courtesy of Paulist Press from *Bread and Justice* (1979).

"Three Levels of Reality" by the Justice/Peace Education Council is reprinted courtesy of the Justice/Peace Education Council from *The Infusion Handbook.*

"Responsibilities of Social Living" by the National Conference of Catholic Bishops is reprinted courtesy of United States Catholic Conference Office of Publishing from *Economic Justice for All* (1986).

"Biblical Perspectives on Justice" by John Donahue, S.J. is reprinted courtesy of Paulist Press from *The Faith that Does Justice*, edited by John Haughey, S.J. (1977).

"The Call to Conversion" by Jim Wallis is reprinted courtesy of *Sojourners* from *The Call to Conversion* (Harper & Row, 1986).

"The Development of Catholic Social Teaching" by John Coleman is reprinted courtesy of Paulist Press from *A Cry for Justice — The Churches and Synagogues Speak*, edited by Robert McAfee Brown and Sydney Thompson Brown (1989).

"From One Earth to One World" by United Nations Commission on Environment and Development is reprinted courtesy of Oxford University Press from *Our Common Future* (1987).

"A Balanced Spirituality" by Donal Dorr is reprinted courtesy of Orbis Books from *Spirituality and Justice* (1984).

"Educating for Peace and Justice" by James McGinnis is reprinted courtesy of Religious Education Association, 409 Prospect Street, New Haven, CT from *Religious Education*, Volume 81, Number 3, Summer 1986.

"Educating for Global Awareness" by Graham Pike and David Selby is reprinted courtesy of Hodder and Stoughton from *Global Teacher, Global Learner* (1988).

"Principles of Liturgy and Social Justice" by J. Frank Henderson, Kathleen Quinn, Stephen Larson is reprinted courtesy of Paulist Press from *Liturgy, Justice, and the Reign of God* (1989).

"Service and Solidarity" by Albert Nolan, O.P. is reprinted courtesy of the Irish Missionary Union.

Part I

Understanding Justice

Overview

This first section explores basic understandings of justice. Such understandings are, necessarily, grounded in Scripture, but have continued to grow and develop as people of faith have worked to do God's will, to bring God's reign of justice closer in their own time and place.

The four components of **Chapter One** fill out a contemporary description of justice. **Daniel Maguire** describes justice as the minimum needed if people are to live together in community with respect for one another's dignity. **James McGinnis** suggests four components of justice: sufficient life-goods, dignity/self-esteem, participation, and solidarity. After exploring the levels on which human life is lived (personal, interpersonal, structural) the chapter concludes with reflections on the responsibilities of social living, excerpted from the United States Bishops' Pastoral Letter, *Economic Justice for All*.

Chapter Two offers biblical perspectives on justice. **John Donahue** presents justice as a central, recurring theme in Scripture. Justice should be equally central in the lives of all God's people. "Engagement in the quest for justice is no more 'secular' than the engagement of Yahweh in the history of God's people, or the incarnation of Jesus into the world of human suffering. The Bible gives a mandate and a testament to Christians that, in their quest for justice, they are recovering the roots of the biblical tradition and seeking to create a dwelling place for the word of God in human history." A "Scriptural Guide to Justice" is appended to the chapter. It should prove to be a valuable resource in identifying key justice references for education, action, and worship programs.

Jim Wallis reflects on the implication of conversion for justice in **Chapter Three**. Biblical conversion, according to Wallis, is always historically specific, that is, it is wrapped up in concrete historical events, dilemmas, and choices. Conversion "marks the movement from a merely private existence into a public consciousness." Wallis presents readers with a challenging, occasionally unsettling, meditation on what it means to be People of the Way today.

If, as Wallis asserts, biblical conversion is historically specific, then the Church's understanding of justice had to grow and develop through time. **John Coleman** traces the development of Catholic social teaching in **Chapter Four**. He suggests seven new elements in Catholic social tradition, elements which have come to expression in the years following the Second Vatican Council. Recent writings of the United States and Canadian bishops are summarized, and similarities as well as differences in their approaches to justice are laid out. Appended to this chapter is a list of "Key Concepts of Catholic Social Teaching," which should be incorporated in the content and structures of our ministry with youth.

Chapter Five takes a serious look at global reality today. The chapter presents a challenging view of the contemporary world and its problems...the time, place and conditions in which Christians are called to work for justice. Authored by the **U.N. World Commission on Environment and Development**, the report examines the pressing problems facing the world community and calls for united action to promote sustainable development. Sustainable development would guarantee that the basic needs of all the world's people are met without compromising the ability of future generations to meet their own needs. The report closes with a message of hope; a hope conditioned on the establishment "of a new era of international cooperation based on the premise that every human being — those here and those who are to come— has the right to life, and a decent life."

This first section closes with **Donal Dorr**'s essay, "A Balanced Spirituality." Dorr uses Micah's oft-quoted call to "act justly, love tenderly, and walk humbly with your God" as a framework for making justice central to one's spirituality. Dorr's approach to a balanced, integrated spirituality reaches beyond individual response to institutional involvement. Spirituality "must be rooted not just in one or two aspects of conversion but in all three — the 'religious,' the 'moral' and the 'political.' It is a distortion of Christian faith to ignore any of them or to fail to work for a full integration of all three."

God speaks in Scripture and tradition, in the privacy of intimate relationships, and in the babble of the marketplace. Though written from different perspectives, these first six chapters provide a remarkably consistent reflection on God's word of justice and a challenge to make God's justice real in our place and time.

Chapter 1

Perspectives
on
Justice

As love and justice are central to God, so too they must be central to all who walk in God's way. The centrality of justice to Christian life has long been recognized. Scholastic theologians referred to justice as a "cardinal" virtue, a virtue on which all of Christian life "hinges." Today, expressing this same thought in less mechanistic terms, one might view justice as the "connective tissue" that holds Christian life together. To act justly is to share in God's great power to accomplish good, happily and hopefully, despite inner turmoil or outside conflict.

The brief essays contained in this chapter offer several complementary perspectives on justice. The first essay offers a simple definition of justice; justice is viewed not as a maximum, but as the minimum necessary to respect the dignity of each person and people. The second essay spells out the implications of this definition of justice; four major categories of rights and duties are suggested as constituting a just response to the needs of contemporary society. The third essay explores the different levels in which life is lived and in which justice needs to be made real. The diagrams included with this essay are particularly helpful in understanding the very real shifts in thinking and action which are necessary as one moves from a personal/interpersonal to a societal/structural outlook on life. The application of justice principles to the economic sphere is explored briefly in the final essay, excerpted from the United States Bishops' 1986 pastoral letter, *Economic Justice for All*. Particular attention is placed on the social dimension of the call to economic justice. Taken together, these four perspectives on justice provide a strong foundation for understanding and doing justice in our time.

Perspective One

A Theory of Justice

Daniel C. Maguire

To speak of justice is to reach for the foundations of human existence. Justice is not one virtue among the lot. It is the cornerstone of human togetherness. To survive and thrive a little we need justice like a body needs blood. To try to define justice is to address the most profound questions ever to challenge the human mind. The American approach has been to dodge these questions. Our public philosophy does not contain an explicit theory of justice. All our laws are, of course, expressions of some concept of justice, but those laws exist in a matrix of confused and contradictory concepts of justice. American scholars have not paid their debts to justice theory. This leaves a gaping hole in the center of our polity.

What I offer here owes many debts to some classical Greek, Hebrew, and medieval theories of justice. There is richness in these theories to be mined and refined and so they are a solid foundation for the theory of justice I develop here. The classical definition begins with deluding simplicity: *Justice is the virtue that renders to each his/her own.* "To each his/her own" is the persistent core formula for justice that has spanned the literature from Homer through Aristotle, Cicero, Ambrose, Augustine, and Roman law, and it is still seen as the axiomatic core of justice theory. (The Latin for "to each his/her own" is *suum cuique* which is neither sexist or clumsy. Our his/her is linguistically ungraceful but morally imperative since justice is all-inclusive and must not be defined in sexist terms.) The simplicity and consistency of this definition are welcomed as a start, but it is only a start. It is like the skin which must then be peeled away to reveal the layers of reality beneath.

Justice is the first assault upon egoism. Egoism would say: "To me my own." Justice says, "Wait. There are other *selves*." Personal existence is a shared glory. Each of those other subjects is of great value and commands respect. The ego has a tendency to declare itself the sun and center of the universe. Justice breaks the news to the ego that there are no solar gods in the universe of persons. Justice is the attitude of mind that accepts the others—all others—as subjects in their own right. Justice asserts that one's own ego is not absolute and that one's interests are related. In the simple concession that each deserves his/her own, the moral self comes to grips with the reality and value of other selves. Justice is thus the elementary manifestation of the other-regarding character of moral and political existence. The alternative to justice is social disintegration because it would mean a refusal to take others seriously.

But let us peel away another layer. When you say, "To each his/her own," you face the question "Why?" Why take others seriously? Why not just "to me my own?" To move from pure egoism to justice is nothing more or less than the discovery of the value of persons, or, in the common term, the discovery of "the sanctity of life." Justice implies indebtedness. You *owe* his/her own to each. But indebtedness is grounded in worth. The each is worth his/her own. Justice is thus founded upon a perception of the worth of persons. We show what we think persons are worth by what we ultimately concede is due to them. Talk of justice would sound like gibberish if we had no perception of the value of persons.

All of which leads to a jarring conclusion. If we deny persons justice, we have declared them worthless! Justice, you see, is not the best we can do in reaction to the value of persons. Friendship is. Aristotle did well to point out that friends have no need of justice. In friendship a higher, more generous dynamism is operative. You don't tell newlyweds they owe one another signs of affection in simple justice. Love will take care of that. Justice, however, is the least we can do for persons. It is the first response to the value of persons, the least we can do in view of that value. In friendship and in love we respond lavishly. Justice is concerned with the minimal due. Less than this we could not do without negating the value of the person. To be perfectly consistent, if we deny justice to persons we ought to kill them because we have declared them worthless. Their liquidation would be perfectly in order.

These are grim tidings in the political order. Love does not make the political world go around; justice is the most we can achieve. Love can flourish at the interpersonal level, but it would be a mad romantic who said that, at this point in moral evolution, love can be the energy of the social order. In the political realm, only justice stands between us and barbarity. In this realm, when justice fails, persons perish. In different words, justice is incipient love and the only form love takes in political life.

Notice, I started out saying "To each his/her own," with a warning that there is more to the phrase than meets the eye. This led to the worth of persons as the only reason why we should acknowledge the other *"eaches"* and render them at least their minimal due. Denying that implies they are worthless, and is thus murderous in intent. And this leads to the next key question: How does *need* relate to justice?

Most would concede that justice means giving to each what each deserves. Justice, in other words, is based upon deserts. Here quickly the ways part between individualists and the defenders of genuine social justice. The individualist would say that your deserts and entitlements come from your own achievements or as gifts from other achievers. The theory of social justice concedes this but goes on to say that you also deserve in accordance with your needs. Needs too give entitlement. The essential needs of each are also "his/her own." "To each his own" translates into "To each according to his/her merits and earned entitlements" and "To each according to his/her needs."

Need gives entitlement because of the worth of the needing person. Needs, of course, like rights, can conflict with one another. *Basic needs issue into rights when their neglect would effectively deny the human worth of the needy.* Or in other words, essential needs create inalienable rights.

The final point on need is this: meeting essential needs in society is not a work of optional charity or benevolence. It is often spoken of this way but this is loose and dangerous talk. Meeting essential needs does not make one a candidate for sainthood; it merely establishes one's credentials as human. It is a minimal manifestation of humanness, the alternative to which is barbarity. If we wish to make it possible for handicapped people, as far as is financially feasible, to move about in society, this is not heroic on our part. It is simply a matter of meeting essential needs of persons as best we can. As soon as we cast this obligation in terms of compassion or charity, we have declared it supererogatory and therefore dispensable. To neglect it would be ungenerous, but not morally wrong. When we are speaking about essential needs, such a view is nonsense. Such a view is also a radical departure from the Judeo-Christian idea of justice, which is supposedly normative for many Americans. In Hebrew and Christian thought, meeting essential needs is the soul of justice.

The heart of the matter is that we are not merely individuals we are *social individuals*, and there are three fundamental modes of sociality to which the three kinds of justice correspond. These three are *individual justice, social justice, and distributive justice.* These are not three different categories but rather three ways in which the one category, justice, is realized. Justice does not admit of partitioning. Failure at any form of justice is injustice. (*The Moral Revolution* 3-4, 8, 10-11, 12)

Perspective Two

Four Components of Justice

James McGinnis

In simple terms, justice has long been understood as giving each person his or her due. And what is due to each person is the fundamental right to live a fully human life. But what does it mean to live a fully human life? I see four major categories of rights and duties that spell out the meaning of justice. Each of these four is closely paralleled by four states of human development. All four components of justice are deeply rooted in the Christian understanding of the human person, reflected not only in the Jewish scriptures and in the New Testament, but also in the social teaching of the Christian churches. This is especially true as that teaching has developed in the last fifteen years. See the diagram on the next page.

SUFFICIENT LIFE-GOODS

The first component of justice is the right of each person to those basic goods without which human life would be impossible. These involve three categories of goods. Food, clothing, and shelter are all items people need for their individual use. Health care and skills development are essential services that are provided by and to the community as a whole. Lastly, the right and need for work—for creative worthwhile labor—is a special life-good. It serves both as a means to fulfilling other needs and as an end in itself. These are the economic rights of persons and parallel the state of human development sometimes called security, where the concern is basically survival.

That these life-goods are matters of justice is clear from the very first chapters of Genesis. God created earth and its fullness for all the people of the earth. The earth is the Lord's, says the psalmist. Its resources are not meant just for those with the economic, political, or military power to take them for themselves. The Scriptures are definite about this. Economic sharing is part of the Judeo-Christian way of life. In the Acts of the Apostles, we read about the early Christian community: "The faithful all lived together and owned everything in common;

Components of Justice	Their Christian Basis	Stages of Human Development
SUFFICIENT LIFE-GOODS — Food, shelter, clothing, health care, skills development, work (economic rights)	The earth is the Lord's; it is for the use of all; stewardship	Security (concern for survival)
DIGNITY/ESTEEM— recognizing, affirming & calling forth the value /uniqueness of each person and each people (cultural rights)	Each person is created in the image and likeness of God	Self-worth (concern for personal recognition)
PARTICIPATION— the right of individuals & peoples to shape their own destinies (political rights)	Each person is called by Jesus to help build His Kingdom in our world	Self determination (concern for control over one's life)
SOLIDARITY— the corresponding duty to promote these rights with & for others (duties as well as rights)	We are created in the image of a God Who is a (community) Trinity of persons	Interdependence (concern for others)

they sold their goods and possessions and shared out the proceeds among themselves according to what each one needed" (2:44-45).

God's wrath toward those who refused to recognize this fundamental human right has troubled Jews and Christians for centuries—from the harsh condemnations of the prophets to St. Matthew's description of the Final Judgment (25:31-46). Amos, for instance, writes:

For the three crimes, the four crimes, of Israel, I have made my decree and will not relent: because they have sold the virtuous man for silver and the poor man for a pair of sandals, because they trample on the heads of ordinary people and push the poor out of their path, . . . See then how I am going to crush you into the ground as the threshing sledge crushes when clogged by straw; flight will not save even the swift, the strong man will find his strength useless, the mighty man will be powerless to save himself. (Amos 2:6-16)

The notion of stewardship has been the core of Christian teaching and practice about property or goods for twenty centuries, in clear continuity with the Jewish tradition of responsibility for the world's resources. The early Christian fathers were equally explicit. To quote St. Ambrose—with regard to the attitude of persons with possessions toward those in need:

You are not making a gift of your possessions to the poor person. You are handing over to them what is theirs. For what has been given in common for the use of all, you have arrogated to [taken for] yourself. The world is given to all, and not only to the rich.

But this is very difficult for most of us to hear. We live in a society where "more is better," where private property means private property in an exclusive sense. That is, we can do with it pretty much what we want. This is true about our national wealth as well as about our personal possessions. The Church's teaching on property—that it must always be used for the common good—is foreign to us. Many of us resist the idea that our national wealth—grain, for instance—is not ours to do with as we please, but belongs to all.

DIGNITY OR ESTEEM

The second component of justice is the right to human dignity. Each person and each people (society or culture) must have their personhood—their uniqueness, values, etc.—recognized, affirmed and called forth. This component embraces what might be called the cultural rights of persons and parallels the self-worth stage of human development. As expressed by the American Baptist Churches, USA, there is both

The right to human dignity, to be respected and treated as a person and to be protected against discrimination without regard to age, sex, race, class, marital status, income, national origin, legal status, culture or condition in society; (and)

The right of ethnic or racial groups to maintain their cultural identity and to develop institutions and structures through which that identity can be maintained. (*Policy Statement on Human Rights* 3)

This second component of justice tells us two things. First, no one is expendable. People with physical or emotional disabilities, people in prison, people half-dead from hunger—all are equal in the sight of God. It may cost us a lot of money, time, and emotional energy to respond to their special needs. But Matthew 25:31-46 will not allow us to conclude that some people are not worth it. "Whatever you do to the least of My brothers and sisters, you do unto Me."

Secondly, to do justice to another person is not to *do for* them. Rather, it is working to enable them to develop and contribute their unique gifts to the human family. This holds true for any classroom, home, community. It also holds true for national and global development. "Helping" means *doing with* and calling forth.

For instance, in working with older people, our purpose should not be just to do for them what they cannot do for themselves. We should also try to identify what their talents, insights, and interests are and seek out opportunities for these to be shared with others. Inviting older persons into our schools as resources to be learned from, rather than needy persons to be cared for, is one step in the right direction. This is equally true of poor people, especially people of different races and cultures.

Each people or culture, just as each individual person, mirrors the infinite truth, beauty, and richness of God. Each is unique. All persons have a dignity and an irreplaceability rooted in their being created in the image and likeness of God. So central is the notion that it forms the basis of the Christian churches' teaching on human rights. Pope John XXIII's *Pacem in Terris* is echoed eloquently by the 1974 Catholic bishops Synodal statement on "Evangelization:"

Human dignity is rooted in the image and reflection of God in each of us. It is this which makes all persons essentially equal. The integral development of persons makes more clear the divine image in them. In our time the Church has grown more deeply aware of this truth; hence she believes firmly that the promotion of human rights is required by the Gospel and is central to her ministry.

PARTICIPATION

This third component of justice means the right of each person and each people to shape their own destinies. That is, we are all entitled to exercise some meaningful control over the political, economic, and cultural forces shaping our lives. In this category come the political rights of persons, like free speech and assembly. Parallel to this component of justice is the self-determination state of human development.

Doing justice to others, then, means working to empower them to be the *agents* of their own development and not just the beneficiaries of someone else's efforts. No one likes to be always cared for. How much greater is our satisfaction when we help design, build, or create something, rather than just being allowed to enjoy it. This is as true of our childhood clubhouses as it is of our adult neighborhood community centers. It is also true in our classrooms. Students invited to help shape what happens there (some of the content of the course, ways of learning that content, the rules of classroom behavior) can develop much more than those who are just the beneficiaries of someone else's knowledge or who have to operate within someone else's rules.

Thus, *how* sufficient life-goods are provided often becomes more important than *that* they are provided. A redistribution of goods often happens only because the poor begin to organize themselves and discover their power.

A redistribution of goods without a redistribution of power is what people mean by "paternalism." "We don't want your hand-outs—we want to be represented on the city council" has a familiar ring. If it is the wealthy and influential who make the rules and who run the economic and political institutions of a society, no matter how well-meaning they may be, the poor cannot expect those rules and institutions to adequately respond to their needs. Those who make the rules get the goods. Thus, it is a redistribution of power even more than a redistribution of goods that justice demands.

The scriptural basis for this basic right is again the image of God. We are made in the likeness of a God who invites us to share in the creative and redemptive work of Jesus—to recreate the earth. We are to be, in Jesus' words, "the salt of the earth" and "the light of the world" (Matthew 5:13-16). We do this not as servants but as friends of Jesus—chosen by Him to go into the world, to bear witness to the truth, and to bear fruit (John 15:12-20). Indeed, we have both a right and a duty to participate in the development of ourselves and of our society. The recent social teaching of the Christian churches strongly emphasizes this participation dimension of justice. A passage from the pastoral letter of the Catholic bishops of Appalachia—*This Land Is Home To Me*—poetically captures this theme:

Throughout this whole process of listening to the people, the goal which underlies our concern is fundamental in the justice struggle, namely, citizen control, or community control. The people themselves must shape their own destiny. Despite the theme of powerlessness, we know that Appalachia is already rich here in the cooperative power of its own people. (7)

INTERDEPENDENCE OR SOLIDARITY

This fourth component of justice—and the final stage of human development—invovles duties as well as rights. Because we are social beings by nature, we have a responsibility to exercise our own rights and avoid frustrating the rights to others. But even more, we have a duty to actively promote these rights with and for others. This component is best expressed in my own religious tradition in Pope Paul VI's encyclical, *On the Development of Peoples*:

But each person is a member of society. Each is part of the whole humankind. It is not just certain individuals, but all persons, who are called to this fullness of development. Civilizations are born, develop and die. But humanity is advancing along the path of history like the waves of a rising tide encroaching gradually on the shore. We have inherited from past generations, and we have benefitted from the work of our contemporaries; for this reason we have obligations toward all, and we cannot refuse to interest ourselves in those who will come after us to enlarge the human family. The reality of human solidarity, which is a benefit for us, also imposes a duty. (#17)

Human solidarity demands action. It is action on behalf of justice, not just studying about justice, that the Gospel requires of us. Matthew's account of the Final Judgment is echoed in Jesus' parable of the Good Samaritan. The letters of John and James repeat this theme again and again—faith demands works of love:

If one of the brothers or one of the sisters is in need of clothes and has not enough food to live on, and one of you says to them, "I wish you well; keep yourself warm and eat plenty," without giving them these bare necessities of life, then what good is that? Faith is like that: if good works do not go with it, it is quite dead. (James 2:15-17)

Like Matthew, Isaiah is more detailed about the kinds of works we are to do: Is this not the sort of fast that pleases me—it is the Lord Yahweh who speaks—to break unjust fetters and undo the thongs of the yoke, to let the oppressed go free, and break every yoke, to share your bread with the hungry, and shelter the homeless poor, to clothe the person you see to be naked and not

turn from your own kin? Then will your light shine like the dawn and your
wound be quickly healed over. . . . If you do away with the yoke, the clenched
fist, the wicked word, if you give your bread to the hungry, and relief to the
oppressed, your light will rise in the darkness, and your shadows become like
noon . . . . (Is. 58:6-12)

Three kinds of action are called for in this passage and all are essential today:
the works of mercy, the works of justice, and changes in our lifestyles. Solidarity
expresses itself in working side-by-side with the victims of injustice, whether it be
the hungry, the unemployed, the imprisoned. Isaiah speaks of sharing bread with
the hungry and sheltering the homeless poor. Such direct service—the traditional
corporal works of mercy—can deepen our commitment to work for justice.
Nothing motivates most of us quite as much as being directly touched by victims
of injustice.

But solidarity means more than caring for the victims. It also means working
with people to change the political, economic, and cultural situations and structures
that victimize them in the first place. These are the works of justice. Such works
are implied in the language of liberation in Isaiah—"break unjust fetters," "undo
the thongs of the yoke," "break every yoke," etc.

As important as they are, the works of mercy are not enough, if we really want
to love our neighbor. Racial minorities in the U.S. need more than the friendship
and hospitality of their white neighbors. They need white people to work with
them to change the policies of businesses, unions, banks, real estate agencies, and
school systems that deprive them of their rights. Prisoners need more than our
letters. They need us to help change the attitudes and practices of employers and
others that often make their return to society very difficult. The hungry need more
than our food distribution centers. They need us to help change laws and
regulations so that jobs and decent wages are available. That way they can get their
own food. "Participation" as well as "sufficient life-goods" is essential.

But there is a third kind of action that is also important. The works of mercy and
the works of justice need to flow out of a growing realization of our oneness as a
human family, especially our oneness with the often voiceless victims of injustice.
Changing our lives toward greater simplicity can help us identify more fully with
the victims of injustice, especially the poor. It is not a matter of "playing at being
poor." Rather, it is a matter of beginning to let go of some of the privileges that
many of us have *at the expense of* those who are economically poor. This process
of relinquishing our privileges may begin with eating and drinking less, buying
fewer gadgets. (Shoemaker 23ff) But it moves beyond these first steps to a more
radical letting go. What is important to realize here is that it is difficult for
materially comfortable people to hunger and thirst for justice. Comfort can dull our
sense of urgency and passion and prevent us from ever really identifying with
those with whom we want to struggle.

Perspective Three

Three Levels of Human Existence

Justice/Peace Education Council

The diagram on page 21 invites us to consider reality as consisting of three levels:
(1) the personal — within the self or between the self and God;

(2) the interpersonal — the relationship of the self to all persons in the family, school, workplace, church, and neighborhood;

(3) the structural — the level of institutions, structures, systems, and patterns (economic, political, social, cultural, and religious).

The swirling openness of the diagram is meant to connote the interdependent and dynamic relationship of the levels. The influence of structural level on our personal and interpersonal reality is a notion that has received little attention until recently. Generally speaking, many persons limit their analysis of issues and their actions to the personal and interpersonal levels. A number of contemporary social scientists and theologians have directed our attention to a systemic or structural level of analysis. They have asked us to examine the major systems of society to ascertain their impact on human dignity and community, on peace, justice, and the ecosphere.

While there is a growing consciousness among people about the effects of societal structures on our lives, this awareness is not yet widespread. Two pervasive mindsets seem to militate against our grasping the implications of the effects of social forces.

Mindset #1 is often expressed as follows, "If only we are all good and kind to each other, then there would be peace in the world."

This reasoning suggests that an aggregation of good persons will always produce good results. We have only to recall that many good Christians owned slaves and never questioned the morality of one human being owning another.

Levels of Reality

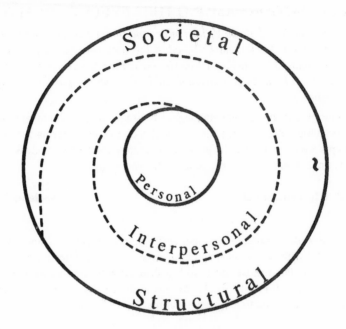

Indeed, growth in personal goodness is essential but it is not sufficient to bring about societal change.

Mindset #2 states the principle of home-first, "I know there are many national and international problems that need attention, but first I must put my own house in order and take care of the needs of those close to me before I can move into structural areas."

Personal striving for holiness is the work of a lifetime and action on behalf of justice and liberation of others is an essential component of that striving. And, this component is not, as some might think, a kind of post-graduate work. If it is not part of one's strivings, the basic message of Yahweh has not been grasped:

This rather, is the fasting I wish; releasing those bound unjustly, untying the thongs of the yoke; setting free the oppressed, breaking every yoke, sharing your bread with the hungry, sheltering the oppressed and the homeless; clothing the naked when you see them and not turning your back on your own. (Isaiah 58: 6-8)

In truth, if we all waited for our perfect conversion before working to change the world, very little progress would take place.

One approach toward creating a better understanding of the levels of reality is to reflect on some terms commonly used. If, for example, we reflect on human needs and suffering, we see on the personal level the victim and we respond by acts of charity. Structural reality directs us to look also at the cause of suffering and to work to change it. (*Dimensions of Justice and Peace in Religious Education* 15-16)

DISTINCTIONS AMONG THE LEVELS OF REALITY

[Editor's Note: The following chart offers additional examples of the shift in understanding and action necessitated by the movement from a personal to a structural approach to justice. In its simplicity the chart is a persuasive argument for a balance of individual and institutional responses to inequity and injustice.]

When moving from an understanding of personal and interpersonal reality toward one which includes structures as well, a double list of terms can help. To the concepts we have used at the personal and interpersonal level, ideas are added to help us understanding the structural level.

Personal & Interpersonal   **Societal-Structural**

Victims   **Cause**
When we look at human needs and suffering on the personal and interpersonal levels, we deal with the *victims*, and aiding the victim occupies our consciousness. The Church has been most successful at dealing with victims through works of mercy. Structural reality asks us also to look at the causes of suffering and work to change them, in addition to aiding the victims.

Mercy   **Justice**
We have always described our aid to victims in terms of virtues like *mercy, charity,* and *compassion.* When practiced on the structural level, these virtues are called *justice* and *peace.*

Conversion   **Influence/Power**
Change takes place on the personal level by *conversion* or *metanoia,* a turning toward a new realization. On the interpersonal level we seek to change others or to be changed ourselves by *influence,* mutual dialogue and listening. At the structural level, change takes place through exercise of *power.*

Attitudes   **Organization**
When working for change on the personal or interpersonal levels, we work to change *attitudes.* On the structural level, we change organizations, systems, *structures.*

Personal Sin   **Social Sin**
Social Sin has been defined by Peter Henriot, S.J. as a sort of institutionalization of *personal* wrong-doing. Greed, violence, domination become part of the culture, system, pattern, or organizational reality.

Guilt/Blame   **Responsibility for Change**
When we see wrong in ourselves, we feel *guilty*. When we see others doing wrong, we often *blame*. When we see wrong on the structural level, we become *responsible* for change.

Programs   **Policy**
On the personal and interpersonal level, we seek to aid victims by *programs*. We address causes on the structural level by a change of *policy*.

Autonomy/Relationship   **Interdependence**
On the personal level, we strive for *autonomy*. On the interpersonal level, for *relationship*. On the structural level, this relationship is called *interdependence*.

Psychology-Humanities   **Social Sciences**
In studying and teaching about the human condition, we have used disciplines like *psychology* and the *humanities*, which deal with the personal and interpersonal realities. In trying to understand and interpret the human condition on the societal or structural level, we must add the disciplines of the *social sciences*: sociology, economics, political science, and anthropology.

(Adapted from *Infusion Leadership Workshop Manual*. Justice and Peace Education Council 1985. The Justice/Peace Education Council authors include Sr. Loretta Carey, R.D.C.; Sr. Eileen Fitzmaurice, C.N.D.; Sr. Joan Hart, O.S.U.; Sr. Kathleen Kanet, R.S.H.M.; and Sr. Rose Sheridan, C.S.J.)

Perspective Four

Economic Justice for All

National Conference of Catholic Bishops

THE RESPONSIBILITIES OF SOCIAL LIVING

63. Human life is life in community. Catholic social teaching proposes several complementary perspectives that show how moral responsibilities and duties in the economic sphere are rooted in this call to community.

A. LOVE AND SOLIDARITY

64. *The commandments to love God with all one's heart and to love one's neighbor as oneself are the heart and soul of Christian morality.* Jesus offers himself as the model of this all-inclusive love: "...Love one another as I have loved you" (Jn 15:12). These commands point out the path toward true human fulfillment and happiness. They are not arbitrary restrictions on human freedom. Only active love of God and neighbor makes the fullness of community happen. Christians look forward in hope to a true communion among all persons with each other and with God. The Spirit of Christ labors in history to build up the bonds of solidarity among all persons until that day on which their union is brought to perfection in the Kingdom of God. Indeed Christian theological reflection on the very reality of God as a Trinitarian unity of persons — Father, Son, and Holy Spirit — shows that being a person means being united to other persons in mutual love.

65. What the Bible and Christian tradition teach, human wisdom confirms. Centuries before Christ, the Greeks and Romans spoke of the human person as a "social animal" made for friendship, community, and public life. These insights show that human beings achieve self-realization not in isolation, but in interaction with others.

B. JUSTICE AND PARTICIPATION

68. Biblical justice is the goal we strive for. This rich biblical understanding

portrays a just society as one marked by the fullness of love, compassion, holiness, and peace. On their path through history, however, sinful human beings need more specific guidance on how to move toward the realization of this great vision of God's Kingdom. This guidance is contained in the norms of basic or *minimal* justice. These norms state the minimum levels of mutual care and respect that all persons owe to each other in an imperfect world. Catholic social teaching, like much philosophical reflection, distinguishes three dimensions of basic justice: commutative justice, distributive justice, and social justice.

69. *Commutative justice calls for fundamental fairness in all agreements and exchanges between individuals or private social groups.* It demands respect for the equal human dignity of all persons in economic transactions, contracts, or promises. For example, workers owe their employers diligent work in exchange for their wages. Employers are obligated to treat their employees as persons, paying them fair wage in exchange for the work done and establishing conditions and patterns of work that are truly human.

70. *Distributive justice requires that all allocation of income, wealth, and power in society be evaluated in light of its effects on persons who basic material needs are unmet.* The Second Vatican Council stated: "The right to have a share of earthly goods sufficient for oneself and one's family belongs to everyone. The fathers and doctors of the Church held this view, teaching that we are obliged to come to the relief of the poor and to do so not merely out of our superfluous goods." Minimum material resources are an absolute necessity for human life. If persons are to be recognized as members of the human community, then the community has an obligation to help fulfill these basic needs unless an absolute scarcity of resources makes this strictly impossible. No such scarcity exists in the United States today.

71. Justice also has implications for the way the larger social, economic, and political institutions of society are organized. *Social justice implies that persons have an obligation to be active and productive participants in the life of society and that society has a duty to enable them to participate in this way.* This form of justice can also be called "contributive," for it stresses the duty of all who are able to help create the goods, services, and other nonmaterial or spiritual values necessary for the welfare of the whole community. In the words of Pius XI, "It is of the very essence of social justice to demand from each individual all that is necessary for the common good." Productivity is essential if the community is to have the resources to serve the well-being of all. Productivity, however, cannot be measured solely by its output in goods and services. Patterns of production must also be measured in light of their impact on the fulfillment of basic needs, employment levels, patterns of discrimination, environmental quality, and sense of community.

72. The meaning of social justice also includes a duty to organize economic and social institutions so that people can contribute to society in ways that respect their freedom and the dignity of their labor. Work should enable the working person to become "more a human being," more capable of acting intelligently, freely, and in ways that lead to self-realization.

73. Economic conditions that leave large numbers of able people unemployed, under-employed, or employed in dehumanizing conditions fail to meet the converging demands of these three forms of basic justice. Work with adequate pay for all who seek it is the primary means for achieving basic justice in our society. Discrimination in job opportunities or income levels on the basis of race, sex, or other arbitrary standards can never be justified. It is a scandal that such discrimination continues in the United States today. Where the effects of past discrimination persist, society has the obligation to take positive steps to overcome the legacy of injustice. Judiciously administered affirmative action programs in education and employment can be important expressions of the drive for solidarity and participation that is at the heart of true justice. Social harm calls for social relief.

74. Basic justice also calls for the establishment of a floor of material well-being on which all can stand. This is a duty of the whole of society and it creates particular obligations for those with greater resources. This duty calls into question extreme inequalities of income and consumption when so many lack basic necessities. Catholic social teaching does not maintain that a flat, arithmetical equality of income and wealth is a demand of justice, but it does challenge economic arrangements that leave large numbers of people impoverished. Further, it sees extreme inequality as a threat to the solidarity of the human community, for great disparities lead to deep social divisions and conflict.

75. This means that all of us must examine our way of living in light of the needs of the poor. Christian faith and the norms of justice impose distinct limits on what we consume and how we view material goods. The great wealth of the United States can easily blind us to the poverty that exists in this nation and the destitution of hundreds of millions of people in other parts of the world. Americans are challenged today as never before to develop the inner freedom to resist the temptation constantly to seek more. Only in this way will the nation avoid what Paul VI called "the most evident form of moral underdevelopment," namely greed.

76. These duties call not only for individual charitable giving but also for a more systematic approach by business, labor unions, and the many other groups that shape economic life — as well as government. The concentration of privilege that exists today results far more from institutional relationships that distribute power and wealth inequitably than from differences in talent or lack of desire

to work. These institutional patterns must be examined and revised if we are to meet the demands of basic justice. For example, a system of taxation based on assessment according to ability to pay is a prime necessity for the fulfillment of these social obligations.

C. OVERCOMING MARGINALIZATION AND POWERLESSNESS

77. These fundamental duties can be summarized this way: *Basic justice demands the establishment of minimum levels of participation in the life of the human community for all persons.* The ultimate injustice is for a person or group to be treated actively or abandoned passively as if they were nonmembers of the human race. To treat people this way is effectively to say that they simply do not count as human beings. This can take many forms, all of which can be described as varieties of marginalization, or exclusion from social life. This exclusion can occur in the political sphere: restriction of free speech, concentration of power in the hands of a few, or outright repression by the state. It can also take economic forms that are equally harmful. Within the United States, individuals, families, and local communities fall victim to a downward cycle of poverty generated by economic forces they are powerless to influence. The poor, the disabled, and the unemployed too often are simply left behind. This pattern is even more severe beyond our borders in the least-developed countries. Whole nations are prevented from fully participating in the international economic order because they lack the power to change their disadvantaged position. Many people within the less developed countries are excluded from sharing the meager resources available in their homelands by unjust elites and unjust governments. These patterns of exclusion are created by free human beings. In this sense they can be called forms of social sin. Acquiescence in them or failure to correct them when it is possible to do so is a sinful dereliction of Christian duty.

78. Recent Catholic social thought regards the task of overcoming these patterns of exclusion and powerlessness as a most basic demand of justice. Stated positively, justice demands that social institutions be ordered in a way that guarantees all persons the ability to participate actively in the economic, political, and cultural life of society. The level of participation may legitimately be greater for some persons than for others, but there is a basic level of access that must be made available for all. Such participation is an essential expression of the social nature of human beings and of their communitarian vocation. (*Economic Justice for All*)

WORKS CITED

Dimensions of Justice and Peace in Religious Education. Justice and Peace Education Council. Washington, DC: NCEA, 1989.

Maguire, Daniel. *The Moral Revolution.* San Francisco: Harper and Row, 1986.

National Conference of Catholic Bishops. *Economic Justice for All*. Washington, D.C.: USCC Publishing, 1986.

Pope Paul VI. *On The Development of Peoples*. Washington, DC: USCC Publishing, 1967.

Policy Statement on Human Rights. American Baptist Churches, USA. Valley Forge: American Baptist Churches.

Synod of Catholic Bishops. "Evangelization Statement." Washington, DC: USCC Publishing, 1974.

Shoemaker, Dennis E. *The Global Connection: Local Action for World Justice*. New York: Friendship Press, 1977.

This Land Is Home To Me. Catholic Bishops of Appalachia. Prestonsburg, KY: Catholic Committee on Appalachia, 1975.

Chapter 2

Biblical Perspectives on Justice

John R. Donahue, S.J.

I. THE OLD TESTAMENT

INTRODUCTION

Contemporary Catholic theology, as well as official Church teaching, is engaged in reflection on problems of the relation of Christian faith to the quest for justice in the modern world. While such reflection has a precedent in the social encyclicals of Leo XIII and his immediate successors, contemporary thought is characterized by rooting the reflection in the biblical heritage rather than in a natural law philosophy. This emphasis in Catholic theology resonates as well with statements of scholars of other denominations. G. von Rad writes: "There is absolutely no concept in the Old Testament with so central a significance for all relationships of human life as that of sedaqah [justice/righteousness]." (von Rad 370) H. H. Schrey, in a study prepared for the World Council of Churches, states: "It can be said without exaggeration that the Bible, taken as a whole, has one theme: The history of the revelation of God's righteousness." (*Biblical Doctrine of Justice and Law* 50)

The centrality as well as the richness of the biblical statements on justice is the very reason why it is difficult to give a "biblical definition" of justice which, in the Bible, is a protean and many-faceted term.[1] Justice is used in the legal codes to describe ordinances which regulate communal life (e.g., Ex. 21:1-23:10) and which prescribe restitution for injury done to person and property, as well as for cultic regulations. The Hebrew terms for justice are applied to a wide variety of things. Scales or weights are called just when they give a fair measure and paths are called just when they do what a path or way should do—lead to a goal. (Pedersen 337-340) Laws are just not because they conform to an external norm or constitution, but because they create harmony within the community. Acting justly consists in avoiding violence and fraud and other actions which destroy communal life and in pursuing that which sustains the life of the community.[2] Yahweh is just not only as lawgiver and Lord of the covenant; Yahweh's saving deeds are called "just deeds" because they restore the community when it has been threatened. The justice of Yahweh is not in contrast to other covenant qualities such as steadfast love (hesed), mercy (rahamin) or faithfulness ('emunah) but, in many texts, is virtually equated with them.[3]

In general terms, the biblical idea of justice can be described as fidelity to the demands of a relationship. In contrast to modern individualism the Israelite is in a world where "to live" is to be united with others in a social context either by bonds of family or by covenant relationships. This web of relationships—king with people, judge with complainants, family with tribe and kinfolk, the community with the resident alien and suffering in their midst and all with the covenant God—constitutes the world in which life is played out. (Achtemeier 80) The demands of the differing relationships cannot be specified *a priori* but must be seen in the different settings of Israel's history.

The present essay will attempt to describe some of these relationships and to indicate how this general notion of justice as fidelity to the demands of a relationship is concretely manifest. We will mention certain ways in which both the individual and Yahweh can be called just and then turn to a characteristic element of Hebrew thought: justice as concern for the marginal people in society, the widow, the alien, the poor. In the second section of the essay we will describe certain transformations of the Old Testament ideas of justice which took place in the intertestamental period, and in the final section we will address certain aspects of a New Testament theology of justice. In doing this we hope to show how the contemporary realization that faith must be involved in the quest for and expression of justice, far from being foreign to biblical thought, recovers a core of the biblical heritage which, when neglected, brings the danger of reducing this heritage to a manual of personal piety.

1. THE JUST INDIVIDUAL

In the Book of Job and in Proverbs the just person preserves the peace and wholeness of the community. (Achtemeier 80) Such a one "upholds the weak hands and the one who was stumbling" (Jb. 4:3-4), cares for the poor, the fatherless and the widow (Jb. 29:12-15; 31:16-19; Prov. 29:7) and defends their cause in court (Jb. 29:16; Prov. 31:9). The just are good stewards of their land and of work animals, and their relations with their workers create peace and harmony (Jb. 31:13). They live at peace with their neighbors and are a joy to their families (Jb. 31:1-12; Prov. 23:24). From justice flows peace and prosperity to the land and to all in the community. In the Psalms the just person is the one who calls upon Yahweh as a source of strength with a confidence which is based on faith in the justice of Yahweh, that is, Yahweh's fidelity to what Yahweh promises. Yahweh rewards according to justice (Ps. 18:20) and "leads me in the paths of righteousness, for Yahweh's name's sake" (Ps. 23:3). The justice of Yahweh is saving help. The psalmist cries "In thy righteousness deliver me" (Ps. 31:1) and vindication comes from the justice of God (Ps. 35:24). The response to this experience of and hope for the saving justice of Yahweh is to praise God, which, in the Psalms, is equivalent to praise of the justice of God (Pss. 35:28; 71:16, 18-19; 89:16). The justice of the individual is summed up in Psalm 112, a wisdom Psalm. The Psalm begins with a command to praise the Lord (Ps. 112:1), and then calls blessed the one who fears the Lord. Such a one will be rich in land and descendants, "wealth and riches are in God's house and God's justice endures forever" (Ps. 112:3). Such a one "conducts affairs with justice" and his or her heart is "firm, trusting in the Lord." The just ones give freely to the poor and their "justice endures forever" (Ps. 112:9). The double statement of justice enduring forever in the context of both possessing wealth and distributing it captures the biblical notion that the goods of this earth are the sign of the right relationship with Yahweh as well as the means to create harmony within the community.

The statements on justice in Job, Proverbs and the Psalms reveal that justice is a harmony which comes from a right relationship to the covenant Lord and to the neighbor to whom a person is related by covenant bond. The realism of biblical thought is expressed by the fact that the sign of justice is peace, prosperity, and fertility on the land. At the same time, biblical thought has a dialectical counter to the naive view of Proverbs 11 that the unjust suffer and the just prosper. Such a view provides the arena for the problem of theodicy in Job. Job has lived a just life and yet he suffers. He is so convinced of his justice that he is ready to call Yahweh unjust (Jb. 39:8). The answer to Job is that Yahweh is Lord even of the destructive powers of nature (Jb. 38:1—40:5; 40:6—41:26). Job is called on to have faith— "Do you have faith in him that he will return?" (Jb. 40:12). He is restored (Jb. 42:10-17) when he discards his last support, his integrity as a claim on God's justice and accepts it as gift. (MacKenzie 533) What Job expresses in mythological and dramatic form, the Psalms express in confessional form—the justice of God is both gift and mystery and the attempt to crystallize it by human standards can result in destroying the proper relation with Yahweh. To live justly is to rejoice in the good things of life and at the same time to be able to recognize that life is a gift even in the faces of loss and destructiveness. To be just is to be open to the world as gift and God as mystery.

2. THE JUSTICE OF YAHWEH

Throughout the Old Testament Yahweh is proclaimed as just (2 Chr. 12:6; Neh. 9:8; Pss. 7:9; 103:17; 116:5; Jer. 9:24; Dan. 9:14; Zech. 3:5; Zech. 8:8). The justice of Yahweh is not deduced from reflection on God's nature, but is intrinsic to the covenant relationship (Hos. 2:19; Jer. 9:24). Breaking of the covenant or turning away from Yahweh is a failure of justice. At the conclusion of the song of the vineyard (Is. 5:1-17), Yahweh indicts the people he "planted" and watched over which Isaiah captures by means of a poetic word play:

And he looked for justice (mispat), but behold bloodshed (mispah); for righteousness (sedaqah), but behold a cry (seaqah). (Is. 5:7)

The justice of God embraces an element of forensic judgment on the sins of the people. Justice is often equated thus with punishment. In Isaiah 10, there is an indictment against the infidelity of Israel which begins:

Woe to those who decree iniquitous decrees
and the writers who keep writing oppressions
to turn aside the needy from justice
and to rob the poor of my people from their right. (Is. 10:2)

The chapter then threatens Israel with the same punishments which were visited upon Assyria when "the Lord will destroy both soul and body" (Is. 10:18). However, from this destruction a remnant will be saved "for destruction is decreed overflowing with righteousness" (Is. 10:22). In like vein, when the rulers have made a covenant with death (Is. 28:14) their faithlessness will be overcome by Yahweh's restoring love:

And I will make justice the line
and righteousness the plummet.
Then your covenant with death will be annulled
and your agreement with Sheol will not stand. (Is. 28:17-18)

The anger of Yahweh leads to a justice which can overcome even the power of death. While Yahweh's justice restores the afflicted and condemns the wicked, caution should be exercised in describing the Lord of the Old Testament as vindictive. Though Yahweh punishes sinners, there is no text in the Old Testament where Yahweh's justice is equated with vengeance on the sinner. Yahweh's justice is saving justice where punishment of the sinner is an integral part of restoration. (Achtemeier 83)

The justice of Yahweh receives special emphasis in the enthronement Psalms (Pss. 47, 93, 95—100). These Psalms are cultic in origin and may have been used either at the enthronement of the king as Yahweh's vice-regent or in an annual festival celebrating the reign of Yahweh. (Mowinckel 16-17, 62, 68-70) Here, as in some other places in the Psalms, justice is virtually personified. *Sedaqah* is a messenger who goes before Yahweh (Ps. 85:14); justice and righteousness are the foundation of Yahweh's throne (Ps. 97:2). In these Psalms Yahweh is hailed as king because Yahweh is victor over hostile powers (Pss. 47:2; 98:2), the world is established or made firm (Pss. 93:1; 96:10), and all creation returns praise (Pss. 96:11-12; 98:4-8). As victorious king, Yahweh will rule in justice. Yahweh is called mighty king "lover of justice" (Ps. 99:4), who "will judge the world with righteousness and the peoples with equity" (Ps. 98:9) and Yahweh's reign will be a dawning of light for the just (Ps. 97:17).

The justice of Yahweh is, therefore, Yahweh's saving power, fidelity to the role of Lord of the covenant. It is also Yahweh's indictment of sin and a call to return or conversion. Justice represents a victory over evil powers which threaten the destruction of the world. It is manifest both in the historical lives of the people and as an object of their eschatological hope.

3. JUSTICE AND THE WIDOW, THE ORPHAN AND THE POOR

Characteristic of all strands of Israel's traditions is concern for the widow, the orphan, the poor, and the sojourner in the land. In the legal traditions, as represented by the covenant code and the Deuteronomic legislation, we find the following texts:

> You shall not wrong a stranger or oppress him. You shall not afflict any widow or orphan. (Ex. 22:21-22)

> ...and the sojourner, the fatherless and the widow who are within your house shall come and be filled; that the Lord your God may bless you and all the work of your hands that you do. (Dt. 14:29, cf. Dt. 15:7)

This concern for the defenseless in society is not a command designed simply to promote social harmony, but is rooted in the nature of Yahweh who is defender of the oppressed. (Miranda 77-106, Berkovits 188-209) There are a series of texts, again from different traditions, which portray Yahweh in this role:

> For the Lord God executes justice for the fatherless and the widow and loves the sojourner giving him food and clothing. (Dt. 10:18)

> Give justice to the week and the fatherless,
> maintain the right of the afflicted and the destitute,
> rescue the weak and the needy. (Ps. 82:3-4)

> The Lord works vindication and justice
> for all who are oppressed. (Ps. 103:6 cf. Pss. 140:23; 146:7)

In one of the earliest texts immediately following the revelation of "I am" at the burning bush, Yahweh is revealed as a compassionate Lord who enters Israel's history to free them from oppression:

> Then the Lord said, "I have seen the affliction of my people who are in Egypt, and have heard their cry because of their taskmasters; I know their sufferings and I have come down to deliver them out of the land of the Egyptians." (Ex. 3:7-8)

Therefore, Yahweh is revealed as a God who is compassionate to the oppressed and their vindicator. When Israel is the oppressed one, Yahweh leads them out of slavery; when they inherit the land, Yahweh again emerges as the protector of the landless.

When Israel forgets the covenant it is the prophets, most explicitly Amos, Isaiah, and Jeremiah, who proclaim to Israel that their fidelity to the covenant Lord must be manifest in concern for the poor and the oppressed. The prophet in Israel is not one who foretells, but one who *forthtells*. The prophet speaks not with foresight into the future but with insight into the ways in which people have broken the covenant. The prophet is one who is called not only to speak on behalf of Yahweh, but one who speaks on behalf of those who have no voice.[4]

Amos, one of the earliest prophets (c. 760-750 B.C.), is one of the strongest to call Israel to return to justice. One of the transgressions of Israel is that:

> They sell the righteous for silver
> and the needy for a pair of shoes,
> they trample the head of the poor into the dust of the earth. (Am. 2:7)

And the people will be punished because:

> You trample upon the poor
> and take from him exactions of wheat. (Am. 5:11)

Amos culminates his judgment against the rich and exploiters of his day by proclaiming that their injustice negates their worship of Yahweh:

I hate, I despise your feasts,
I take no delight in your solemn assemblies . . .
but let justice roll down like waters
and righteousness like an ever-flowing stream. (Am. 5:21, 24)

The imagery here is striking. One function of the cult (feasts and solemn assemblies) was to pray for the waters and flowing steams which would assure fertility and hence life to the land. But comparing justice and righteousness with water and a stream, Amos, speaking in the name of Yahweh, shows that without justice the totality of life is barren.

Two of the most striking texts which affirm Yahweh's concern for the poor and show that faith in God involves the doing of justice are from Jeremiah and Isaiah. In these texts the core of Israel's faith, knowing God and praising God in the cult, is equated with the doing of justice. In Chapter 22 Jeremiah is commanded to deliver a word of the Lord to the king:

Thus says the Lord: Do justice and righteousness, and deliver from the hand of the oppressor him who has been robbed. And do no wrong or violence to the alien, the fatherless and the widow. (Jer. 22:3-4)

Later in the same chapter the king, Jehoiakim, is censured for not following the way of his father Josiah:

Woe to him who builds his house by unrighteousness,
and his upper rooms by injustice.
Did not your father eat and drink
and do justice and righteousness?
Then it was well with him.
He judged the cause of the poor and the needy;
then it was well.
Is this not to know me? says the Lord. (Jer. 22:13, 15-16)

The conclusion of this passage is one of the strongest in the Old Testament for equating true religion with the doing of justice. Josiah, the one king who is praised by Jeremiah and the Deuteronomic school, is remembered not simply for his reform of the cult or promulgation of the Torah (2 Kgs. 22:1—23:25). He is the one who "knew" Yahweh, and the knowing of Yahweh is taking the cause of the poor and the needy. Here there is no division between *theoria* and *praxis*, between faith and the doing of justice.[5] Justice is concrete. It combines non-exploitation of the poor and taking their cause. The doing of justice is not the application of religious faith, but its substance; without it, God remains unknown.

Isaiah 58 begins with a cry to declare to the people their transgression. The people assemble for worship and ask of Yahweh righteous judgments (Is. 58:2). They come in fasting and prayer, but hear no answer (Is. 58:3). The answer of Yahweh appears in verses 4 - 7. The cultic fast which the people choose is a charade because "in the day of your fast you seek your own pleasure and oppress your workers." Then the true fast demanded by Yahweh is described:

Is this not the fast I choose:
to loose the bonds of wickedness,
to undo the thongs of the yoke,
to let the oppressed go free and to break every yoke?
Is it not to share your bread with the hungry,
and bring the homeless poor into your house;
when you seek the naked, to cover him,
and not to hid yourself from your own flesh? (Is. 58:6-7)

In verse 8 the request of the people for "righteous judgments" is then answered. If they observe the fast as called for by Yahweh:

Then shall your light break down like the dawn,
and your healing shall spring up speedily;
and your righteousness shall go before you
and the glory of the Lord shall be your rear guard. (Is. 58:8)

In these texts justice, as fidelity to the demands of a relationship, is described most concretely. A people cannot be just before the covenant God, they cannot know or worship God, when they do not heed God's call to take the cause and defend the rights of the poor and oppressed in the community.

CONCLUDING REMARKS ON THE OLD TESTAMENT

1. To live in Old Testament terms is to be open to relationships. For the Israelite death is not simply the cessation of life but the end of a relation to Yahweh, to fellow Israelites, and to the land. In most general terms justice is fidelity to this threefold relationship by which life is maintained. What these relationships concretely involve assumes different forms in different literary traditions as the social and religious world of the Old Testament evolves. For example, in the early period the command to take the cause of the widow, etc., is given to the whole community; with the rise of the monarchy it becomes a royal task, and when the monarchy fails, ethically and historically, Yahweh becomes the defender. (Fahlgren 89-93)

2. While justice is central to the Old Testament, it is impossible to view texts on justice in isolation from a host of other concepts such as loving mercy, truth, covenant fidelity, vindication, and saving deed, as well as law and statute. A reading of the Old Testament which seeks the path of justice leads one into many other paths of Israel's faith.

3. *Realism* characterizes Israel's view of justice. Injustice is not simply a bad moral attitude but a social cancer which destroys society and a physical force which can bring chaos to the goods of the earth. So, too, the fruits of justice are portrayed most realistically—harmony and peace in personal relations (Job, Proverbs); fertility and rain in due season (Joel); freedom from slavery and oppression (Deutero-Isaiah); hope in the face of sinfulness (Psalms).

4. Although human justice may fail, Yahweh's endures. The Lord's justice has a forensic quality in that God calls people to account when they forget or break the covenant relationship. It is also salvific in that Yahweh restores harmony to the world, intervenes on behalf of the people, forgives their sin, and saves them from bondage.

5. The marginal groups in society—the poor, the widows, the orphans, the aliens—become the scale on which the justice of the whole society is weighed. When they are exploited or forgotten neither worship of God nor knowledge of God can result in true religion.

6. The religious world of the Old Testament is not our world. We have difficulties with both the anthropomorphism of the picture of Yahweh and the interventionist or salvation history perspective of the Old Testament. Nor is our world the social world of the tribal confederacy, the centralized monarchy, or the community of exile and restoration. Old Testament statements on justice need not only application, but interpretation. Despite the gulf between the Old Testament and our world certain constants remain. The expression of religious faith by confrontation with the evils which destroy the social fabric of society is no new phenomenon but as old as the eight-century prophets. The God who spoke long ago as one compassionate to the oppressed and vindicator of the poor remains the Lord of the Jewish and Christian heritage. The call to see the quest for justice as integral to faith in the God of Abraham, Moses, and the prophets must be heard by all who claim this book as either Bible or Testament.

II. THE INTERTESTAMENTAL PERIOD

A general description of the meanings of justice in the period from the exile to the time of Jesus is helpful not only in noting the transformations of the notions of justice within Judaism itself, but also in providing a context for New Testament statements on justice. During this period the Hebrew terms for justice and Greek translations retain the same wide connotations which we find in the early period. (Cronbach 85-91) Justice is associated with mercy (2 Esd. 8:36; Tb. 3:2; Sir. 44:10), goodness of heart (Tb. 14:11; Wis. 1:1), love of neighbor (Jub. 7:20; 20:2), compassion for the poor and weak (Asmp. Mos. 11:17), truth (Tb. 1:3; 3:2; 4:6; Wis. 5:6; 1 Mc. 7:18; 4 Ezr. 7:114), harmony in family and social relations (Jub. 7:20; 31:12; 7:26). Along with these, justice is closely identified with a number of individual qualities—integrity, courage, constancy, self-control, steadfastness amid poverty and illness, intelligence and knowledge.

While maintaining continuity with the meanings of justice in the Old Testament, justice in this period undergoes three major transformations: (1) emphasis on the justice of the individual and a sectarian stress between the just and the unjust, (2) the establishing of justice as a characteristic of the end time, or the influence of eschatology on justice (3) the shift in language whereby *sedaqah* means almsgiving or care for the poor.

1. THE JUST INDIVIDUAL

During the intertestamental period reflection on the call to be just before the Lord, coupled with a growing awareness of the transcendence of God, leads to a theology where God alone is just (Sir. 18:2; 1QH. 1:4) and that man alone is devoid of justice (Dan. 9:18; Sir. 5:8). The justice of the individual is a striving for innocence and purity in the face of Hellenization and religious syncretism. This individualization of justice is vividly portrayed in the departure address of Tobit to his son, Tobias (Tb. 4:1-21). Tobit tells his son:

Remember the Lord our God all your days, and refuse to sin or transgress his commandments. Live uprightly all the days of your life, and do not walk in the ways of wrongdoing. (Tb. 4:5)

Tobit goes on to counsel his son to give alms and share his goods with the poor, but the social motive is absent. Instead:

For charity delivers from death and keeps you from entering the darkness. (Tb. 4:10)

The son is also urged to avoid immorality, to marry a woman from the Jewish people, to avoid pride, to honor the dead, and to persevere in prayer. What in the earlier period were manifestations of justice incumbent on the whole community become, for Tobias, a rule of life.

In this context the rise of Pharisaic notions of justice can be understood.[6] The Pharisees originated in the movement of the pious or "separated ones" who were conscious of the evils of Hellenization and sought to preserve the sanctity of God by careful observance of God's revelation, the Torah. In observing the Law the Pharisee did not hope to merit or gain salvation, but attempted to recognize that the sovereignty of God applied to every area of human life and that the Torah made present to daily life the distant God. Nonetheless, Pharisaic piety fosters the individualization of justice.

Allied to the individualization of justice is the rise of the motif of suffering as a sign of justice. In the Old Testament the command was to remain faithful to the covenant God amid suffering and see God's saving power as the vindication of God's justice. In the intertestamental period suffering itself becomes a sign of a just person. This emphasis culminates in the *Wisdom of Solomon*. (Ruppert 16-22)

Suffering, itself, becomes a stage in the manifestation of God's judgment on sinners and a prelude to the hope of vindication. This conjunction of justice and suffering provides the background for the Pauline idea of the cross as a stumbling block (1 Cor. 1:23) as well as a manifestation of the saving justice of God (Rom. 4:25).

2. ESCHATOLOGICAL JUSTICE

A very important development in the intertestamental period is the motif that the true justice of God will be manifest only at the end time. This motif is anticipated in the Old Testament, especially in the "Messianic" oracles of Isaiah 9:2-7 and 11:1-9 in the Isaiah Apocalypse (24:1—27:13). Such prophetic sayings provide the matrix for the view that justice is no longer something that Yahweh will establish in the sphere of history, but will be reserved to the end time and be characteristic of the new age.[7]

Eschatological justice assumes different forms. One form is the revelation of justice by a final judgment of God.

The final judgment is, simultaneously, revelation and vindication. It uncovers the sins of the unjust and vindicates the just. Eschatology does not function simply as speculation on the end time. It provides a double answer: (a) to the problem of theodicy—how a just and loving God can permit the unjust to prosper; and (b) to the problem of salvation history—what the history of God's saving acts means to a people who experience oppression and loss of political power. Therefore, in eschatological thought not only are the faithful "justified" at the end time, but God is shown to be just and faithful. The meaning of history is seen not simply from the course of events but from the perspective of the goal or end of history. The "God who acts" of the Old Testament is here the Lord of hope. This type of eschatology is important for understanding Paul's teaching in the New Testament on the contrast between this age and the age to come and his statements that the end time, that is, the judgment on the powers of the age, has come in Jesus Christ.

3. JUSTICE AS ALMSGIVING

One of the more interesting transformations of older biblical notions of *sedaqah* during this period is that the word comes to mean "almsgiving" and is translated by the Greek *eleemosyne*. (Cronbach 86, Miranda 14-18) Justice in the sense of almsgiving is found in Tobit 1:3; 12:8-9 and 14:11, and while the Greek text of Ben Sirach employs *eleemosyne* in such sayings as "almsgiving atones for sins" (3:30) and "do not be fainthearted in your prayers, nor neglect to give alms" (7:10), the Hebrew original has *sedaqah* in these places. The change in meaning of the term can be seen from a comparison of Proverbs 10:2 with Tobit 12:9:

Righteousness (sedaqah) delivers from death. (Prov. 10:2)
Almsgiving (eleemosyne) delivers from death. (Tb. 12:9)

J. Lauterbach describes the significance of this development when he says that in later Judaism charity and concern for neighbor are conceived as justice and not simply as an excess of love. (Lauterbach 292)

The roots of this view lie in the Old Testament identification of doing justice with concern for the poor, the widow, the orphan and, the sojourner. The development lives on in both Christianity and Judaism. In Judaism it produced a large system of care for the poor in the community. In the New Testament it is mirrored in Paul's concern for the poor and for the collection and in the view of the relation of faith and works in the letter of James where true faith demands acts of charity (Jas. 2:16-17). Also, in the early Church, the command to give alms and share the goods of the earth is seen as a manifestation of justice rather than an act of unselfish charity, crystallized in Augustine's statement: "Assisting the needy is justice (Justitia est in subveniendo miseris)."[8]

This development represents a very important facet of biblical thought which was obscured by later distinctions between justice and charity. Concern for the poor and a desire to lessen the inequality between rich and poor either individually or collectively, in a biblical perspective, should not proceed simply from a love for or compassion with the sufferings of others, but is rooted in claims of justice, i.e., how one can be faithful to the Lord who has given the goods of the earth as common possession of all and be faithful to others in the human community who have equal claim to these goods.

III. THE NEW TESTAMENT

New Testament statements on justice are neither as rich nor as direct as the Old Testament witness. Nonetheless, justice is central to the New Testament. In Matthew Jesus says, "Seek first God's [the Father's] Kingdom and justice" (Mt. 6:33), and Jesus criticized the scribes because they have neglected the weightier matters of the Law, "justice and mercy and faith" (Mt. 23:23). The early Church proclaims the risen Jesus as the just one (Acts 3:13ff; 7:52). A major emphasis of Paul is the justice of God and the justice given to the world in faith. The Book of Revelation takes up the tradition of justice as the eschatological vindication of the faithful (Rev. 19:11), and the letter of James, as well as 1 John, is concerned about care for the suffering members of the community. Since the new element in the New Testament is the linking of the revelation of God's justice to the life and death of Jesus, we will make some initial observations about the relation of the Kingdom proclamation of Jesus to the quest for justice. Secondly, we will call attention to certain aspects of the theology of Matthew and Luke which contribute to a theology of justice.

THE TEACHING AND LIFE OF JESUS

In 1 Corinthians 1:30 Paul says that Jesus has become our wisdom, justice, sanctification, and redemption. The question is: How does Paul's theological statement mirror the life and career of Jesus? Answering this question has become increasingly difficult in light of the intense debate on the "historical Jesus." Virtually all scholars admit that the Synoptic Gospels are not biographies of Jesus but presentations of a "faith image" of Jesus which reflect the theological concerns of the evangelists and their traditions. What Jesus actually did and said must be reconstructed by source and form criticism. Such a reconstruction is beyond the scope of the present discussion. What we can do is to indicate certain elements of the Jesus tradition which are agreed on by all scholars as authentic Jesus material and from these elements make certain observations on Jesus as the revelation of God's justice.

1. THE KINGDOM PROCLAMATION

In the Gospels Jesus begins his ministry with a proclamation: "The Kingdom of God is at hand. Repent" (Mk. 1:15; Mt. 4:17). The Kingdom is proclaimed as a present reality active and calling for a response from the hearers (Mt. 3:2; 4:23; 5:3; 10; 9:35; Lk. 10:9; 11:20; 17:21: "The Kingdom of God is in your midst"); at the same time, it is a future reality, the object of hope and prayer: "Thy Kingdom come" (Mt. 6:10).[9] The meaning of Kingdom is much debated. Older exegesis tended to interpret it in a spatial sense—the place where the king dwells—and identified Kingdom with ecclesiastical or political realities. The Liberal Protestantism saw it as a purely spiritual reality dwelling only in the hearts of men, urging them to love of the neighbor as brother and God as Father. A certain breakthrough was achieved when Kingdom was understood in the Old Testament sense as the active exercise (Yahweh is king or reigns) of God's sovereignty. (Schnackenburg 13) While this insight is helpful, it too runs the danger of being overly spiritualized. Kingdom, while denoting the active rule of God, never loses its spatial dimension as active rule calling for a place or area in which this rule finds a home. (Hodgson 181-185)

The relation of Kingdom to justice may not be immediately apparent, but a connection is suggested by the observation of N. Perrin that, in the New Testament, Kingdom is a "symbol." (Perrin 29-32) As a symbol, Kingdom carries with it all the overtones of meanings it has in the Old Testament and in the intertestamental literature. As we have seen in the enthronement Psalms, Yahweh's rule and the establishment of justice are closely joined (Pss. 97:1-2; 96:10). In the apocalyptic literature the coming of the time of the Messiah will inaugurate the victory of God's justice and mercy. By identifying the advent of God's Kingdom with his ministry and teaching, Jesus proclaims the advent of God's justice.

Jesus, as the eschatological proclaimer of God's Kingdom and God's justice, shows that this Kingdom is to have effect in the everyday events of life. The Kingdom is the power of God active in the world, transforming it and confronting the powers of the world. It is to find a home among the poor (Mt. 5:3) and the persecuted (Mt. 5:4), and only with difficulty will the rich enter it (Mk. 10:23). The person who can summarize the whole Law as love of God and neighbor is not far from the Kingdom of God (Mk. 12:34). The exorcisms of Jesus represent Jesus' confrontation with a victory over the powers of evil and are signs that "the Kingdom of heaven has come upon you" (Lk. 11:20). The Kingdom and therefore God's justice — God's fidelity and call to fidelity — are to be manifest in history no less than the proclaimer of the Kingdom, Jesus, who was incarnate in history.

2. FELLOWSHIP WITH TOLL COLLECTORS

Jesus manifested the meaning of God's Kingdom by his close association and table fellowship with sinners and toll collectors, the ritual and legal outcasts of his time.[10] He is the one who has come not to call the just, but sinners (Mk. 2:17). By his fellowship with the toll collectors and sinners, Jesus makes present the love and saving mercy of God to those whom the social structures of his time would classify as unjust and beyond the pale of God's loving concern. Jesus' association with these groups is a form of symbolic activity which proclaims that those ritual laws which were designed to protect the sanctity and justice of God concealed the revelation of the true God. In associating with these groups Jesus is a parable of God's justice where mercy (*hesed*) and justice (*sedaqah*) are not in opposition, but in paradoxical agreement.

3. THE CALL TO DISCIPLESHIP

In the Gospels the proclamation of the Kingdom is followed by the calling of disciples. Response to this call is not simply a hearing of Jesus' teaching but involves following and mission. The disciple is called to be with Jesus, to have the same authority, to preach, heal, and confront the power of evil in the same way that Jesus did (Mk. 3:13). Like Jesus the disciple is not to be a person of power, but is to be a servant of all and give his life for others (Mk. 10:35-45). The disciple is to be a person who is free of the care and anxiety which centers on length of days and wealth (Mt. 6:25-33). Discipleship involves commitment to the kind and quality of life Jesus led as well as dedication to a mission of compassion and mercy to the outcast along with a prophetic stance which confronts the power of evil in the world.

Therefore, as the proclaimer of God's Kingdom, Jesus is also the sacrament of God's justice in the world. In Jesus' life this involved engagement with the social world of his time, the offer of mercy to the outcasts of his time, and the calling of others to continue this mission.

THE JESUS OF THE SYNOPTICS

As indicated, the Jesus of history is elusive. However, the Gospels, though viewed from the perspective of the Christ of faith, present a theology in which an evangelist presents to a community the religious meaning of the life and teaching of Jesus. In this sense, the question of the historical Jesus is not as important as how the Jesus of Matthew or Luke may become a "pioneer of faith" (Heb. 12:2) for the contemporary believer. In the following section we will indicate some ways in which the Jesus of Matthew and the Jesus of Luke speak to the concerns of faith and justice.

1. MATTHEW: THE NEW RIGHTEOUSNESS

While Matthew contains some of the harshest statements in the New Testament against the Pharisees (Mt. 23:1-39), his Gospel is the most Jewish of the Gospels. In Matthew Jesus is a teacher of the new righteousness. Jesus is the New Moses who addresses his community in five large discourse blocks, like the five books of the Pentateuch, and his initial thematic sermon is given from a mountain. Like Moses, he is to found a new community (*ekklesia*) which is to follow the new Torah.[11]

Two examples from Matthew are presented to show that, for Matthew, the new righteousness is qualified by mercy which reaches out to the marginal ones in the world. The parable of the unmerciful servant (Mt. 18:23-34) shows justice qualified by mercy. (Linnemann 105-113) The parable is placed by Matthew at the end of a section where Jesus proclaims a series of regulations for life in the community—a community which is concerned about the problem of forgiveness. The parable is familiar. A man who received remission of a huge debt then goes out and demands payment of a minor debt from a fellow servant. When this action is brought to the master's attention he punishes the first servant and says to him:

"Should you not have had mercy on your fellow servant, as I had mercy on you?" (Mt. 18:33). Though on one level the parable seems to be an exhortation to forgiveness, on another level it is a parable of justice qualified by mercy. When the first servant approaches the master for remission of the debt, he thinks that the way to be free of his predicament is to satisfy the demands of strict justice: "I will pay you everything" (Mt. 18:26). Given the size of the debt this is impossible, and the master "out of pity" (literally "out of compassion—Mt. 18:27) forgives the debt. When forgiven he meets a fellow servant who owes him a minor debt and makes the same request: "I will pay you" (Mt. 18:29). The dramatic tragedy in the parable hinges on why the first servant acted as he did. Unless he is to be considered as totally unfeeling, the only explanation for his action was that he was a person who thought in terms of strict justice. He uses in his request to the master this language and uses it with his fellow servant. The reason he treated his fellow servant as he did is that he is one who was never able to interiorize the forgiveness he received nor make it a norm of action in his life. (Via 137-144) He experiences a gift without the conversion which comes with having received a gift. This is, therefore, not an example of how one should forgive but is a parable about the condition necessary for forgiveness—the realization that one can be merciful because one has received mercy. In the parable also the master emerges as the vindicator of the one who is treated unjustly. He restores true justice, which is justice qualified by mercy. Therefore, in the context of Matthew's theology the new law of the Christian community is that the just are those who meet the demands of fellow men because they live in a covenant relationship with a Lord who has given them mercy.

The dramatic scene of the final judgment in Matthew 25:31-46 shows Matthew's concern for the marginal ones in the community. The location of this scene is significant since it is the last discourse of Jesus before the passion narrative. In this section the reader is taken beyond the passion and the death to the return of the Son of Man as vindicator. It looks back to the Matthean interpretation of the parable of the weeds and the wheat (Mt. 13:36-43) where the final separation of the good and bad will take place at the Last Judgment; until then the Church is a mixed state. The scene in Matthew 25 unfolds with dramatic intensity. After the judgment and separation the Lord will say to the blessed (called the just in verse 37): "Inherit the Kingdom." The reason for their inheritance is:

I was hungry and you gave me food, I was thirsty and you gave me drink. I was a stranger and you welcomed me, I was naked and you clothed me. I was sick and you visited me, I was in prison and you came to me. (Mt. 25:35-36)

The just ones seem puzzled about how and when they did these things to the Lord, and he answers: "Truly, I say to you, as you did it to one of the least of these my brethren, you did it to me" (Mt. 25:40). In the second half of the scene the structure of the first part is repeated but now it becomes a structure of condemnation. The unjust are condemned because they did not do those things which the just did. The condemnation does not take place because the goats do not know the commands to feed, clothe, etc. Their response and question in verse 44 presupposes familiarity with these.

In effect, they knew what justice demanded; they simply did not know or recognize where its demands were to be met in the world. In the scene it is the marginal and suffering in the world who reveal the place where the Son of Man, Lord and Judge, is, as it were, hidden in the world. The parable is a warning to Christians of all ages that they must discover not only what the doing of justice is but where justice is to be located. As in the Old Testament, the marginal ones become the touchstone for the doing of justice.

2. THE GOSPEL OF LUKE

More than any other evangelist, Luke is concerned with the life of the Christian in the world. His Gospel is written at a time when hope of the imminent parousia or return of Jesus had waned, and his two volume work (Luke-Acts) wants to present the ministry of Jesus and the life of the early Church as a paradigm for Christian life.[12] Luke is the evangelist who is most interested in what we could call today "social justice," and the Jesus of Luke is very much a prophet in the Old Testament model.

The infancy narratives in Luke form a diptych where John and Jesus are both compared and contrasted. John is a prophet of the old age. He will walk in the "spirit of Elijah and turn the disobedient to the wisdom of the just" (Lk. 1:17). John is the last of Old Testament prophets (Lk. 16:16). Jesus is to be the first of the prophets of the new order. (Yoder 22-63) Like Hannah, the mother of Samuel (1 Sam. 2:1-10), Jesus' mother, Mary, sings a canticle at the announcement of his birth. In the canticle Jesus is proclaimed as one who is to show the saving mercy and justice of God: he will put down the mighty and will exalt the lowly and fill the hungry with good things. This prophetic motif is taken up by Jesus in his inaugural sermon (Lk. 4:18-19) where he applies to himself the role of the servant prophet of Isaiah 61:1-2 who will proclaim release to the captives, recovery of sight to the blind, and liberty to the oppressed. This incident is a combination of a prophetic mandate and a prophetic rejection recalling the rejection of Elijah (Lk. 4:25-27—only in Luke). Jesus says, in reference to his own death, that a prophet should not perish away from Jerusalem (Lk. 13:33), and, after his death, his disciples speak of him as a prophet mighty in word and work (Lk. 24:19). Like the prophets of the Old Testament Jesus speaks on behalf of God (Lk. 6:7, 20-49); he performs symbolic actions and mighty works (the miracles); he shows concern for a widow (Lk. 7:11ff), and takes the cause of the stranger in the land (the Samaritan—Lk. 10:29-37). The Lukan Jesus speaks to his Church with the same prophetic voice for justice with which the Old Testament prophets spoke.

Allied to this is a prophetic critique of wealth which runs throughout the Gospel of Luke. In biblical thought generally, wealth is evil on two grounds: (a) when it becomes a source of dominating power over others, and (b) when it dominates the one who possesses it. For Luke, wealth seems incompatible with the Gospel. Observation of material which is found *only in Luke* illustrates this special Lukan concern. John's preaching includes an address to special social groups (Lk. 3:10-14). Would-be followers are to give away one of two coats; the toll collectors are to collect only "what is due" and the soldiers are to avoid violence, robbery, and greed. As mentioned, Luke cites Isaiah 61:1-2, the good news to the poor, at the beginning of Jesus' ministry. When Levi follows Jesus "he leaves everything" (Lk. 5:28). In his sermon on the plain Luke has the "Beatitudes" in the form of prophetic oracles of blessing followed by oracles of woe (Lk. 6:20-26). The "poor" blessed in Luke are the literal poor, not the "poor in spirit." The first two woes are directed against the rich and those who are full. Luke adds a saying on lending, even to enemies, without hope of return (Lk. 6:35). He places the parable of the rich fool (Lk. 12:16-21) after the saying "Beware of all covetousness, for a man's life does not consist in the abundance of possessions" (Lk. 12:15). The disciple in Luke is one who is to "sell your possessions and give alms" (Lk. 12:33). In the parable of the great supper, those invited after the initial refusal are "the poor, the maimed, the lame, and the blind" (Lk. 14:21; cf. Lk. 14:13). Discipleship involves renouncing all that you have (Lk. 14:33). The Pharisees are "lovers of money" (Lk. 16:14). Luke alone has the parable of the unjust steward and the sayings which follow (Lk. 16:1-14), as well as the parable of the rich man and Lazarus (Lk. 16:19-31). Zacchaeus, the chief toll collector, is praised at his conversion as a true son of Abraham because he gives half of his goods away and does not defraud (Lk. 19:1-10). It is to Luke that we owe the picture of the early Church as a group which "held all things in common, and sold their possessions and distributed them to all, as any had need" (Acts 2:45; 4:34-36). Having observed these characteristics of Luke's Gospel, Malcom Tolbert writes:

> Luke was convinced that the Gospel was applicable to the great social issues of his day and his presentation is colored throughout with a compassion for the exploited and despised. The study of the third Gospel should be a reminder that violence is done to the message of Jesus when it is severed from a concern for man's social problems. (Tolbert 451)

THE PREACHING OF PAUL

It is a paradox, in contemporary discussions of faith and justice, that while the Old Testament and the teaching of Jesus are called on to construct a theology of social justice, Paul, who cites the Old Testament "The just man lives by faith" (Rom. 1:17; Hab. 2:4), and who struggles with the relation of faith and justice in Romans and Galatians, is rarely treated in this context. A variety of reasons explain this neglect. Since the Reformation, Paul's teaching on the justice of God has been seen under the problematic of how the individual sinner can be accepted by a just God. This has led to an exegesis where Paul is, as Krister Stendahl has remarked, "the introspective conscience of the West." (Stendahl 199-215) Though there is no doubt that Paul's language resonates with a modern quest for personal freedom and a struggle with guilt, much of the individualized and existential study of Paul was based on a misreading of his understanding of justice. Recent exegesis has located Paul's thought not so much in the Pharisaic problem of the just individual, but in the context of Old Testament and apocalyptic thought about the justice of God.[13]

1. PAUL'S ESCHATOLOGY

In his use of the terminology "this age," Paul shows himself to be an heir of apocalyptic Judaism. (Furnish 115-116) He exhorts his community: "Do not be conformed to this age" (Rom. 12:2). The present age is transitory (1 Cor. 7:31); it is an evil age (Gal. 1:4) which is characterized by suffering and tribulation (Rom. 8:18). Paul does not root the evil of this age only in an empirical description of sin, but sees this age as held captive by evil power.

However, Paul parts company from apocalyptic Judaism in not contrasting this age with the age to come which will bring victory over sin and death, but in locating the sending of Jesus as the turning of the age when this victory is inaugurated. (Kertlege 135-143) Jesus "gave himself for our sins to deliver us from the present evil age" (Gal. 1:4). The Christians are those who live in the period of the "eschatological now" and the end of the age has come upon them (1 Cor. 10:11).[14] For the Christian the old has passed away and the new has come (2 Cor. 5:17). Therefore, Paul has in one sense a "realized eschatology." The events of the hoped for end time have arrived in Christ.

While emphasizing the "already" in the event of Jesus, Paul has also an eschatological reservation. (Kasemann, *New Testament Questions* 170) Though the evil powers have been broken by Christ who is now Lord of all creation (Phil. 2:10-11), the Christian lives between the times, a period when evil and injustice will continue to exercise their influence until the final victory.

When a discussion of justice in Paul is put in the context of his eschatology certain conclusions are suggested. If the sending of Christ is salvation from the present evil age, and if this is a manifestation of the justice of God (Rom. 4:25), then justice is not simply the quality of God as righteous judge over against sinful man, but a relation of the saving power of God to a world captured by evil. God's justice is a fidelity which inaugurates a saving victory over the powers that enslave and oppress man. Paul's eschatology suggests a Christian response to being in the world. On the one hand, if the world is still under the reign of sin and death, a prophetic stance of opposition to these powers is demanded. Such a stance demands an accurate diagnosis of what the powers are in contemporary experience. Along with the prophetic stance is an eschatological stance which sees that the quest for realization of God's saving justice is always held in hope and anticipation. Paul sees the world in process of transformation and Christians as co-workers in the process. However, precisely because the world is in process, is "groaning," no one crystallization of God's saving justice will be adequate, nor will any system ever be the final system.

2. THE SAVING SIGNIFICANCE OF THE CROSS

The concrete event which Paul sees as a manifestation of God's justice—God's fidelity to self and people—is the death and resurrection of Jesus. The cross and resurrection have a two-fold significance. First of all, Jesus' death exposes and unmasks the powers (1 Cor. 1:18). The death of Christ reveals the true nature of evil powers. This theology continues the motif from the Old Testament that the suffering of the just one exposes the evil of the unjust people. The suffering and death of the innocent is a sign that the power of injustice is at work.

Secondly, in more positive terms Paul portrays the effect of the cross by four metaphors of salvation, among which is justification. (Kummel 185)

The metaphors of salvation deal with those events in the Old Testament—redemptive liberation, sanctification, reconciliation—by which God dealt with a people as a whole. Paul's idea of justification has a social dimension. The second Adam theology of Romans 5 and 1 Corinthians 15, as well as the discussion about the salvation of Israel in Romans 9—11, shows that the result of justification is not simply individual acceptance and freedom but incorporation into a new social structure, the body of Christ (1 Cor. 12; Rom. 12:1-8) and the household of faith (Gal. 6:10; cf. Eph. 2:19, "household of God"). Those who are justified by faith are called on to be faithful not only to the demands of the relationship with God, but faithful to the relationships with all people.

3. EFFECTS OF JUSTIFICATION

The effects of justification in Paul are generally classed as freedom from sin, from the Law, and from death (Rom. 6—8). Freedom in Paul is not simply the absence of obligation or of limitations on human activity. It is a transfer of loyalties:

> Having been set free from sin, you have become slaves of righteousness. (Rom. 6:18)

> For the one who was called in the Lord as a slave is a freeman of the Lord. Likewise the one who was free when called is a slave of Christ. (1 Cor. 7:22)

Sin is the desire and tendency of humans to live for themselves alone in a world of social and religious isolation; it is the equivalent of living according to the flesh. Freedom from sin is then found when the believer sees his or her life as one ransomed, as one who does not belong simply to self, but lives free of care, and lives open to the Lord:

> None of us lives to himself and none of us dies to himself. If we live, we live to the Lord, if we die, we die to the Lord. (Rom. 14:7)

The one who is free from sin is one who now is called "through love to be servants of one another" (Gal. 5:13) and is "a slave to all" (1 Cor. 9:19). Such a one is now free to walk according to the Spirit (Gal. 5:25) and to live according to the fruits of the Spirit—love, joy, peace, patience, kindness, goodness, faithfulness, gentleness, self-control. Therefore, sin is social isolation, and freedom from sin is openness to others. Those things which characterize life, according to the Spirit, are the things which make human social life possible.

The Christian is also free from Law (Rom. 6:14; 10:4). Paul sees in legalism an exclusiveness which would make Christianity into a set of norms and customs, rather than a gift to be shared. Legalism would make the Church simply into a society rather than into a community where membership transcends all norms and social custom:

For as many of you were baptized into Christ have put on Christ. There is neither Jew nor Greek, there is neither slave nor free, there is neither male nor female; for you are all one in Christ Jesus. (Gal, 3:28, cf. 1 Cor. 12:13)

This indicative of freedom from the Law brings with it also the imperative: "Bear one another's burdens and so fulfill the Law of Christ" (Gal. 6:2). The Christian is to owe no one anything except to love one another, "for the one who loves the neighbor has fulfilled the Law" (Rom. 13:8). For Paul freedom *from* the Law is also freedom *for* the law of love.

The Christian is also free of death (Rom. 6:23; 7:5-16; 1 Cor. 15:56). The victory over death is a victory over the power of death to destroy hope, to limit and be the lord of human life. Such a view is the ultimate basis of the Pauline paradoxes of 1 Corinthians 4:12 and 2 Corinthians 6:9ff, "dying, behold we live." It is also the basis of those places where Paul glories in his weaknesses that the power of Christ may be evident in him (2 Cor. 12).

4. FAITH AND JUSTICE

There are two sets of texts in Paul which group faith and justice. In the first set justice is joined with faith and Jesus Christ (e.g., Rom. 3:22, "the justice of God through faith in Jesus Christ"; cf. Phil. 3:9; Rom. 3:26; Gal. 2:16). In the second set there is the conjunction of simply faith and justice (Rom. 3:28, 30; 4:5, 9, 11, 13; 9:30; 10:6; 10:10). (Kertlege 161-166) Since faith in Paul is primarily faith in what God has done in Jesus, the difference between the two sets of texts is not significant. What is significant is what Paul means when he says that justice comes through faith.

Faith for Paul is akin to the metanoia or conversion of the Synoptic Gospels which demands a turning to the demands of the Kingdom and engagement in the mission of the Kingdom. Faith looks to the past: "I live by faith in the Son of God who loved me and gave himself for me" (Gal. 2:20); it also characterizes the present life of the individual: "I live by faith" (Ga. 2:20) and of the community: "Your faith is proclaimed in the whole world" (Rom. 1:8), and, as Paul's description of the faith of Abraham in Romans 4 shows, faith is living under a promise which must prove itself in the Christian life. (Kasemann, *Perspectives on Paul* 82)

The faith which justifies is the faith which leads to knowledge of Jesus Christ—a knowledge which involves personal sharing in the life and death of Jesus. The life and death of Jesus is his emptying (Phil. 2:5-11), his renunciation of grasping, and the giving of his life for others. Therefore, the justice of God which comes from faith in Jesus is fidelity to the demands of a relationship—the relationship that the Christian is to have with Christ by being "in Christ" (over 165 times in Paul) and putting on Christ and the mind of Christ.

To be justified by faith is to walk in the trust that God through Christ offers grace and redemption to a sinful world; that God is at work in history. A quest for justice which is from faith proceeds with the faith that the kind and quality of life Jesus lived and proclaimed still has meaning.

5. THE ETHICS OF THE COMMUNITY

Neither Paul's doctrine of justification by faith nor his eschatological reservation led him to a flight from concern for the world or to an inactive fideism. In his own life Paul was a minister of reconciliation (2 Cor. 5:18) and a servant of justice (Rom. 6:18). The hortatory parts of Paul's letter turn to everyday concerns of the community. Though these concerns may seem archaic to us today (e.g., discussion of goods offered to idols, of appearance before pagan courts—1 Cor. 8 and 6), they show that Paul's deepest theological reflection touched on the problems of how Christians were to relate to each other. Paul's theological insights touch on the lives of the community through (a) concern for the weak in the community, (b) the bearing of one another's burdens, (c) concern for the poor and the collection, and (d) concern for peace and harmony in the community.

These aspects of Paul's ethics of everyday life are not exhaustive but indicative that Paul writes as a pastor for a world he sees in process of transformation, but where the transformation is revealed in the creation of structures of interpersonal relations in the community. Paul's ethics are simultaneously an ethics where decisions are made in response to the felt needs of others and an ethics where the goal of Christian life determines its present shape. Today, no less than in the time of Paul, the justice and freedom which comes as gift through faith must be a gift shared and realized in Church and world.

SUMMARY OF PAUL

1. Paul's statements on justice and on justification must be seen in a Christological context. Paul sees salvation in the event of the incarnation and the cross and resurrection of Jesus. This is the revelation of the justice of God which is God's fidelity to creation and the saving victory over the evil in creation.

2. Paul's statements about the salvation and justification of the individual are in context of the salvation and justification of the world. Evangelization for Paul is not simply kerygmatic preaching, but involves the ministry of reconciliation, the service of justice, and concern for the suffering members of the community.

3. The metaphors which Paul uses for salvation all convey a nuance of the restoration of broken relationships and the creation of a new people. In this sense they are descriptions of the *sedaqah* or justice of God.

4. The access to salvation is faith. Faith is the obedient surrender to the love of God manifest in Christ. It is a walking under a promise which frees one from the power of evil. In this sense, faith frees both the oppressor and the oppressed.

5. The Christian is to live in the new creation, is to fulfill the Law of Christ by love of neighbor, and to be in a union where the sufferings and joys of others are his or her sufferings and joys.

IV. CONCLUSIONS

The Bible proclaims what it means to be just and to do justice; it is less interested in what justice is in the abstract. It gives concrete instances of justice and injustice in the lives of people. The task of translation is to make alive in our present age the vision of justice which formed the lives of the biblical writers. Interpretation of the Bible is always determined by the social context of the interpreter. Luther wrestled with the late medieval problem of a just God and sinful creation and translated the God of justice into a God of love. The task of our age may well be the reverse—to translate the love of God into the doing of justice.

The God of the Old Testament is a God who loves justice and righteousness. What God loves, God brings to pass. As a just Lord, God is faithful to the covenant by revealing to people how they may turn to God and return when they fail. God's justice is manifest both in the saving deeds whereby God frees people from slavery and oppression and in God's indicting of sinfulness. In God justice and mercy are not in opposition, but, as Heschel states: "God is compassion without compromise; justice, though not inclemency." *(The Prophets* 16)

To be just is to be faithful to the covenant God as this God is revealed in history, in the Law, and in the prophets. Covenant faithfulness means that justice is shown to the neighbor as a sign of the saving justice received from God. Peace and harmony are the fruits of justice as well as its signs.

Particular to Israel's faith is the revelation of God as protector of the helpless, the poor, and the oppressed in the community. In order to become a faithful and just people, Israel is summoned to true knowledge and true worship of God which is not simply the recognition that another person has equal rights to the goods of God's creation, but is active engagement in securing these goods for them.

In the development of biblical faith the quest for justice is always present gift and demand, and the full realization of the quest is always future hope. The heir of biblical faith lives "between the times" with a mission both to confront the evils of injustice and to offer to the world visions of justice.

In the New Testament the revelation of God's justice is Christological. God shows fidelity to creation by the offer of love and mercy in the life and teaching of Jesus. This offer represents the reclamation of the world to the sovereignty of God. The world of human history is God's world. Faith is the recognition of God's claim. It is expressed in love and care for all those claimed by God. Faith frees people to be people of compassion because they have received compassion; it frees them to care for the weak and the prodigal because they have been accepted by God, though weak and prodigal.

The cause of the poor, the hungry, and the oppressed is now the cause of Jesus. He is the Son of Man, present in the least of his brethren. Christians are called on to bear one another's burdens. This is to fulfill the law of Christ, to be a just people.

Engagement in the quest for justice is no more "secular" than the engagement of Yahweh in the history of God's people or the incarnation of Jesus into the world of human suffering. The Bible gives a mandate and a testament to Christians that, in their quest for justice, they are recovering the roots of the biblical tradition and are seeking to create a dwelling place for the word of God in human history.

END NOTES

[1]F. Notscher, "Righteousness (Justice)." *Sacramentum Verbi*, ed. J. B. Bauer (New York: Herder and Herder, 1970) II, 780. Hebrew has two main terms for justice, *sedaqah* and *mispat*, usually translated as "righteousness" and "justice." In this essay we will follow the R.S.V. in its translation of the terms but with the caution that the terms are often used synonymously in the Old Testament and that righteousness has a much wider connotation than moral innocence.

[2]K. H.-J. Fahlgren, *Sedaka, nahestehende und entgegengesetze Begriffe im Alten Testament* (Uppsala: Almquist und Wiksells, 1932) 81. Fahlgren describes justice as *Gemeinschafttreue*, i.e., fidelity in communal life.

[3]See Hosea 2:19; Isaiah 16:5; Psalm 38:4-5.

[4]A. Heschel, *The Prophets* (New York: Harper and Row, 1962). On page 5 Heschel calls prophecy "a voice to the plundered poor;" see also page 205.

[5]Jose Miranda, *Marx and the Bible*, trans. John Eagleson (Maryknoll: Orbis Books, 1974) 44-53. "Know" in the Bible is not simply intellectual awareness but involves intimate knowledge and personal commitment.

[6]On Pharisaic notions of justice, see G. F. Moore, *Judaism in the First Three Centuries of the Christian Era* (Cambridge: Harvard University Press, 1963) II, 180-197, and J. Lauterbach, "The Pharisees and Their Teaching," *Rabbinic Essays* (Cincinnati: Hebrew Union College, 1951) 87-159.

[7]"Eschatology" is a general term for statements about the end time when Yahweh intervenes to bring history to fulfillment or conclusion. "Apocalyptic" represents a particular form of eschatology which stresses symbolic revelation of the future and depicts a detailed scenario of the end time and the new age. Jewish eschatological thought in the intertestamental and New Testament periods is very often expressed in apocalyptic categories. See *Journal for Theology and Church*, Vol. 6, *Apocalypticism*, ed. R. Funk (New York: Herder and Herder, 1969), and K. Koch, *The Rediscovery of Apocalyptic*, Studies in Biblical Theology, New Series, No. 22 (London: S.C.M. Press, 1972).

[8]Cited by Miranda, *Marx and the Bible*, trans. John Eagleson (Maryknoll: Orbis Books, 1974) 16. See also M. Hengel, *Property and Riches in the Early Church*, trans. J. Bowden (Philadelphia: Fortress Press, 1974).

[9]N. Perrin, *The Kingdom of God in the Teaching of Jesus* (London: S.C.M. Press, 1963) 74-78, 81-87, discusses the evidence for Kingdom as present and as future in the teaching of Jesus.

[10]"Toll collector" is used in place of the more familiar but less accurate "publican" or "tax collector," since these men were not the rich publicans of classical antiquity but were petty functionaries. They were scorned because of ritual uncleanliness from contact with Gentiles, because they were thought to be dishonest, and because they were seen as "quislings" of the Roman occupation.

See J. Donahue, "Tax Collectors and Sinners: An Attempt of Identification," *Catholic Biblical Quarterly* 33 (1971): 39-61.

[11]For a survey of Matthew's theology, see J. Rohde, *Rediscovering the Teaching of the Evangelists*, trans. D. B. Barton (Philadelphia: Westminster Press, 1967) 47-113.

[12]On the theology of Luke, see Rohde, *Rediscovering the Teaching of the Evangelists*, trans. D. B. Barton (Philadelphia: Westminster Press, 1967) 159-239, and M. Tolbert, "Leading Ideas of the Gospel of Luke," *Review and Expositor* 64 (1967): 441-453.

[13]*Miranda, Marx and the Bible*, trans. John Eagleson (Maryknoll: Orbis Books, 1974) 174-177; E. Kasemann, "'The Righteousness of God' in Paul," *New Testament Questions of Today* (Philadelphia: Fortress Press, 1969) 169-182; E. Kasemann, "Justification and Salvation history in the Epistle to the Romans," *Perspectives on Paul* (Philadelphia: Fortress Press, 1971) 60-78; K. Kertlege, *"Rechtfertigung" bei Paulus*, Neutestamentliche Abhandlungen, 3 (Munster: Aschendorf, 1967); P. Stuhlmacher, *Gerechtigkeit Gottes bei Paulus, FRLANT*, 87 (Gottingen: Vandenhoeck und Ruprecht, 1965). Miranda and Kertlege are Catholic, and Kasemann and Stuhlmacher are Lutheran, which shows an ecumenical consensus on the social dimension of Paul's teaching on justification.

[14]Paul uses the "eschatological now" to stress that the new era has been inaugurated in Christ; see. J. A. Fitzmyer, "The Letter to the Romans," *JBC* II, 301; "Pauline Theology," *JBC* 809-810.

WORKS CITED

Achtemeier, E. "Righteousness in the Old Testament." *Interpreter's Dictionary of the Bible*. Nashville: Abingdon Press, 1962.

Berkovits, E. "The Biblical Meaning of Justice." *Judaism* 18 (1969): 188-209.

The Biblical Doctrine of Justice and Law. Ecumenical Biblical Studies, No. 3. London: S.C.M. Press, 1955.

Cronbach, A. "Righteousness in Jewish Literature, 200 B.C.—A.D. 100," *IDB* IV: 85-91.

Fahlgren, K. H.-J. *Sedaka, nahestehende und entgegengesetze Begriffe im Alten Testament*. Uppsala: Almquist und Wiksells, 1932.

Furnish, V. *Theology and Ethics in Paul*. Nashville: Abingdon Press, 1968.

Heschel, A. *The Prophets*. New York: Harper and Row, 1962.

Hodgson, P. *Jesus as Word and Presence*. Philadelphia: Fortress Press, 1971.

Kasemann, E. "'The Righteousness of God' in Paul." *New Testament Questions of Today*. Philadelphia: Fortress Press, 1969.

Kasemann, E. "The Faith of Abraham in Romans 4." *Perspectives on Paul*. Trans. M. Kohl. Philadelphia: Fortress Press, 1971.

Kertlege, K. *"Rechtfertigung" bei Paulus*. Neutestamentliche Abhandlungen, 3. Munster: Aschendorf, 1967.

Kummel, W. G. *The Theology of the New Testament*. Trans. J. Steely. Nashville: Abingdon Press, 1973.

Lauterbach, J. "The Ethics of the Halakah." *Rabbinic Essays*. Cincinnati: Hebrew Union College, 1951.

Linnemann, E. *Jesus of the Parables*. Trans. J. Sturdy. New York: Harper and Row, 1967.

MacKenzie, R. A. F. "Job," *Jerome Biblical Commentary*. Ed. R. E. Brown, J. A. Fitzmyer, R. E. Murphy. Englewood Cliffs: Prentice Hall, 1968.

Miranda, Jose. *Marx and the Bible*. Trans. John Eagleson. Maryknoll: Orbis Books, 1974.

Mowinckel, S. *The Psalms in Israel's Worship*. Nashville: Abingdon Press, 1967.

Pedersen, J. *Israel: Its Life and Culture*. Vols. I-II. London: Oxford University Press, 1926.

Perrin, N. *Jesus and the Language of the Kingdom*. Philadelphia: Fortress Press, 1976.

Ruppert, L. *Jesus als der leidende Gerechte*. Stuttgarter Bibel-studien, 59. Stuttgart: Katholisches Biblewerk, 1972.

Schnackenburg, R. *God's Rule and Kingdom*. Trans. J. Murray. New York: Herder and Herder, 1963.

Stendahl, K. "The Apostle Paul and the Introspective Conscience of the West." *Harvard Theological Review* 56 (1963): 199-215.

Tolbert, M. "Leading Ideas of the Gospel of Luke." *Review and Expositor* 64 (1967): 441-453.

Via, Dan O. *The Parables: Their Literary and Existential Dimension*. Philadelphia: Fortress Press, 1967.

von Rad, G. *Old Testament Theology*. Trans. D. M. G. Stalker. New York: Harper and Bros., 1962.

Yoder, J. H. *The Politics of Jesus*. Grand Rapids: Eerdmans, 1972.

Chapter 2A

Scriptural Guide to Justice

<table>
<tr><td colspan="2" align="center">HEBREW SCRIPTURES</td></tr>
<tr><td>Gn 1:1-31</td><td>The story of creation; call to stewardship of the earth</td></tr>
<tr><td>Gn 4:9-10</td><td>Am I my brother's keeper?</td></tr>
<tr><td>Ex 3:1-20</td><td>God reveals himself as liberator; sends Moses to free his people from economic and political oppression</td></tr>
<tr><td>Ex 6:2-13</td><td>God the liberator</td></tr>
<tr><td>Ex 16:1-36</td><td>The manna and the quails</td></tr>
<tr><td>Ex 17:1-7</td><td>Water from the rock</td></tr>
<tr><td>Ex 22:20-24</td><td>Justice and mercy toward stranger, orphan, widow</td></tr>
<tr><td>Ex 22:25-27</td><td>Mercy and kindness toward neighbor</td></tr>
<tr><td>Ex 23:6-8</td><td>Legal systems should judge fairly</td></tr>
<tr><td>Ex 23:9</td><td>Don't oppress strangers</td></tr>
<tr><td>Lv 19:9-18</td><td>Treat your neighbor with justice and mercy; love your neighbor as yourself</td></tr>
<tr><td>Lv 19:23-24</td><td>Don't oppress strangers</td></tr>
<tr><td>Lv 19:32-34</td><td>Respect for the elderly and foreigners</td></tr>
<tr><td>Lv 25:8ff</td><td>Holy year of jubilee; economic restoration</td></tr>
<tr><td>Lv 25:23-28</td><td>The land belongs to the Lord; you are strangers and guests</td></tr>
<tr><td>Lv 27:32</td><td>Tithing</td></tr>
<tr><td>Dt 1:16-17</td><td>Judge impartially</td></tr>
<tr><td>Dt 10:16-20</td><td>Don't oppress strangers</td></tr>
<tr><td>Dt 15:1-15</td><td>Periodic cancellation of debts and release of slaves; let there be no poor among you</td></tr>
<tr><td>Dt 24:17-22</td><td>Justice toward strangers, orphans, widows</td></tr>
<tr><td>Dt 24:19-22</td><td>Remember the poor while harvesting; gleaning</td></tr>
<tr><td>Dt 26:12-13</td><td>Tithing and concern for the poor</td></tr>
</table>

Dt 27:19	Don't oppress strangers
Dt 30	A nation that chooses the Lord chooses life
1Ch 29:10-14	We only give back to God what God has first given us
1 Sm 15:22	Excessive formalism vs. obedience to God
Tb 4:16-17	Treat others as you would be treated
Jb 1:21	Naked I came from my mother's womb, naked I shall return
Ps 8:1-9	Placed over all creation
Ps 9:7-12, 18	God rules the world with justice
Ps 9:9	Strength for the oppressed; justice toward all
Ps 241ff	The earth is the Lord's
Ps 25:6-18	The Lord hears and protects the just
Ps 41:1-3	Regard for the lowly and the poor
Ps 65:9-13	God's care for creation
Ps 68:5-6	God's care for the helpless and homeless
Ps 72	God liberates and defends the poor and oppressed; justice flourishes in God's day
Ps 82	No more mockery of justice
Ps 96:10-13	God judges the people with justice
Ps 103	Yahweh is always on the side of the oppressed
Ps 103:6-7	God judges in favor of the oppressed
Ps 140:12	God defends the cause of the poor
Ps 146:1-10	Creator and God of the oppressed
Ps 146:6-9	The Lord gives justice and liberty
Prv 17:15	In making fun of the poor you insult the Creator
Prv 19:17	The Lord will pay back what you give to the poor
Prv 21:3	Justice is more pleasing than sacrifice
Prv 21:13	Listen to the cry of the poor or your cry for help will not be heard
Prv 22:22-23	Do not rob or injure the poor
Prv 31:8-9	Be an advocate for the voiceless
Eccl 4:1-3	The power of oppressors and the weak
Sir 3:30; 4:11	Charity toward the poor
Is 1:10-28	Religious hypocrisy, its punishment and cure
Is 2:1-5	Turn swords into ploughshares
Is 3:13-15	Grinding the face of the poor
Is 5:1-7	God's people produce the bitter fruit of injustice
Is 5:8-9	Woe to those who hoard riches
Is 10:1-2	Bad legislators; denial of human rights
Is 29:13	Change of heart requires more than lip service
Is 32:16-17	Justice will bring peace
Is 58:1-12	God doesn't want empty worship but a conversion of heart that produces justice, love, and mercy
Is 61:1-2	Mission of Christ foretold, good news to the poor;

	liberation
Jer 6:13-16	They cry, "Peace!" but there is none
Jer 6:19-20	Worship is not acceptable without obedience
Jer 7:1-11	The temple is no haven for evildoers
Jer 22:3	Rescue the victim from the oppressor
Jer 22:16	To know the Lord is to act justly
Ez 34	Responsibilities of religious and civil leaders and authorities
Ez 37	God raises up a new people from "dry bones"
Dn 9:1-19	The nation is called to repent
Hos 6:6	Love, not empty worship
Am 2:6-7	The unjust trample on the heads of ordinary people
Am 5:10-15	Hate what is evil, do right; establish justice
Am 5:21-24	God wants worship that expresses true conversion and renewal that produces justice
Am 6:1, 3-6	Woe to the complacent and oppressive rich
Am 8:4-7	The powerful trample on the poor and needy
Mi 2:1-2	Woe to the oppressor
Mi 4:1-4	God's universal reign of peace; swords beat into plows
Mi 6:8	Act justly, love tenderly, walk humbly with God
Mi 6:9-14	Dishonesty condemned
Mi 7:18-20	God's constant love
Hb 2:6-9	Trouble will come to those who exploit
Zec 7:9-10	Justice and mercy

CHRISTIAN SCRIPTURES

Mt 4:1-10	The temptation of Jesus
Mt 5:13-16	Salt and light for the world
Mt 5:23-25	Forgiveness and reconciliation
Mt 5:38-48	Give your coat; walk the extra mile
Mt 6:1-4	Don't make a show of your generosity
Mt 6:19-21	Your heart is where your treasure is
Mt 6:25-34	Set your hearts on God's kingdom first
Mt 7:21; Lk 6:46-49	Combine prayer with action
Mt 8:20	Christ lived in poverty
Mt 10:37-39	Take up the cross daily; lose life to gain life
Mt 11:2-6	The signs for recognizing the Messiah and his followers
Mt 12:46-50	Do God's will
Mt 12:15-21	God's chosen servant, persistent until justice triumphs
Mt 15:32	Compassion and a sense of responsibility
Mt 19:16-30	The rich young man
Mt 20:26-28	Christians must be servants
Mt 23:11	Be a servant

Mt 23:23-24	Don't neglect justice and mercy
Mt 25:12-30	The parable of the three servants
Mt 25:31-46	The last judgement; whatever we do to our neighbor, we do to Christ
Mk 6:30-37	Give them something to eat yourselves
Mk 8:1-9	Jesus feeds four thousand people
Mk 9:35; 10:41-45	To be first before God, be a servant
Mk 10:17-31	The rich young man refuses invitation to voluntary poverty
Mk 12:41-44	The widow's offering
Lk 1:52-53	Mary's song of praise; God exalts the poor and lowers the rich
Lk 3:10-18	John the Baptist's call to share extra clothing, food; for honesty in work
Lk 4:16-30	Jesus announces his mission to liberate people
Lk 6:20-26	Beatitudes, condemnation of oppressive and complacent rich
Lk 6:27-35	Make peace through nonviolence and love of enemies
Lk 7:18-23	Tell John what you see; the blind see, the Good News is preached
Lk 10:25-37	The Good Samaritan
Lk 11:40-42	Pharisaism; need justice and love
Lk 12:13-21	A person's worth is not determined by how much one owns
Lk 12:32-34	Sell and give alms; your heart will be where your riches are
Lk 14:7-14	Humility and hospitality
Lk 15:1-7	Jesus associated with the outcasts of society; the lost sheep
Lk 16:19-31	The story of Lazarus and the rich man
Lk 19:7-9	Zaccheus; conversion, repentance, and restitution
Lk 19:41	Jesus weeps over Jerusalem
Lk 22:24-27	Be a servant
Lk 24:49	Christ empowers us to continue his work
Jn 6:5-13	Christ feeds the hungry
Jn 6:35	Jesus the Bread of Life
Jn 10:1-18	Jesus the Good Shepherd
Jn 13:1-15	Jesus, the Suffering Servant, washes the feet of the disciples.
Jn 13:34-35	Love - the distinctive characteristic of Christians
Jn 14:10-17	Those who believe in Christ will do the same and greater works through the power of the Spirit
Jn 16:33	Christ has overcome the world
Acts 1:4	The power we need to do Christ's work

Acts 1:6-8	Our job is to be Christ's witness
Acts 2:43-47; 5:12-16	The first Christian community shared everything; no one was in need
Acts 4:18-22	Obey God rather than people
Acts 4:32-35	True Christian community; possessions shared
Acts 6:1-6	Deacons appointed for service
Acts 10:34-35	God shows no favoritism
Acts 16:16-24; 17:1-9	Paul thrown into jail for preaching Jesus and calling for change
Rom 5:6-11	Friends with God through Christ
Rom 8:14-17	We have been given a spirit of freedom, not slavery
Rom 12:9-13, 16-17	One body in Christ, serving others
Rom 12:10-18	Make hospitality your special care; make friends with the poor
Rom 13:8-10	Our only debt is to love one another
Rom 14:17-19	The kingdom is justice, peace, and joy
1Cor 11:17-34	Dishonoring the Lord's supper, division in the community
1 Cor 12:7-11	The gifts of the Holy Spirit are tools for building Christian community
1 Cor 12:24-26	If one suffers, all suffer
1 Cor 13	Love as the Christian life style
1 Cor 16:1-4	Set aside money to aid others
2 Cor 4:7	God's power working in and through us
2 Cor 6:6	The qualities of a servant
2 Cor 8:1-15	Be generous in sharing with the needy; Christ became poor to enrich us
2 Cor 9:1-15	Give gladly
Gal 3:28	There are no distinctions, all are one in Christ
Gal 5:1	You have been called to live in freedom
Gal 5:13-15	Use your freedom to serve others; love fulfills the law
Gal 5:22-23	The fruits of the Holy Spirit
Gal 6:2	Bear one another's burdens
Eph 2:8-10	Saved through faith in Christ, created for a life of good deeds
Eph 4:11-16	The base for ministry is the community; the whole body grows and is built up by love
Eph 4:23-24	Put aside old misdirected ways for a new, fresh way of thinking
Phil 2:1-11	Unity and service; be a servant like Christ
Col 3:10-12	On racial discrimination
Col 3:17	Do all in Christ's name
1 Thes 5:12-18	The demands of community life
Gal 6:9-10	Do not tire of doing good

1 Tm 6:1-10	Love of money is the root of all evil
1 Tm 6:17-19	Tell the rich not to be proud
Heb 10:24-25	Concern in Christian community
Heb 13:1-3	Welcome strangers, remember those imprisoned
Heb 13:5	Be satisfied, God is with you
Jas 1:22-27	Be doers, not only hearers of the word
Jas 2:1-9	Love your neighbor, treat all with dignity
Jas 2:14-17	Faith without actions is dead
Jas 3:13-18	Peacemakers follow true wisdom
Jas 5:1-6	Riches obtained unjustly bring misery
1 Pt 4:7-11	Put your gifts at the service of others
1 Jn 3:17	Selfishness precludes love
1 Jn 4:7-12	If we love one another, God's love is made perfect in us
1 Jn 4:19-21	We can't love God without loving neighbor
Rev 21:1-6	The new heaven and the new earth

Chapter 3

The Call to Conversion

Jim Wallis

The people who sat in darkness have seen a great light, and for those who sat in the region and shadow of death light has dawned. From that time Jesus began to preach, saying, "Repent, for the kingdom of heaven is at hand." (Matthew 4:16-17)

Just as light breaks into the darkness, the kingdom of God has arrived. This is how the prophet Isaiah, quoted here by Matthew, said it would be. The times into which Jesus came were dark indeed. Political domination at the hands of Rome, economic oppression by the rich, and human sinfulness on every side—these were the experiences of the common people. But where there was no light, God's new order would shine for all to see in the person of Jesus Christ. No wonder the word *gospel* means "good news!" The people had been waiting a long time.

Jesus inaugurated a new age, heralded a new order, and called the people to conversion. "Repent!" he said. Why? Because the new order of the kingdom is breaking in upon you and, if you want to be a part of it, you will need to undergo a fundamental transformation. Jesus makes the need for conversion clear from the beginning. God's new order is so radically different from everything we are accustomed to that we must be spiritually remade before we are ready and equipped to participate in it. In his Gospel, John would later refer to the change as a "new birth." No aspect of human existence is safe from this sweeping change—neither the personal, nor the spiritual, social, economic, or political. The kingdom of God has come to change the world and us with it. Our choice is simply whether or not we will offer our allegiance to the kingdom.

As he walked by the Sea of Galilee, he saw two brothers, Simon who is called Peter and Andrew his brother, casting a net into the sea; for they were fishermen. And he said to them, "Follow me, and I will make you fishers of men." Immediately they left their nets and followed him. And going on from there he saw two other brothers, James the son of Zebedee and John his brother, in the boat with Zebedee their father, mending their nets, and he called them. Immediately they left the boat and their father, and followed him (Matt. 4:18-22).

Jesus called people to follow him. The first disciples took him quite literally. They were young Jewish men with established occupations and family responsibilities who, nevertheless, left everything to follow him. Jesus called them to himself, and he called them to a mission. "Follow me, and I will make you fishers of men." Their calling was not just for their own sake. From the outset, Jesus' disciples were—and are—called for a purpose.

To leave their nets was no light choice for these Galilean fishermen. Their fishing nets were their means of livelihood and the symbol of their identity. Now Peter and the others were leaving not only their most valued possessions; they were leaving their former way of life. This is what it meant to follow Jesus. Old ties were broken, former things left behind. Peter said, "Lo, we have left everything and followed you." (Matt 19:27)

Four simple fishermen heard the call of Jesus. They were the first to obey and follow. They would not be the last. Others too would forsake all previous commitments to join Jesus' band. They would become his disciples and share his life. From then on they were bound to Jesus and to his Kingdom; nothing would ever be the same for them again. They had made a clear choice with very real consequences. Jesus told potential converts to count the cost:

> As they were going along the road, a man said to him, "I will follow you wherever you go." And Jesus said to him, "Foxes have holes, and birds of the air have nests; but the Son of man has nowhere to lay his head." To another he said, "Follow me." But he said, "Lord let me go and bury my father." But he said to him, "Leave the dead to bury their own dead; but as for you, go and proclaim the kingdom of God." Another said, "I will follow you, Lord; but first let me say farewell to those at my home." Jesus said to him, "No one who puts his hand to the plow and looks back is fit for the kingdom of God." (Luke 9:57-62)

In the Bible, conversion means "turning." "To convert" in the King James Bible is translated "to turn" in the Revised Standard Version.

The Old Testament word for conversion (*shub*) means "to turn, return, bring back, restore." It occurs more than one thousand times and always involves turning from evil and to the Lord.[1] The prophets continually called Israel to turn from its sins and worship of idols and return to Yahweh, the true and living God. This call to conversion was both individual and corporate in the Old Testament. These people of God were much like us, always falling away from their Lord and getting themselves into trouble. Conversion meant to come back, to come home again, to wander no longer in sin, blindness, and idolatry. To convert meant to be again who you really were and to remember to whom you really belonged.

The New Testament words for conversion (*metanoein* and *epistrephein*) mean "to turn around."[2] Turning around involves stopping and proceeding in a new direction. The New Testament stresses the necessity of a radical turnabout and invites us to pursue an entirely different course of life. Thus, fundamental change of direction is central to the meaning of the words. The assumption—from the preaching of John the Baptist through Jesus to the first apostles—is that we are on the wrong path, moving away from God. The Bible refers to our self-determined course as walking in sin, darkness, blindness, dullness, sleep, and hardness of heart. To convert is to make an about-face and take a new path.[3]

Correct intellectual belief was a major concern of the Greeks. The early Christians, in contrast, were more concerned with transformation. The first evangelists did not simply ask people what they believed about Jesus; they called upon their listeners to forsake all and to follow him. To embrace his kingdom meant to radically change not only in outlook but in posture, not only in mind but in heart, no only in worldview but in behavior, not only in thoughts but in actions. Conversion for them was more than a changed intellectual position. It was a whole new beginning.

Thus conversion is far more than an emotional release and much more than an intellectual adherence to correct doctrine. It is a basic change in life direction. If the key to conversion in the biblical stories is a turning from and a turning to, it is always appropriate to ask what is being turned from and what is being turned to in the account of any conversion.

Conversion begins with repentance, the New Testament word for which is metanoia. Our word *repentance* conjures up feelings of being sorry or guilty for something. The biblical meaning is far deeper and richer. In the New Testament usage, repentance is the essential first step to conversion. In the larger rhythm of turning from and turning to, repentance is the turning away from. Repentance turns us from sin, selfishness, darkness, idols, habits, bondages, and demons, both private and public.[4] We turn from all that binds and oppresses us and others, from all the violence and evil in which we are so complicit, from all the false worship that has controlled us. Ultimately, repentance is turning from the powers of death. These ominous forces no longer hold us in their grip; they no longer have the last word.

Having begun with repentance, conversion proceeds to faith. The call to repentance is the invitation to freedom and the preparation for faith. Just as John the Baptist prepared the way of Jesus, so repentance makes us ready for faith in Christ. As repentance is the turning from, faith is the turning to. Repentance is seeing our sin and turning from it; faith is seeing Jesus and turning toward him. Together, repentance and faith form the two movements of conversion.[5]

Faith is turning to belief, hope, and trust. As repentance dealt with our past, faith opens up our future. Faith opens us to the future by restoring our sight, softening our hearts, bringing light into our darkness. We are converted to compassion, justice, and peace as we take our stand as citizens of Christ's new order. We see, hear, and feel now as never before. We enter the process of being made sensitive to the values of the new age, the kingdom of God. The victory of Jesus Christ over the powers of death has now been appropriated to our own lives; we are enabled to live free of their bondage. Christ has vanquished the powers that once held us captive and fearful; we now stand in the radical freedom he bought for us with his own blood. "So if the Son makes you free, you will be free indeed" (John 8:36). Our freedom, like Jesus', will now become a threat to the existing order of things. It is no mere coincidence that immediately after Jesus says, "You will be free indeed," he says, "Yet you seek to kill me" (John 8:37).

Conversion in the Bible is always firmly grounded in history; it is always addressed to the actual situation in which people find themselves. In other words, biblical conversion is historically specific. People are never called to conversion in an historical vacuum. They turn to God in the midst of concrete historical events, dilemmas, and choices. That turning is always deeply personal, but it is never private. It is never an abstract or theoretical concern; conversion is always a practical issue. Any idea of conversion that is removed from the social and political realities of the day is simply not biblical.

In the biblical narratives, the "from" and "to" of conversion are usually quite clear. Conversion is from sin to salvation, from idols to God, from slavery to freedom, from injustice to justice, from guilt to forgiveness, from lies to truth, from darkness to light, from self to others, from death to life, and much more.[6] Conversion always means to turn to God. But what it means to turn to God is both universal and particular to each historical situation. We are called to respond to God always *in the particulars* of our own personal, social, and political circumstances. But conversion is also universal: it entails a reversal of the historical givens *whatever they may be* at any place and time—first-century Palestine, sixteenth-century Europe, or the United States in the 1990s. As such, conversion will be a scandal to accepted wisdoms, status quos, and oppression arrangements. Looking back at biblical and saintly conversions, they can appear romantic. But in the present, conversion is more than a promise of all that might be; it is also a threat to all that is. To the guardians of the social order, genuine biblical conversion will seem dangerous.

In both the Old and New Testaments conversion involved a "change of lords."[7] Conversion from idolatry is a constant biblical theme: false gods enter the household of faith; alien deities command an allegiance that rightly belongs to God alone. The people, then as now, resisted the naming of their idols and stubbornly clung to them. What were the idols that lured the people to God? Which were the false gods that demanded service and fidelity? Our contemporary idols are not so different from those of biblical times: wealth, power, pride of self, pride of nation, sex, race, military might, etc. Conversion meant a turning away from the reigning idolatries and turning back to the true worship of the living God.

There are no neutral zones or areas of life left untouched by biblical conversion. It is never solely confined to the inner self, religious consciousness, personal morality, intellectual belief, or political opinion. Conversion in Scripture was not a self-improvement course or a set of guidelines to help people progress down the same road they were already traveling. Conversion was not just added to the life they were already living. The whole of life underwent conversion in the biblical accounts. There were no exceptions, limitations, or restrictions.

If we believe the Bible, every part of our lives belongs to the God who created us and intends to redeem us. No part of us stands apart from God's boundless love; no aspect of our lives remains untouched by the conversion that is God's call and God's gift to us. Biblically, conversion means to surrender ourselves to God in every sphere of human existence: the personal and social, the spiritual and economic, the psychological and political.

Conversion is our fundamental decision in regard to God. It marks nothing less than the ending of the old and the emergence of the new. "When anyone is united to Christ, there is a new world; the old has gone, and a new order has already begun" (2 Cor. 5:17, New English Bible). Heart, mind, and soul, being, thinking, and doing—all are remade in the grace of God's redeeming love. This decision to allow ourselves to be remade, this conversion, is neither a static nor a once-and-finished event. It is both a moment and a process of transformation that deepens and extends through the whole of our lives. Many think conversion is only for nonbelievers, but the Bible sees conversion as also necessary for the erring believer, the lukewarm community of faith, the people of God who have fallen into disobedience and idolatry.[8]

The people of God are those who have been converted to God and to God's purposes in history. They define their lives by their relationship to the Lord. No longer are their lives organized around their own needs or the dictates of the ruling powers. They belong to the Lord and serve God alone. They have identified themselves with the kingdom of God in the world, and the measure of their existence is in doing God's will. Transformed by God's love, the converted experience a change in all their relationships: to God, to their neighbor, to the world, to their possessions, to the poor and dispossessed, to the violence around them, to the idols of their culture, to the false gods of the state, to their friends, and to their enemies. The early church was known for these things. In other words, the early Christians were known for the things their conversion wrought. Their conversion happened in history; and, in history, the fruits of their conversion were made evident.

Biblical conversion is never an ahistorical, metaphysical transaction affecting only God and the particular sinner involved. Conversion happens in individuals in history; it affects history and is affected by history. The biblical accounts of conversion demonstrate that conversion occurs *within* history; it is not something that occurs in a private realm apart from the world and is then *applied* to history.[9]

The goal of biblical conversion is not to save souls apart from history but to bring the kingdom of God into the world with explosive force; it begins with individuals but is for the sake of the world. The more strongly present that goal is, the more genuinely biblical a conversion is. Churches today are tragically split between those who stress conversion but have forgotten its goal, and those who emphasize Christian social action but have forgotten the necessity for conversion. Today's converts need their eyes opened to history as much as today's activists need their spirit opened to conversion. But first, both need to recover the original meaning of conversion to Jesus Christ and to his kingdom. Only then can our painful division be healed and the integrity of the church's proclamation be restored. Only then can we be enabled to move beyond the impasse that has crippled and impoverished the churches for so long.

Conversion in the New Testament can only be understood from the perspective of the kingdom of God. The salvation of individuals and the fulfillment of the kingdom are intimately connected and are linked in the preaching of Jesus and the apostles. The powerful and compelling call to conversion in the Gospels arose directly out of the fact of an inbreaking new order. To be converted to Christ meant to give one's allegiance to the kingdom, to enter into God's purposes for the world expressed in the language of the kingdom. The disciples couldn't have given themselves to Jesus and then ignored the meaning of his kingdom for their lives and the world. Their conversion, like ours, can only be understood from the vantage point of the new age inaugurated in Jesus Christ. They joined him, followed him, transferred their allegiance to him, and, in so doing, became people of the new order. His gospel was the good news of the kingdom of God. There is no other gospel in the New Testament. The arrival of Jesus was the arrival of the kingdom.

Our conversion, then, cannot be an end in itself; it is the first step to entry into the kingdom. Conversion marks the birth of the movement out of a merely private existence into a public consciousness. Conversion is the beginning of active solidarity with the purposes of the kingdom of God in the world. No longer preoccupied with our private lives, we are engaged in a vocation for the world. Our prayer becomes, "Thy kingdom come, they will be done, on earth as it is in heaven." If we restrict our salvation to only inner concerns, we have yet to enter into its fullness. Turning from ourselves to Jesus identifies us with him in the world. Conversion, then, is to public responsibility—but public responsibility as defined by the kingdom, not by the state. Our own salvation, which began with a personal decision about Jesus Christ, becomes intimately linked with the fulfillment of the kingdom of God. The connection between conversion and the kingdom cannot be emphasized enough.[10]

But what if our particular conversion is misshaped by an inadequate preaching of the Gospel or the church's lack of faith? What if our particular conversion event knows little of the intimate connection between conversion and the kingdom? We must submit our conversion to the standard of Scripture. Having stressed the importance of the kingdom, we will now turn to Jesus' own description of it.

The preaching of John the Baptist set the stage for Jesus. His radical call to repentance was clearly in the prophetic tradition, which always called the people of God to return. Jesus' preaching followed directly upon John's call to the people to repent and believe the good news of the kingdom which he came to announce. Both called for the fundamental turning that is always the substance of conversion. After the announcement of the kingdom, Jesus called his disciples and quickly moved on to set forth the meaning of his kingdom. His description of the new order is found in the Sermon on the Mount (Matt. 5-7; Luke 6). The Sermon explains what the kingdom is all about. Its message is clear and compelling. The Sermon is a practical vision of how to live in the new order and of what it will mean to follow Jesus. It is not a new law, but it is a vivid description of the kind of behavior involved in accepting the good news of the kingdom.

In fact, the Sermon on the Mount is the declaration of the kingdom of God, the charter of the new order. It describes the character, priorities, values, and norms of the new age Jesus came to inaugurate. The early church took it to be a basic teaching on the meaning of the kingdom; the Sermon was used to instruct new converts in the faith.

Examining the content of the Sermon, we quickly realize that this new order is not as theoretical and abstract as we might have hoped. It has to do with very concrete things. Jesus speaks to the basic stuff of human existence. He concerns himself with money, possessions, power, violence, anxiety, sexuality, faith and the law, security, true and false religion, the way we treat our neighbor, and the way we treat our enemies. At stake are not just religious issues. These are the basic questions that every man and woman must come to terms with and make choices about. The way we respond to these issues will determine our allegiance to the kingdom of God.

Yet, the Sermon begins not with a list of obligations but with a series of blessings. The beatitudes, as they are called, reveal the heart of Jesus and the core values of the kingdom. Jesus' blessings are for the poor, both in spirit and in substance. They know their need of God. He promises comfort to those who have learned how to weep for the world. Those with a meek and gentle spirit will have the earth for their possession. He blesses both those who are hungry for justice and those who show mercy; they will receive satisfaction and obtain mercy. It is the pure in heart, he says, who will see God. Jesus blesses the peacemakers and says they will be called God's own children. Finally, he blesses all those who suffer unjustly for the cause of right; the kingdom of heaven will be theirs. This is the personality of the kingdom. It is straightforward. It is both gentle and strong.

Jesus goes on to counsel his disciples to live simply and without hypocrisy. He tells them to trust God for their care and security rather than relying on the accumulation of possessions. In Luke's account of the beatitudes, Jesus pronounces a series of "woes" upon the rich and warns of the judgment that awaits them. He tells his followers to turn the other cheek when attacked and to go the extra mile when prevailed upon. Jesus instructs his disciples to love their enemies and not to return evil for evil. If they live this way, they will be like salt and light to the world. If they seek the kingdom of God first and value it above all else, everything they ever need will be theirs as well.

Jesus concludes by saying that his disciples, like good and bad trees, will be known by the fruit they bear. Not everyone who calls him Lord will enter the kingdom, but only those who obey his words. They will be like the wise person who builds a house solidly, on a good foundation; when the rains come, that person will be prepared. Those who don't listen to Jesus' words will be washed away because their houses are built on sand.

Blessing and cursing in the Bible are matters of life and death. Blessing is life and the power of God poured into our lives. Cursing is, inevitably, to die. Clear in the Sermon is the fact that the specific things that Jesus blesses are the very things we most try to avoid. On the other hand, the things that are so opposite to the description of the kingdom are the things we seek most eagerly. We can only conclude that the values of the kingdom of God are utterly incompatible with our own values and the way of the world. Our culture rejects those who live in the way Jesus calls blessed. Only those who are willing to be despised by the world are ready to enter the kingdom of God. The Sermon reveals that God's will for us is completely different from our own inclinations and social training.

The kingdom indeed represents a radical reversal for us. Aggrandizement, ambition, and aggression are normal to us and to our society. Money is the measure of respect, and power is the way to success. Competition is the character of most of our relationships, and violence is regularly sanctioned by our culture as the final means to solve our deepest conflicts. The scriptural advice "Be anxious for nothing" challenges the heart of our narcissistic culture, which, in fact, is anxious over everything. To put it mildly, the Sermon on the Mount offers a way of life contrary to what we are accustomed. It overturns our assumptions of what is normal, reasonable, and responsible. To put it more bluntly, the Sermon stands our values on their heads.

Not everyone responded to this upside-down value system the way the fishermen did. The chief priests and scribes were critical and unbelieving from the beginning. These leaders of society, the holders of wealth and power, plotted against Jesus, mocked him, and sought to destroy him. They wielded religious and political authority. Jesus showed no respect or deference toward any of them. Some of his harshest words were reserved for them. He called them "hypocrites" and "vipers;" referred to his political rulers as a "fox." Jesus' teaching and behavior created conflict with the ruling authorities wherever he went. The kingdom he proclaimed undermined their whole system. His confrontation with the religious and economic powers in the temple was the incident that led to his crucifixion.[11]

To receive his kingdom, Jesus said we had to become as open as children (Mark 10:13-15). Wealth would be a great obstacle (Mark 10:21-25). Pride, self-satisfaction, and complacency would be enemies of his kingdom. Jesus said he came not to save those who already considered themselves righteous, but to call sinners to repentance (Mark 2:17). Humility would be necessary for conversion (Luke 18:10-14).

The Gospels and the book of Acts record examples of many conversions. The theme is constant. The good news of salvation created a changed heart and life in those who heard and received. Whether in Paul's language of being justified by faith instead of works, or in John's picture of passing from darkness to light, the movement is one from death to life.

The early Christians were referred to as the people of "the Way."[12] There is a lot in a name.

First, it is highly significant that they were called the people of *the Way*. Christians at the beginning were associated with a particular pattern of life. Their faith produced a discernible lifestyle, a way of life, a process of growth visible to all. This different style of living and relating both grew out of their faith and gave testimony to that faith. To all who saw, Christian belief became identified with a certain kind of behavior. Unlike our modern experience, there was an unmistakable Christian lifestyle recognized by believers and nonbelievers alike. That style of life followed the main lines of Jesus' Sermon on the Mount and his other teaching. To believe meant to follow Jesus. There was little doubt in anyone's mind: Christian discipleship revolved around the hub of the kingdom. The faith of these first Christians had clear social results. They became well known as a caring, sharing, and open community that was especially sensitive to the poor and the outcast.

Their love for God, for one another, and for the oppressed was central to their reputation. Their refusal to kill, to recognize racial distinctions, or to bow down before the imperial deities was a matter of public knowledge.

Aristides described the Christians to the Roman emperor Hadrian in this way: They love one another. They never fail to help widows; they save orphans from those who would hurt them. If they have something, they give freely to the man who has nothing; if they see a stranger, they take him home, and are happy, as though he were a real brother. They don't consider themselves brothers in the usual sense, but brothers instead through the Spirit, in God.[13]

The early Christians were known for the way they lived, not only for what they believed. For them, the two were completely intertwined.[14] The earliest title given to them reflected the importance of their kingdom lifestyle. They were not called the people of "the experience" or the people of "right doctrine" or even the people of "the church." Rather, they were the people of "the Way."

Second, it is equally significant that the Christians were known as *the people of the Way*.[15] More than just individuals who have been converted, they were now a people, a new community of faith, which has embarked together on a new way of life. The first thing Jesus did after announcing the kingdom was to gather a community. To follow Jesus meant to share Jesus' life and to share it with others. From the beginning, the kingdom would be made manifest through a people who shared a common life. Their visible fellowship would be the sign and the first fruits of God's new order begun in Jesus Christ. Those who had left everything to follow Jesus were given the gift of community with one another. Henceforth they would belong to Jesus and be inextricably bound together as brothers and sisters in the family of God. The call of Jesus was not only to a new commitment; it was also to a new companionship, a new community established by conversion.

The quality of life shared in the Christian community was a vital part of the evangelistic message of the early church. Christian fellowship became the companion of the Christian Gospel; demonstration was vitally linked to proclamation. The oneness of word and deed, dramatically evident in their life together, lent power and force to the witness of the early Christians. In a classic study of evangelism in the early church, Michael Green concludes: "They made the grace of God credible by a society of love and mutual care which astonished the pagans and was recognized as something entirely new. It lent persuasiveness to their claim that the New Age had dawned in Christ."[16] The word was not only announced but seen in the community of those who were giving it flesh.

The message of the kingdom became more than an idea. A new human society had sprung up, and it looked very much like the new order to which the evangelists pointed. Here love was given daily expression; reconciliation was actually occurring. People were no longer divided into Jew and Gentile, slave and free, male and female. In this community the weak were protected, the stranger welcomed. People were healed, and the poor and dispossessed were cared for and found justice. Everything was shared, joy abounded, and ordinary lives were filled with praise. Something was happening among these Christians that no one could deny. It was very exciting. According to Tertullian, people looked at the early Christians and exclaimed, "See how they love one another!"[17] The fervent character of Christian love not only bound them to one another; it also spilled over the boundaries of their own communities and extended to all in need. The economic sharing practiced by the early Christians, together with their generosity toward the poor, was one of the most evangelistic characteristics of their life. Radical, practical love became the key to their public reputation.

The basic movement of conversion is a change of allegiance to the kingdom of God, the good news which Jesus brings. To convert means to commit our lives unreservedly to Jesus Christ, to join his new order, and to enter into the fellowship of the new community. Our sins are forgiven, we are reconciled to God and to our neighbor, and our destiny becomes inextricably bound to the purposes of Christ in the world.

Evangelism is to this end. The purpose of evangelism is to call for conversion and to call for it in its wholeness. The most controversial question at stake in the world, and even in the church, is whether we will follow Jesus and live under the banner of his kingdom. The evangelist asks that question and aims it right at the heart of each individual and at the heartbeat of our society. Evangelism confronts each person with the decisive choice about Jesus and the kingdom, and it challenges the oppression of the old order with the freeing power of a new one. The gospel of the kingdom sparks a fundamental change in every life and is an intrusion into any social order, be it first-century culture or our twentieth-century world. Evangelism that is faithful to the New Testament will never separate the salvation of the individual from visible witness to God's kingdom on earth. Rather, biblical evangelists will show people how to "cast off the works of darkness" and how to live "as in the day" (Rom. 13:12, 13), in the light of the kingdom that is coming and has already begun in Christ Jesus.

In every renewal movement since the time of the early church, the true nature of conversion has been freed from the narrow limitations and restrictions imposed by the world, and the wholeness of conversion recovered. The power of evangelism is restored and the Gospel again becomes a message that turns things upside down. The task of the evangelist is not to make the Gospel easy but to make it clear. Instead of merely passing on knowledge or imparting an experience, evangelism should call for (and expect) a radical change in behavior and lifestyle.

The unequivocal assertion of the evangelist is that we are saved only through Jesus Christ. Evangelism refutes every ideological prescription for the salvation of the world, defying the suggestion that we can, after all, save ourselves.

The recovery of the fullness and centrality of conversion is essential to genuine renewal. The monastic movements of the Middle Ages, the radical reformation of the sixteenth century, and the evangelical revivals in eighteenth-century England and nineteenth-century America were each marked by a primary emphasis on conversion. That emphasis continues today in the revolutionary consciousness of Third World Christians. Gustavo Gutierrez calls conversion "the touchstone of all spirituality."[18]

Our need, in the rich countries of the northern hemisphere, is for a fresh consciousness of conversion. In the midst of social conditions so oppressive to others and to ourselves, we must again turn to Jesus. Then will authentic evangelism flower and genuine revival break forth in this land once more. But first we must examine and honestly face up to the ways our evangelism has been corrupted and our conversion distorted.

END NOTES

[1] See the article on "Conversion" by F. Laubach, J. Goetzmann, and U. Becker, in *The New International Dictionary of the New Testament*, ed. Colin Brown, 3 vols. (Grand Rapids: Zondervan, 1975-78) 1:353-362 (hereafter cited as NIDNT); and the article on "Strepho" by G. Bertram in the *Theological Dictionary of the New Testament*, ed. Gerhard Friedrich, trans. and ed. Geoffrey W. Bromiley, 10 vols. (Grand Rapids: Eerdmans, 1964-1976) 7:714-29 (hereafter cited as TDNT). Both of these New Testament dictionaries discuss the Hebrew roots of conversion.

The Hebrew verb *shub* is basically one of motion and preserves much of the real meaning of conversion as an actual turning around, a *reversal from* and *turning toward* something. The concept of conversion, however, is not exhausted by this one word. Walter Eichrodt shows that there are at least twenty common phrases used to indicate conversion and a return of God, including: to seek God, to humble oneself before God, to soften one's heart, to seek the good and hate the evil, to break up the fallow ground, etc. *Shub*, though, sums up all those other descriptions in a single, pregnant word.

The metaphor was an especially suitable one, for not only did it describe the required behavior as a real act—"to make a turn"—and so preserve the strong personal impact; it also included both the negative element of turning away from the direction taken hitherto and the positive element of turning towards, and so, when combined with prepositions, allowed the rich content of all the many other idioms to be reproduced tersely yet unmistakably (*Theology of the Old Testament*, Vol. 2, trans. J. A. Baker [London: SCM Press, 1967] 465-466).

[2] See Laubach, Goetzmann, and Becker, "Conversion," *NIDNT*, 1:353-362; Bertram, "Strepho," *TDNT*, 7:714-29; J. Behm and E. Wurthwein, "Metanoia," *TNDT*, 4:975-1008. The process of conversion is expressed in the New Testament by three primary word groups, which deal with its various aspects: *epistrephein*, *metamelomai*, and *metanoein*. Since *metamelomai* expresses the feeling of sorrow for sin without necessarily encompassing a turn to God, the other two terms become the predominant word groups that carry the central meaning of conversion in the New Testament. *Strephein* is the root for ten basic terms in the New Testament that refer to conversion and, in different contexts, may mean turn, return, turn around, turn back, be converted, change, turn away from, or conversion. *Metanoia* means conversion or repentance—in verb form, to repent or be converted.

The New Testament is full of other symbols that describe conversion. The fact that these two primary word groups do not occur often in Paul or John does not mean that the idea of conversion is not present there, but only that in the time between the writing of the Gospels and the epistles a more specialized terminology had developed. Both Paul and John convey the idea of conversion through the imagery of faith. Paul speaks of conversion as "being in Christ," as the "dying and rising with Christ," as the "new creation," or as "putting on the new man." John represents the new life in Christ as "new birth," as passing from death to life and from darkness to light, as the victory of truth over falsehood, and of love over hate.

[3]Karl Barth describes conversion as a twofold call to "halt" and then to "proceed" out of our sleep. Once awakened, we realize we are going down the wrong road and need to have our feet set upon a new one. Our former movement is halted, and we are told to proceed in another direction. The two movements of halting and proceeding belong together says Barth, and form the essential unity of conversion. Karl Barth, "The Awakening to Conversion," in *Church Dogmatics*, trans. G. W. Bromiley (Edinburgh: T. & T. Clark, 1958) IV/2:560-561.

[4]What did Jesus mean when he said "repent?" Joachim Jeremias tries to answer this question by looking especially at the parables. See his *New Testament Theology* (New York: Scribner's, 1971) 153. Jeremias notes that Jesus demands repentance in its breadth and depth by presenting a whole series of new pictures. The pictures are always concrete and specific to the person's situation. Jesus "expects the publican to stop cheating (Luke 19:8), the rich man to turn away from his service of Mammon (Mark 10:17-31), the conceited man to turn away from pride (Matt. 6:1-18). If a man has dealt unjustly with another, he is to make good (Luke 19:8). From hence forward, life is to be ruled by obedience to the word of Jesus (Matt. 7:24-27), the confession of him (Matt. 10:32f.), and by discipleship that comes before all other ties (verse 37).

[5]Gabriel Fackre, *Word in Deed: Theological Themes in Evangelism* (Grand Rapids: Eerdmans, 1975) 84-94. Fackre's chapter on conversion is a well-organized summary of the meaning of conversion as it is understood in this book. Conversion is primarily a turning, which always involves a "turning from something" and a "turning toward something." Conversion is turning to Christ in repentance and faith. *Epistrephein* always includes the element of faith. Since the connotation of metanoia is less broad (it refers to repentance), faith is often expressly used in a complementary way with it. If there is a distinction to be made between the two New Testament words, then *metanoia* emphasizes somewhat more strongly the element of turning away from the old, and *epistrephein* emphasizes turning toward the new (see Fackre 85).

[6]This is only a partial listing of the innumerable threads that are part of the whole cloth of conversion. A more exhaustive list might include: from fear to hope, from spiritual blindness to the light of Christ, from idolatry to true worship, from control to relinquishment, from despair to joy, from wealth to simplicity, from the Bomb to the Cross, from alienation to reconciliation, from domination to servanthood, from anxiety to prayer, from false security to trust, from selfishness to sacrifice, from superiority to equality, from chauvinism to mutuality, from

consumption to conservation, from accumulating to giving away, from hate to love of enemies, from swords to plowshares, from mammon to the God of the poor, from violence to peace, from exploitation to justice, from hardness to heart to compassion, from oppression to liberation, from individualism to community, from America first to Jesus first.

[7]Laubach, Goetzmann, and Becker, "Conversion," *NIDNT*, 1:355. "Conversion involves a change of lords. The one who until then has been under the lordship of Satan (cf. Eph. 2:1f.) comes under the lordship of God, and comes out of darkness into light (Acts 26:18; cf. Eph. 5:8)."

[8]See Walter E. Conn, ed., *Conversion: Perspectives on Personal and Social Transformation* (Staten Island, N.Y.: Alba House, 1978). The overall thrust of this book is that conversion is a progressive, integrative process that has consequences in society—not merely in the spiritual life of the individual. Conversion is not a single event, but an ongoing process in which the totality of a person's life is transformed. Also see Orlando E. Costas, "Conversion as a Complex Experience: A Personal Case Study," in *Down to Earth: Studies in Christianity and Culture*, ed. John R. W. Stott and Robert Coote (Grand Rapids: Eerdmans, 1980). In addition to showing that conversion is a continuous process, Costas emphasizes the "challenge of conversion inside the church. . . . In order to call others to conversion, it must be converted itself." Conversion is most often used for the turning of unbelievers for the first time to God (Acts 3:19; 26:20), but sometimes it is linked to erring believers (James 5:19f.) who are brought back into a right relations with God (see G. Bertram, "Epistrepho," *TDNT*, 7:727). Repentance (metanoia) can likewise be used of believers, and is found in reference to the problem of apostasy inside the church (Rev. 2:5, 16, 21, 22; 3:3, 19).

[9]See Lesslie Newbigin, *The Finality of Christ* (Richmond: John Knox Press, 1969) 93-94. Newbigin describes the historical characteristic of the call to conversion as found in the prophets and in John:

It is a call to concrete obedience here and now in the context of the actual issues of the day.... Conversion is [not] some sort of purely inward and spiritual experience which is later followed by a distinct and different decision to act in certain ways. The idea that one is first converted, and then looks round to see what one should do as a consequence, finds no basis in Scripture. And yet this idea (perhaps not usually expressed so crudely) is very common.... A careful study of the biblical use of the language of conversion, of returning to the Lord, will show that, on the contrary, it is always in the context of concrete decisions at the given historical moment.

[10]According to Newbigin, one of the "very practical and indeed painful" questions that conversion brings to a focus is the relation of Christ to our secular history:

Conversion has always an ethical content; it involves not only joining a new community but also accepting a new pattern of conduct. Conversion implies that the convert accept this new pattern of conduct as that which is relevant for the doing of God's will and the fulfillment of his reign at this particular juncture of world history. Every conversion is a particular event shaped by the experience of the convert and by the life of the church as it is at that place and time (Newbigin, *The Finality of Christ* 91).

[11]See Richard J. Cassidy, *Jesus, Politics and Society: A Study of Luke's Gospel* (Maryknoll: Orbis Books, 1980). A good summary of relevant material about Jesus' relationship to the authorities can be found in chapter 4, "Jesus and His Political Rulers" (50-62). Several appendices provide helpful historical background about the Romans and the religious rulers of Jesus' day.

[12]See Acts 9:2; 19:9, 23; 22:4, 24:14, 22. While the word *way* is used, both literally and figuratively, more than one hundred times in the New Testament, its use in an unconditional and absolute sense as a name for the Christian movement is unique to these six passages in Acts. English translations usually capitalize it as "the Way," which becomes a designation for the Christian community and its preaching. G. Ebel, "Way," *NIDNT*, 3:933-947; Wilhelm Michaelis, "Hodos," *TDNT*, 5:42-114.

While the origin of the self-designation has not yet been fully explained, most scholars would agree that the Christian's unique lifestyle contributed to the name. The dictionaries mentioned above emphasize this term as a "designation for Christians and their proclamation of Jesus Christ, which includes the fact that this proclamation also comprises a particular walk or life or way," and refer to "the mode of life which comes to expression in the Christian fellowship."

[13]From Aristides, *Apology 15*, in The Ante-Nicene Fathers, ed. Allan Menzies, 5th edition (New York: Charles Scribner's Sons, 1926) 9:263-279.

[14]The pagan religions of the day stood in stark contrast to Christian faith both in their separation of belief from behavior and in their refusal to require exclusive loyalty to any one god. As we have seen, biblical conversion demanded a total change of life direction: it forged the vital connection between faith and discipleship, and it called for absolute allegiance to the true and living God. The claim on the lives of Christian converts was total, unlike the partial and syncretistic observances of the pagan deities. In an atmosphere of lukewarm religious pluralism, the single-minded commitment of Christian conversion "stood out like a sore thumb," says Michael Green. There is a good study of this contrast in the "conversion" chapter (chapter 6) of Green's *Evangelism in the Early Church* (Grand Rapids, Mich.: Eerdmans, 1970): "Hellenistic man did not regard ethics as part of religion.... This separation of belief from behavior was one of the fundamental differences between the best of pagan philosophical religion and Christian religion.... Conversion, then, in our sense of an exclusive change of faith, of ethnic, of cult was indeed utterly foreign to the mentality of the Graeco-Roman world" (146).

A. D. Nock's classic study, *Conversion* (London: Oxford University Press, 1933), comes to the same conclusion: Christian conversion "demanded a new life in a new people" and was a radical change in behavior as well as belief (p. 7f.). This all-encompassing quality of conversion is stressed by Nock's contrast between Christian conversion and what he calls general religious "adhesion." Adhesion is the label-changing kind of conversion that was characteristic of other religious cults.

[15]One recent study concludes that the amazing spread of early Christianity was due to "a single, over-riding *internal factor* . . . the radical sense of Christian community—open to all, insistent on absolute and exclusive loyalty, and concerned for every aspect of the believer's life. From the very beginning, the one distinctive gift of Christianity was this sense of community." J. G. Gager, *Kingdom and Community: The Social World of Early Christianity* (Englewood Cliffs, N.J.: Prentice Hall, 1975) 140.

[16]Michael Green, *Evangelism in the Early Church*, (Grand Rapids: Eerdmans, 1970) 120.

[17]This is quoted from Tertullian's *Apology 39* in William J. Walsh and John P. Langan, "Patristic Social Consciousness: The Church and the Poor," *The Faith That Does Justice: Examining the Christian Sources for Social Change*, ed. John C. Haughey (New York: Paulist Press, 1977) 138.

[18]Gustavo Gutierrez, *A Theology of Liberation*, trans. and ed. by Sr. Caridad Inda and John Eagleson (Maryknoll: Orbis Books, 1973) 205.

Chapter 4

The Development of Catholic Social Teaching

John A. Coleman, S.J.

The American Catholic bishops issued their influential document, *Economic Justice for All: Catholic Social Teaching and the U.S. Economy*, in 1986. Three years earlier, the Canadian bishops upset (some said, "intruded upon") the Canadian political debate with their pastoral letter, *Ethical Reflections on the Economic Crisis.*

Confronted with these two events, many commentators have wondered aloud, "Why this new Catholic voice on social issues?"

A LONG TRADITION OF SOCIAL CONCERNS

In 1991, worldwide Catholicism celebrates a hundred years of Catholic "social encyclicals," beginning with Pope Leo XIII's letter, *Rerum Novarum* in 1891, which endorsed the labor movement's struggle for unions and a just wage. In that first modern Catholic social charter, Leo stated:

When there is a question of defending the rights of individuals, the poor and badly-off have a claim to special consideration. The richer class have many ways of shielding themselves... whereas the mass of the poor must chiefly depend upon the assistance of the state.

Forty years later, Pope Pius XI added to this corpus of Catholic social thought with his 1931 encyclical, *Quadragesimo Anno.* Writing during the great depression, Pius XI deplored monopoly capitalism and the replacement of a free market by economic domination. The pope brought a cautious suspicion to bear on both capitalism and socialism. He approved, under certain conditions, the nationalization of basic industries to serve the common good.

Reflecting on the church's critical attitude toward both liberal capitalism and Marxist collectivism, Ricardo Antoncich notes in his commentary on Catholic social teaching, *Christians in the Face of Injustice*, "Not only the Marxist ideology but the liberal as well — *and I mean the system itself and not simply the abuses of it (which might be corrected)* — call for great caution."

All the popes of the present century — notably John XXIII, Paul VI, and John Paul II — have added their distinctive contributions and updating to Catholic social thought.

Nor was the American bishops' letter of 1986 their first attempt to address economic issues. In 1919 they issued the provocative "Bishops' Program on Social Reconstruction" to address American post-war economic adjustments. Again, in 1940 and 1976 the American bishops issued major pastorals underscoring three persistent Catholic themes: (1) *A championing of the common good*, which means more than just the sum of disparate individual interests and common preferences. The common good structures society around notions and institutions that guarantee distributive justice, equality, and the claims of the needy. This common good undercuts purely utilitarian trade-offs or false individualism. (2) *A call to solidarity with the labor movement*. The bishops embrace unions, the right to strike, a just wage, and worker co-ownership and determination in industry. (3) *A recognition of the right to private property*, which includes a wide dispersion of property ownership. Moreover, as John Paul II states, "There is a social mortgage on all private property." The right to private property intends a collective good, however. The goods of the earth were created to serve all. Individual ownership and use of property makes sense only if it furthers this original creative purpose.

NEW ELEMENTS IN CATHOLIC SOCIAL TEACHING
SINCE VATICAN COUNCIL II

Despite this long history of Catholic social thought (which, of course, extends back beyond 1891 to the earliest times in the life of the church), there exist truly new elements in the tradition since Vatican Council II (1962-1965). It is possible, then, to speak of "a new Catholic voice in social issues." Seven of these elements provide background to the American and Canadian bishops' letters of the 1980s.

1. *A new humanism.* Catholic social thought has always been open to dialogue with non-Christian wisdom. An older understanding of "natural law" assumed that fundamental truths about economic justice and a social good could be known by all men and women of good will. Unfortunately, early Catholic "natural law" thought often saw society as a pre-ordained static order, untouched by historical development.

At Vatican II, however, especially in the document on "The Church in the Modern World" (#55), the Catholic bishops argued that creating a just society is a human project, discerned in the struggles for justice in history. Human beings are defined, above all, by their joint responsibility for history and one another. The "natural law" on this reading is dynamic; it unfolds in history and demands that Catholics cooperate with other Christians, Jews, and men and women of good will.

Since John XXIII, the papal social encyclicals have addressed themselves not just to Catholics but to "all persons of good will." Catholics recognize a rightful autonomy to the temporal order. If popes make ethical judgments about economic and political systems, they do not pretend to have some "Catholic blueprint" for just economies. The common good is a joint social project. Dialogue and the consensus of all citizens concerned for a common good characterize this new political humanism. While the church goes public with its ethical wisdom in its social training, it must at the same time respect the nature of a public and pluralistic common good.

2. *A liberationist perspective.* Since the late 1960s, influential bishops and theologians, mainly from Latin America, have criticized taking the advanced industrial nations as the unique model for economic development, since they signal a subtle (or not so subtle) neo-colonialism in the world market economy, so that the poor remain dependent on the rich. Since Vatican II, Catholic social thought speaks of "the signs of the times," secular trends of hope or despair, of improvements or failures in justice arrangements, which call for gospel corrective or approval. It points to the emancipatory movements of social justice and human rights as signs of hope for a more just economic order, and calls upon Catholics to show solidarity with these movements. Moreover, this new tradition places great emphasis on the so-called "north-south debate" about a more just world trade, aid, transfer of technology, and debt policy.

Catholic thought insists, following Pope Paul VI in his 1967 encyclical, *Populorum Progressio*: "Today the principal fact that we must all recognize is that the social question has become worldwide." A liberationist perspective underscores interdependence of economies, and calls for wide-reaching structural reforms in the world market. This view distrusts (as John Paul II underscores in his recent encyclical, *Sollicitudo Rei*) those who would systematically subordinate the north-south debate to the power conflicts between the east-west blocs, or totally reduce justice to security concerns.

3. *A social structural dimension to sin.* Since Vatican II, popes and bishops refer to the classic Christian notion of sin in social and structural terms. When sin is seen uniquely as an individual failing, it can be overcome by individual moral change, a conversion of the heart. But when sin is understood in structural terms, liberation from sin involves structural, as well as moral, change and conversion. In his new encyclical, John Paul II states the relation between individual and structural sin:

> Structures of sin . . . are rooted in personal sin and thus always linked to the concrete acts of individuals who introduce these structures, consolidate them and make them difficult to remove. And thus they grown stronger, spread and become the source of other sins, and so influence people's behavior. (#36)

The pope cites examples of structural sin rooted in cultural distortions (for example, consumerism as a way of life) as well as instances in economic structures (for example, systemic unemployment or homelessness). Liberation from sin calls for a change of structures as well as a change of heart.

4. *A new openness to socialism.* Catholic social thought has long distrusted most forms of socialism because of their anti-religious bias, their over-exaggerated sense of class conflict which verges on hatred of the enemy, their notion of economic determinism which denies that history remains open to human choices, and their substitution of a centralized bureaucracy for economic initiative and decentralized units for planning and economic action. Catholicism espouses instead a doctrine of *subsidiarity* (to be discussed later), which champions decentralization. Still, especially since Paul VI, the church's social teaching has refused to condemn socialism as a possible economic option. Indeed, in his ground-breaking 1981 encyclical on human work, *Laborem Exercens*, John Paul II took as his starting point the characteristic economic questions of socialism.

If the answers of Catholic social thought about the economic order differ from many versions of socialism (as they differ from most versions of capitalism), the tradition frequently agrees with the socialist analysis of the situation of injustice. Speaking of western liberal capitalism and Marxist collectivism, John Paul II states in his latest encyclical that "the church does not show preference for one or the other, provided that human dignity is properly respected and promoted" and religious freedom granted. The pope wants to avoid the manipulation of the church by those, frequently in our own country, who use its aura to legitimate the reigning capitalist economic system. The pope continues:

> The church's social doctrine is not a "third way" between liberal capitalism and Marxist collectivism.... Nor is it an ideology but rather the accurate formulation of the results of a careful reflection on the complex realities of human existence, in society and in the international order, in the light of faith and of the church's tradition. Its main aim is to interpret these realities, determining their conformity with or divergence from the lines of the Gospel teaching on the human person and his vocation.... Its aim is thus to guide Christian behavior. (#41)

Catholic social thought, in this view, must combine careful social analysis with Gospel judgment. Neither alone will suffice.

5. *A preferential option for the poor.* In biblical thought, the litmus test for any society consists in the way it treats windows, orphans, alien farm workers — in short, the poor — in its midst. In the teaching of Jesus, the poor are called "God's poor," and to meet the poor is to meet Christ. Even the medieval church countered the right to private property with the "rights of the poor." First strongly enunciated by the Latin American bishops in their meeting at Puebla, Mexico, in 1979, this biblical idea of "a preferential option for the poor" has

become firmly grafted onto Catholic social thought. Pope John Paul II has endorsed it, as have the American and Canadian bishops. Hence, when the American bishops look at the U.S. economy, they state:

> Decisions must be judged in the light of what they do *for* the poor, what they do *to* the poor, and what they enable the poor to do *for themselves.* The fundamental moral criterion for all economic decisions, policies and institutions is this: they must be at the service *of all people, especially the poor.* (#24)

6. *The priority of labor over capital.* In his 1981 encyclical on work, John Paul II enunciates a Catholic version of the labor theory of value. He stresses, first, that "the basis for determining the value of human work is not primarily the kind of work being done, but the fact that the one doing it is a person. . . . In the first place work is 'for man' and not man 'for work.'" (#6) The prime error in early capitalism (and later socialism), in the pope's view,

> can be repeated wherever the human person is in a way treated on the same level as the whole complex of the material means of production, as an instrument, and not in accordance with the true dignity of his or her work — that is to say, where he or she is not treated as subject and maker, and for this very reason as the true purpose of the whole process of production. (#7)

Finally, against every reduction of persons to things, John Paul asserts the priority of labor over capital:

> We must emphasize and give prominence to the primacy of the human in the production process, the primacy of persons over things. Everything contained in the concept of capital, in the strict sense, is only a collection of things. Humans, as the subject of work and independent of work, in all that they do — humans alone are persons. (#12)

The pope expands the narrow Marxist notion of work to include the entrepreneur, the artist, the business manager. All have their place in the economy. Ultimately, the final judge of an economy is not an impersonal, technical criterion, but a personal judgment about what the economy does to the workers in it.

The American bishops were very conscious of John Paul's principle of the priority of labor over capital when they wrote their pastoral. Hence, they begin with three questions that reflect this priority:

> Every perspective on economic life that is human, moral and Christian must be shaped by three questions: What does the economy do for people? What does it do to people? And how do people *participate* in it? The economy is a human reality: men and women working together to

develop and care for the whole of God's creation. All this work must
serve the material and spiritual well-being of people. (#1)

(We have already seen that the bishops ask the same questions about the poor.)
And if this is what the economy is, in its essential reality — the human reality of
men and women working together to develop the goods of our earth — then
ordinary men and women have a legitimate say about the development of the
economy. They cannot leave it just to the experts.

7. *A new contextualism.* A final new element in Catholic social thought since
   Vatican II can be called a new contextualism. Each national church must
   address its own social and economic context, taking the wider Catholic social
   teaching's principles and applying them with bite and impact in their own
   context. Thus, the Brazilian bishops address justice issues connected with land
   development in the Amazon where large multinational firms drive small farmers
   from their ancestral land, or the Canadian bishops assess Canada's giant oil
   development projects in the northwest which displace the Indian tribes and
   cause environmental destruction. The charter for this new contextualism is Pope
   Paul VI's pastoral letter, *Octogesima Adveniens*:

   It is up to the Christian communities to analyze with objectivity the situation
   which is proper to their own country, to shed on it the light of the Gospel's
   unalterable words and to draw principles of reflection, norms of judgment
   and directives for action from the social teaching of the church. (#4)

THE AMERICAN BISHOPS' LETTER ON THE ECONOMY

In the American Catholic bishops' letter on the economy, the bishops seek to
take the above advice of Paul VI seriously and to provide "principles of reflection,
norms of judgment and directives for action" in the American context.

Before announcing their principles of reflection, the bishops first state why they
speak to the issue of the American economy. This church in its pastoral ministry
sees every day the faces of the poor, of young people struggling for jobs, of new
immigrants, of conscientious business people seeking new and more equitable
ways to organize resources and the workplace. The economy enters the rectories of
parishes in homeless persons asking for a place to sleep, in hungry persons asking
for food, in unemployed persons seeking resources to find work. Moreover, the
bishops themselves are managers of complex economic systems including schools,
hospitals, and agencies of charity outreach. Churches are investors and employers
in the American system, and cannot be excluded from the discussions about the
directions the American economy might take.

They assert the need to bring an *ethical perspective* to any discussion of the
economy and new economic policies:

Economic arrangements can be sources of fulfillment, of hope, of
community — or of frustration, isolation and even despair. They teach
virtues — or vices — and day by day help mold our characters. They

affect the quality of people's lives; at the extreme, even determining
whether people live or die. Serious economic choices go beyond merely
technical issues to fundamental questions of value and human purpose.
(#5)

Theirs is a new humanism that seeks "an ethical framework that can guide
economic life today in ways that are both faithful to the Gospel and shaped by
human experience and reason." (#61) They look to dialogue and consensus
with the wider public for "in the absence of a vital sense of citizenship among
the businesses, corporations, labor unions and other groups that shape
economic life, society as a whole is endangered." (#66) They root their hope
for structural renewal in "our belief that the country can attain a renewed
moral vision." (#27)

Five basic principles govern the bishops' moral assessment of the U.S.
economy:

1. *The principle of human dignity.* "The principles of the dignity of the human
person, realized in community with others, is the criterion against which all
aspects of economic life must be measured." (#28) Human dignity is both
personal and communal. Personal dignity flows from the creation of all humans
in the image of God. Communal dignity is rooted in the biblical concept of a
covenant, which is more than a mere utilitarian contract, since it entails a
relationship with God, with others in such extra-contractual relationships as
mercy and compassion, and with the earth's resources.

2. *The principle of solidarity.* Human life is life in community (#63). Thus:
What the Bible and Christian tradition teach, human wisdom confirms.
Centuries before Christ the Greeks and Romans spoke of the human
person as a 'social animal,' made for friendship, community, and public
life. These insights show that human beings achieve self-realization not in
isolation but in interaction with others. (#65)
So the bishops endorse neither rugged individualism as a cultural virtue, nor the
mindless tolerance of "do your own thing."

3. *The principle of justice and participation.* Here the bishops employ traditional
but important distinctions: (a) "Commutative justice calls for fundamental
fairness in all agreements and exchanges between individuals or private social
groups." (#69) Workers owe their employers diligent work; employers owe their
workers a fair wage and humane conditions of work. (b) "Distributive justice
requires that the allocation of income, wealth and power in society be evaluated
by its effects on persons whose basic material needs are unmet." (#70) Basic
human needs take preference over superfluous wants and luxury preferences. (c)
"Social justice implies that persons have an obligation to be active and
productive participants in the life of society and that society has a duty to enable
them to participate in this way." (#71)

Thus the bishops champion a version of economic democracy that would bring together the best of our American political and economic wisdom. Theirs is a radical proposal. We cannot leave the economy simply to technical experts, although they have a legitimate role to play. Justice itself, the bishops are saying, calls for a society in which all share in the decision-making. "Basic justice demands the establishment of minimum levels of participation in the life of the human society for all persons." (#76) This leads directly to the next principle.

4. The principle of *"the preferential option for the poor."* The principle, which we have already encountered, is best put in the bishops' own words:
    The prime purpose of this special commitment to the poor is to enable them to become active participants in the life of society. It is to enable all persons to share in and contribute to the common good. The option for the poor, therefore, is not an adversarial slogan that pits one group or class against another. Rather it states that the deprivation and powerlessness of the poor wounds the whole community. The extent of their suffering is a measure of how far we are from being a true community of persons. (#87)

5. *The principle of subsidiarity.* The bishops do not endorse a statist economy. They follow Catholic thought in championing initiatives by voluntary groups in the private sector, such as business, unions, and local community groups. The state is not the whole of society, nor has it a monopoly on defining the common good. Still, subsidiarity — a bias toward local initiative and intermediary groups between the state and the individual — must be counter-balanced. "The teachings of the church insist that government has a moral function: protecting the human rights and security basic justice for all members of the common-wealth." (#119) Catholic thought is not preoccupied with "getting government off our backs," nor does it subscribe to the notion that "that government is best which governs least." On the contrary, government has a moral responsibility to make sure the common good of justice for all is achieved.

Using these five basic principles, the bishops turn to selected economic policy issues: unemployment, poverty, food and agriculture, and the impact of the U.S. economy on developing nations. Here the bishops move from overall principles and norms to specific directives for action. For example: "Vigorous action should be undertaken to remove barriers to full and equal employment for women and minorities," (#196) since poverty and unemployment fall unequally on them. Again: "The tax system must be reformed to reduce the burden on the poor." (#199) And again: "Moderate sized farms operated by families on a full-time basis should be preserved and their economic viability protected." (#230)

It is important to note that, before writing their letter, the bishops held hearings at which economists, business and union leaders, welfare mothers, community organizers, and many others testified to what the economy was doing for, to — and against — people. James Tobin, Nobel Prize winner in economics, has stated that the bishops got their economics right because they provided a forum where representatives of *all* the voices in the land could be heard. But in their letter, the bishops carefully state that when they move from general principles to directions for action (relying on social science data), their teaching authority diminishes and is more open to debate and dissent. This is consistent with their acknowledgement of a rightful autonomy to the temporal and technical, so long as the latter does not become an amoral determinism.

Throughout the letter the aim is not only "to provide guidance for members of our own church as they seek to form their consciences about economic matters," but also to influence a larger public debate and discussion about the ethical quality of American economic life:

> We want to add our voice to the public debate about the directions in which the U.S. economy should be moving. We seek the cooperation and support of those who do not share our faith or tradition.... The questions are basic and the answers often elusive, but it is now time for serious and sustained attention to economic justice. (#27)

CANADA VS. THE UNITED STATES

The Canadian Catholic bishops, to whom reference was made at the beginning of this chapter, also want to contribute to "serious and sustained attention to economic justice." Rather than issuing one long and technical document on the economy, Canada's bishops have contributed to the Canadian economic discussion with a sustained series of reflections spanning more than fifteen years, on such topics as "Sharing Nation Income" (1972), "On Decent Housing for All" (1976), "Social Ethical Guidelines for Investment" (1979), "Toward a New International Economic Order" (1981), "Ethical Reflections on the Economic Crisis" (1982) and "Defending Workers' Rights: A New Frontier" (1985). (See *Do Justice* for this collection of letters.)

Like the U.S. bishops, the Canadians root their thought and reflections in earlier consultations with their people. They differ from their U.S. counterparts, however, in asserting "a much larger structural crisis in the international system of capitalism", and underscoring that social justice involves a struggle, even a conflict, in society. They also place great stress, beyond reformist tinkering, in facing alternative possibilities:

> What would it mean to develop an alternative economic model that would place emphasis on: socially useful forms of production; labour-intensive industries; self-reliant models of economic development; community ownership and control of industries; new forms of worker ownership and management; and greater use of the renewable energy sources in industrial production?

The Canadian priorities for ethical judgment are succinct and unequivocal:

> The needs of the poor have priority over the wants of the rich; the rights of workers are more important than the maximization of profits; the preservation of marginalized groups has precedence over the preservation of a system which excludes them.

(The history of these priority principles is quite interesting. They were first coined by David Hollenbach, S.J. in a book on human rights, *Claims in Conflict*, Paulist Press, 1979. Although he was one of the principal drafters of the American letter on the economy, modesty kept Hollenbach from quoting his own maxims in the American letter, although their spirit obviously pervades the American bishops' reflections. In speeches made during his visit to Canada, Pope Paul II adopted these principles as his own.)

Canada's bishops raise issues about the extent of foreign ownership of Canadian industry, and, more generally, the unregulated rule by multinational corporations whose wealth and power surpass that of many sovereign states. They squarely face elements of the third world in their own country, especially in parts of Quebec and the Maritime provinces, and address the flight of industry and jobs through plant closings.

Canadian Catholic social teaching is more ecumenical than in the United States. The Catholic bishops frequently issue joint statements and engage in common action with other Canadian churches. Moreover, speaking of socialism in Canada is not a taboo, as it frequently appears to be in the United States, and Canada has its own indigenous non-Marxist band of socialism in the NDF party, originally founded by Protestant social gospel thinkers.

The Canadian bishops teach a fivefold *method* for devising an appropriate church social teaching and action. We in the American churches could learn from it:

(1) being present with and listening to the experience of the poor, the marginalized, the oppressed in our society;

(2) developing a critical analysis of the economic, political and social structures that cause human suffering;

(3) making judgments in the light of Gospel principles and the social teachings of the church;

(4) stimulating creative thought and action regarding alternative visions and models for social and economic development;

(5) acting in solidarity with popular groups in their struggles to transform economic, political and social structures.

The latter two principles go beyond anything found in the American bishops' letter.

CONCLUSION

The Canadian and American Catholic bishops, taking a lead from international Catholic social thought, want to stimulate and contribute to a renewal of active citizenship and economic justice in our countries and world. They want to add, not impose, their voices in a wider dialogue about the quality of national economic life and international community. There are no indications that this new Catholic voice on social issues will soon fall silent. But to move from principles and directives to action will take the creative imaginations and applications of people in the pews and at their work benches and business offices.

That dialogue — widespread and involving every strand of active citizenship upon which our countries depend — had barely begun.

WORKS CITED

Antoncich, Ricardo. *Christians in the Face of Injustice*. Maryknoll: Orbis Books, 1987.

Canadian Conference of Catholic Bishops. *Ethical Reflections on the Economic Crisis*. Ottawa: CCCB Publications Service, 1983.

NCCB. *Economic Justice for All: Catholic Social Teaching and the U.S. Economy*. Washington, DC: USCC Publishing, 1986.

Pope John Paul II. *The Social Concern of the Church*. Washington, D.C.: USCC Publishing Office, 1989.

Sheridan S.J., E.F., ed. *Do Justice! — The Social Teaching of the Canadian Catholic Bishops*. Toronto: Jesuit Centre for Social Faith and Justice, 1987. (947 Queen St. East, Toronto, Ont. M4M 1J9)

Chapter 4A

Key Concepts
of
Catholic Social Teaching

Any summary of the major or key concepts of Catholic social teaching is difficult to draw up because there is such a large body of church teaching, and dangerous to publish since it is so likely that important items may be left out. Offered with all due caution, therefore, is the following list of key concepts which characterize Catholic social teaching today. This summary provides a useful tool for viewing what the Catholic Church has been teaching and for ensuring that our curriculum and programming embodies the central concepts of Catholic social teaching.

1. **Human Dignity** — The preeminent value placed on women and men, uniquely fashioned in God's image. This dignity must be affirmed by all individuals and institutions.

2. **Community** — Vital relationships that shape people and their world. People are created through and for community. Human dignity can be recognized and protected only in community with others.

3. **Interdependence** — The necessary linkage of all aspects of God's creation. Political and environmental crises proclaim on a large scale our dependence upon and basic interconnectedness with all of life.

4. **Cooperation** — Working with others toward a common goal. True cooperation demands that the goal and the means used to reach it be just.

5. **The Common Good** — A community approach to assessing ultimate value. Individual rights are not the only measure of goodness. Program and policy decisions made on both the local and international levels, (economic, political, cultural, social) must be weighed in light of their impact on the growth and development of all people.

6. **Multicultural Understanding** — The uniqueness, values, and traditions of every culture which deserve to be recognized, affirmed, and celebrated in community. Contemporary life demands and openness to and appreciation of other cultures.

7. **Global Solidarity** — The responsibility shared by all to promote the human rights, integration, and development of all the world's people. National and international structures have a special role to play in the promotion of human rights and the development of people.

8. **Stewardship** — The duty or responsibility to use the world's resources responsibly. All property has a "social mortgage," that is, is entrusted to individuals by God so that the needs of all people may be met.

9. **Change** — The continual process of growth or modification basic to life. As the pace of change quickens, openness to new ways of thinking, acting, and relating is essential so that all people may survive and thrive.

10. **Development** — The process of fulfilling human potential, particularly of those who are subject to hunger, poverty, or illness or who suffer from oppression and powerlessness.

11. **Transformation** — Change on the personal, relational, and structural levels which promotes the development of individuals and cultural or national groups.

12. **Distribution** — Equitable allocation of the world's resources (natural, property, income) to guarantee that the basic needs of all are met. Just distribution of resources is a pressing contemporary issue given the growing scarcity of natural resources and the increasing economic disparity among nations.

13. **Human Rights** — The minimum conditions necessary for the healthy growth of individuals and peoples. Minimum human rights include sufficient life goods, availability of education and work, cultural acceptance, economic justice, and the right to political participation.

14. **Political Participation** — Democratic participation in the decisions impacting one's life, expressed for example through freedom of speech and voting.

15. **Subsidiarity** — A principle of participation affirming the involvement of all individuals in the decision-making process who are likely to be impacted by the decisions made. Individuals and communities have a right and responsibility to be involved in the policies and programs that effect their lives.

16. **Empowerment** — Development and support of people's leadership skills aimed at breaking the dependency cycle and giving people greater control over their lives.

17. **Economic Justice** — Application of church social teaching to the economic sphere. Economic decisions should be made not just with an eye to profit but with careful consideration of the impact of such decisions on people's lives.

18. **Peace** — The natural fruit of justice between people and between nations. Justice is a prerequisite for true peace among peoples. The promotion of peace demands respect for human dignity, international cooperation, a more equitable distribution of the world's resources, and an end to the arms race.

19. **Simpler Lifestyle** — Limiting one's possessions and consumption of resources in order to live in greater solidarity with the poor of the world; sharing generously of one's resources so that others might live more fully.

20. **Option for the Poor** — A preferential active concern for the poor, whose needs and rights are given special attention in God's eyes. "Poor" is understood not just those who are economically deprived, but all who suffer from oppression or powerlessness.

Chapter 5

From One Earth
to One World

United Nations World Commission
on Environment and Development

AN OVERVIEW

In the middle of the 20th century, we saw our planet from space for the first time. Historians may eventually find that this vision had a greater impact on thought than did the Copernican revolution of the 16th century, which upset the human self-image by revealing that the Earth is not the center of the universe. From space, we see a small and fragile ball dominated not by human activity and edifice but by a pattern of clouds, oceans, greenery, and soils. Humanity's inability to fit its doings into that pattern is changing planetary systems, fundamentally. Many such changes are accompanied by life-threatening hazards. This new reality, from which there is no escape, must be recognized — and managed.

Fortunately, this new reality coincides with more positive developments new to this century. We can move information and goods faster around the globe than ever before; we can produce more food and more goods with less investment of resources; our technology and science give us at least the potential to look deeper into and better understand natural systems. From space, we can see and study the Earth as an organism whose health depends on the health of all its parts. We have the power to reconcile human affairs with natural laws and to thrive in the process. In this our cultural and spiritual heritages can reinforce our economic interests and survival imperatives.

This Commission believes that people can build a future that is more prosperous, more just, and more secure. Our report, *Our Common Future*, is not a prediction of ever increasing environmental decay, poverty, and hardship in an ever more polluted world among ever decreasing resources. We see instead the possibility for a new era of economic growth, one that must be based on policies that sustain and expand the environmental resource base. And we believe such growth to be absolutely essential to relieve the great poverty that is deepening in much of the developing world.

But the Commission's hope for the future is conditional on decisive political action now to begin managing environmental resources to ensure both sustainable human progress and human survival. We are not forecasting a future; we are serving a notice — an urgent notice based on the latest and best scientific evidence — that the time has come to take the decisions needed to secure the resources to sustain this and coming generations. We do not offer a detailed blueprint for action, but instead a pathway by which the peoples of the world may enlarge their spheres of co-operation.

THE GLOBAL CHALLENGE

SUCCESSES AND FAILURES

Those looking for success and signs of hope can find many: infant mortality is falling; human life expectancy is increasing; the proportion of the world's adults who can read and write is climbing; the proportion of children starting school is rising; and global food production increases faster than the population grows.

But the same processes that have produced these gains have given rise to trends that the planet and its people cannot long bear. These have traditionally been divided into failures of 'development' and failures in the management of our human environment.

There are also environmental trends that threaten to radically alter the planet, that threaten the lives of many species upon it, including the human species.

There has been a growing realization in national governments and multilateral institutions that it is impossible to separate economic development issues from environment issues; many forms of development erode the environmental resources upon which they must be based, and environmental degradation can undermine economic development. Poverty is a major cause and effect of global environmental problems. It is therefore futile to attempt to deal with environmental problems without a broader perspective that encompasses the factors underlying world poverty and international inequality.

Through our deliberations and the testimony of people at the public hearings we held on five continents, all the commissioners came to focus on one central theme: many present development trends leave increasing numbers of people poor and vulnerable, while at the same time degrading the environment. How can such development serve next century's world of twice as many people relying on the same environment? This realization broadened our view of development. We came to see it not in its restricted context of economic growth in developing countries. We came to see that a new development path was required, one that sustained human progress not just in a few places for a few years, but for the entire planet into the distant future. Thus 'sustainable development' becomes a goal not just for the 'developing' nations, but for industrial ones as well.

THE INTERLOCKING CRISES

Until recently, the planet was a large world in which human activities and their effects were neatly compartmentalized within nations, within sectors (energy, agriculture, trade), and within broad areas of concern (environmental, economic, social). These compartments have begun to dissolve. This applies in particular to the various global 'crises' that have seized public concern, particularly over the past decade. These are not separate crises: an environmental crises, a development crisis, an energy crisis. They are all one.

The planet is passing through a period of dramatic growth and fundamental change. Our human world of 5 billion must make room in a finite environment for another human world.

Economic activity has multiplied to create a $13 trillion world economy, and this could grow five- or tenfold in the coming half-century. Industrial production has grown more than fiftyfold over the past century, four-fifths of this growth since 1950. Such figures reflect and presage profound impacts upon the biosphere, as the world invests in houses, transport, farms, and industries. Much of the economic growth pulls raw material from forests, soils, seas, and waterways.

A mainspring of economic growth is new technology and while this technology offers the potential for slowing the dangerously rapid consumption of finite resources, it also entails high risks, including new forms of pollution and the introduction to the planet of new variations of life forms that could change evolutionary pathways. Meanwhile, the industries most heavily reliant on environmental resources and most heavily polluting are growing most rapidly in the developing world, where there is both more urgency for growth and less capacity to minimize damaging side effects.

These related changes have locked the global economy and global ecology together in new ways. Ecology and economy are becoming ever more interwoven — locally, regionally, nationally, and globally — into a seamless net of causes and effects.

Over the past few decades, life-threatening environmental concerns have surfaced in the developing world. Countrysides are coming under pressure from increasing numbers of farmers and the landless. Cities are filling with people, cars, and factories. Yet, at the same time, these developing countries must operate in a world in which the resources gap between most developing and industrial nations is widening, in which the industrial world dominates in the rule-making of some key international bodies, and in which the industrial world has already used much of the planet's ecological capital. This inequality is the planet's main 'environmental' problem; it is also its main 'development' problem.

The recent crisis in Africa best and most tragically illustrates the ways in which economics and ecology can interact destructively and trip into disaster. Triggered by drought, its real causes lie deeper. They are to be found in part in national policies that gave too little attention, too late, to the needs of smallholder agriculture and to the threats posed by rapidly rising populations. Their roots extend also to a global economic system that takes more out of a poor continent than it puts in. Debts that they cannot pay force African nations relying on commodity sales to overuse their fragile soils, thus turning good land to desert. Trade barriers in the wealthy nations — and in many developing ones — make it hard for Africans to sell their goods for reasonable returns, putting yet more pressure on ecological systems. Aid from donor nations has not only been inadequate in scale, but too often has reflected the priorities of the nations giving the aid, rather than the needs of the recipients. The production base of other developing world areas suffers similarly both from local failures and from the workings of international economic systems.

A majority of developing countries now have lower per capita incomes than when the decade began. Rising poverty and unemployment have increased pressure on environmental resources as more people have been forced to rely more directly upon them. Many governments have cut back efforts to protect the environment and to bring ecological considerations into developing planning.

The deepening and widening environmental crisis presents a threat to national security — and even survival — that may be greater than well-armed, ill-disposed neighbors and unfriendly alliances.

Globally, military expenditures total about $1 trillion a year and continue to grow. In many countries, military spending consumes such a high proportion of gross national product that it itself does great damage to these societies' development efforts.

The arms race — in all parts of the world — pre-empts resources that might be used more productively to diminish the security threats created by environmental conflict and the resentments that are fuelled by widespread poverty.

Many present efforts to guard and maintain human progress, to meet human needs, and to realize human ambitions are simply unsustainable — in both the rich and poor nations. They draw too heavily, too quickly, on already overdrawn environmental resource accounts to be affordable far into the future without bankrupting those accounts. They may show profits on the balance sheets of our generation, but our children will inherit the losses. We borrow environmental capital from future generations with no intention or prospect of repaying. They may damn us for our spendthrift ways, but they can never collect on our debt to them. We act as we do because we can get away with it: future generations do not vote; they have no political or financial power; they cannot challenge our decisions.

But the results of the present profligacy are rapidly closing the options for future generations.

SUSTAINABLE DEVELOPMENT

Humanity has the ability to make development sustainable — to ensure that it meets the needs of the present without compromising the ability of future generations to meet their own needs. The concept of sustainable development does imply limits — not absolute limits but limitations imposed by the present state of technology and social organization on environmental resources and by the ability of the biosphere to absorb the effects of human activities. But technology and social organization can be both managed and improved to make way for a new era of economic growth. The Commission believes that widespread poverty is no longer inevitable. Poverty is not only an evil in itself, but sustainable development requires meeting the basic needs of all and extending to all the opportunity to fulfill their aspirations for a better life. A world in which poverty is endemic will always be prone to ecological and other catastrophes.

Meeting essential needs requires not only a new era of economic growth for nations in which the majority are poor, but an assurance that those poor get their fair share of the resources required to sustain that growth.

In the end, sustainable development is not a fixed state of harmony, but rather a process of change in which the exploitation of resources, the direction of investments, the orientation of technological development, and institutional change are made consistent with future as well as present needs. We do not pretend that the process is easy or straightforward. Painful choices have to be made. Thus, in the final analysis, sustainable development must rest on political will.

THE INSTITUTIONAL GAPS

The objective of sustainable development and the integrated nature of the global environment/development challenges pose problems for institutions, national and international, that were established on the basis of narrow preoccupations and compartmentalized concerns. Governments' general response to the speed and scale of global changes has been a reluctance to recognize sufficiently the need to change themselves. The challenges are both interdependent and integrated, requiring comprehensive approaches and popular participation.

There is a growing need for effective international co-operation to manage ecological and economic interdependence.

The ability to anticipate and prevent environmental damage requires that the ecological dimensions of policy be considered at the same time as the economic, trade, energy, agricultural, and other dimensions. They should be considered on the same agendas and in the same national and international institutions.

This reorientation is one of the chief institutional challenges of the 1990s and beyond. Meeting it will require major institutional development and reform. Many countries that are too poor or small or that have limited managerial capacity will find it difficult to do this unaided. They will need financial and technical assistance and training. But the changes required involve all countries, large and small, rich and poor.

INTERNATIONAL CO-OPERATION
AND INSTITUTIONAL REFORM

THE ROLE OF THE INTERNATIONAL ECONOMY

Two conditions must be satisfied before international economic exchanges can become beneficial for all involved. The sustainability of ecosystems on which the global economy depends must be guaranteed. And the economic partners must be satisfied that the basis of exchange is equitable. For many developing countries, neither condition is met.

Growth, in many developing countries, is being stifled by depressed commodity prices, protectionism, intolerable debt burdens, and declining flows of development finance. If living standards are to grow so as to alleviate poverty, these trends must be reversed.

The present level of debt service of many countries, especially in Africa and Latin America, is not consistent with sustainable development. Debtors are being required to use trade surpluses to service debts, and are drawing heavily on non-renewable resources to do so. Urgent action is necessary to alleviate debt burdens in ways that represent a fairer sharing between both debtors and lenders of the responsibilities and burdens.

MANAGING THE COMMONS

Traditional forms of national sovereignty raise particular problems in managing the 'global commons' and their shared ecosystems — the oceans, outer space, and Antarctica. Some progress has been made in all three areas; much remains to be done.

There are growing concerns about the management of orbital space, centering on using satellite technology for monitoring planetary systems, on making the most effective use of the limited capacities of geosynchronous orbit for communications satellites, and on limiting space debris. The orbiting and testing of weapons in space would greatly increase this debris. The international community should seek to design and implement a space regime to ensure that space remains a peaceful environment for the benefit of all.

PEACE, SECURITY, DEVELOPMENT, AND THE ENVIRONMENT

Among the dangers facing the environment, the possibility of nuclear war is undoubtedly the gravest. Certain aspects of the issues of peace and security bear directly upon the concept of sustainable development. The whole notion of security as traditionally understood — in terms of political and military threats to national sovereignty — must be expanded to include the growing impacts of environmental stress — locally, nationally, regionally, and globally. There are no military solutions to 'environmental insecurity.'

Governments and international agencies should assess the cost-effectiveness, in terms of achieving security, of money spent on armaments compared with money spent on reducing poverty or restoring a ravaged environment.

But the greatest need is to achieve improved relations among those major powers capable of deploying weapons of mass destruction.

GETTING AT THE SOURCES

Governments must begin now to make the key national, economic, and sectorial agencies directly responsible and accountable for ensuring that their policies, programs, and budgets support development that is economically and ecologically sustainable.

All major international bodies and agencies should ensure than their programs encourage and support sustainable development, and they should greatly improve their coordination and co-operation.

DEALING WITH THE EFFECTS

Governments should also reinforce the roles and capacities of environmental protection and resource management agencies. This is needed in many industrialized countries, but most urgently in developing countries, which will need assistance in strengthening their institutions.

ASSESSING GLOBAL RISKS

The capacity to identify, assess, and report on risks of irreversible damage to natural systems and threats to the survival, security, and well-being of the world community must be rapidly reinforced and extended.

A new international program for co-operation among largely non-governmental organizations, scientific bodies, and industry groups should be established.

MAKING INFORMED CHOICES

Making the difficult choices involved in achieving sustainable development will depend on the widespread support and involvement of an informed public and of non-governmental organizations, the scientific community, and industry. Their rights, roles, and participation in development planning, decision making, and project implementation should be expanded.

PROVIDING THE LEGAL MEANS

National and international law is being rapidly outdistanced by the accelerating pace and expanding scale of impacts on the ecological basis of development. Governments now need to fill major gaps in existing national and international law related to the environment, to find ways to recognize and protect the rights of present and future generations to an environment adequate for their health and well-being.

INVESTING IN OUR FUTURE

Over the past decade, the overall cost-effectiveness of investments in halting pollution has been demonstrated. The escalating economic and ecological damage costs of not investing in environmental protection and improvement have also been repeatedly demonstrated — often in grim tolls of flood and famine. But there are large financial implications: for renewable energy development, pollution control, and achieving less resource-intensive forms of agriculture.

Multilateral financial institutions have a crucial role to play.

Given the limitations on increasing present flows of international aid, proposals for securing additional revenue from the use of international commons and natural resources should now be seriously considered by governments.

A CALL FOR ACTION

Over the course of this century, the relationship between the human world and the planet that sustains it has undergone a profound change.

When the century began, neither human numbers nor technology had the power to radically alter planetary systems. As the century closes, not only do vastly increased human numbers and their activities have that power, but major, unintended changes are occurring in the atmosphere, in soils, in waters, among plants and animals, and in the relationships among all of these. The rate of change is outstripping the ability of scientific disciplines and our current capabilities to assess and advise. It is frustrating the attempts of political and economic institutions, which evolved in a different, more fragmented world, to adapt and cope. It deeply worries many people who are seeking ways to place those concerns on the political agendas.

The onus lies with no one group of nations. Developing countries face the obvious life-threatening challenges of desertification, deforestation, and pollution, and endure most of the poverty associated with environmental degradation. The entire human family of nations would suffer from the disappearance of rain forests in the tropics, the loss of plant and animal species, and changes in rainfall patterns. Industrial nations face the life-threatening challenges of toxic chemicals, toxic wastes, and acidification. All nations may suffer from the releases by industrialized countries of carbon dioxide and of gases that react with the ozone layer, and from any future war fought with the nuclear arsenals controlled by those nations. All nations will have a role to play in changing trends, and in righting an international economic system that increases rather than decreases inequality, that increases rather than decreases numbers of poor and hungry.

The next few decades are crucial. The time has come to break out of past patterns. Attempts to maintain social and ecological stability through old approaches to development and environmental protection will increase instability. Security must be sought through change.

This Commission has been careful to base our recommendations on the realities of present institutions, on what can and must be accomplished today. But to keep options open for future generations, the present generation must begin now, and begin together.

A THREATENED FUTURE

The Earth is one but the world is not. We all depend on one biosphere for sustaining our lives. Yet each community, each country, strives for survival and prosperity with little regard for its impact on others. Some consume the Earth's resources at a rate that would leave little for future generations. Others, many more in number, consume far too little and live with the prospect of hunger, squalor, disease, and early death.

Yet progress has been made. Throughout much of the world, children born today can expect to live longer and be better educated than their parents. In many parts, the new-born can also expect to attain a higher standard of living in a wider sense. Such progress provides hope as we contemplate that improvements are still needed, and also we face our failures to make this Earth a safer and sounder home for us and for those who are to come.

The failures that we need to correct arise both from poverty and from the short-sighted way in which we have often pursued prosperity. Many parts of the world are caught in a vicious downwards spiral. Poor people are forced to overuse environmental resources to survive from day to day, and their impoverishment of their environment further impoverishes them, making their survival ever more difficult and uncertain. The prosperity attained in some parts of the world is often precarious, as it has been secured through farming, forestry, and industrial practices that bring profit and progress only over the short term.

Societies have faced such pressures in the past and, as many desolate ruins remind us, sometimes succumbed to them. But generally these pressures were local. Today, the scale of our interventions in nature is increasing and the physical effects of our decisions spill across national frontiers. The growth in economic interaction between nations amplifies the wider consequences of national decisions. Economics and ecology bind us in ever-tightening networks. Today, many regions face risks of irreversible damage to the human environment that threaten the basis for human progress.

These deepening interconnections are the central justification for the establishment of this Commission. We travelled the world for nearly three years, listening.

We found everywhere deep public concern for the environment, concern that has led not just to protests but often to changed behavior. The challenge is to ensure that these new values are more adequately reflected in the principles and operations of political and economic structures.

We also found grounds for hope: that people can cooperate to build a future that is more prosperous, more just, and more secure; that a new era of economic growth can be attained, one based on policies that sustain and expand the Earth's resource base; and that the progress that some have known over the last century can be experienced by all in the years ahead. But for this to happen, we must understand better the symptoms of stress that confront us, we must identify the causes, and we must design new approaches to managing environmental resources and to sustaining human development.

SYMPTOMS AND CAUSES

Environmental stress has often been seen as the result of the growing demand on scarce resources and the pollution generated by the rising living standards of the relatively affluent. But poverty itself pollutes the environment, creating environmental stress in a different way. Those who are poor and hungry will often destroy their immediate environment in order to survive: they will cut down forests; their livestock will overgraze grasslands; they will overuse marginal land; and, in growing numbers, they will crowd into congested cities. The cumulative effect of these changes is so far-reaching as to make poverty itself a major global scourge.

On the other hand, where economic growth has led to improvements in living standards, it has sometimes been achieved in ways that are globally damaging in the longer term. Much of the improvement in the past has been based on the use of increasing amounts of raw materials, energy, chemicals, and synthetics and on the creation of pollution that is not adequately accounted for in figuring the costs of production processes. These trends have had unforeseen effects on the environment. Thus today's environmental challenges arise both from the lack of development and from the unintended consequences of some forms of economic growth.

POVERTY

There are more hungry people in the world today than every before in human history, and their numbers are growing. In 1980, there were 340 million people in 87 developing countries not getting enough calories to prevent stunted growth and serious health risks. This total was very slightly below the figure for 1970 in terms of share of the world population, but in terms of sheer numbers, it represented a 14 percent increase. The World Bank predicts that these numbers are likely to go on growing.

The number of people living in slums and shanty towns is rising, not falling. A growing number lack access to clean water and sanitation and hence are prey to the diseases that arise from this lack. There is some progress, impressive in places. But, on balance, poverty persists and its victims multiply.

The pressure of poverty has to be seen in a broader context. At the international level there are large differences in per capital income, which ranged in 1984 from $190 in low-income countries (other than China and India) to $11,430 in the industrial market economies.

Such inequalities represent great differences not merely in the quality of life today, but also in the capacity of societies to improve their quality of life in the future.

These pressures are reflected in the rising incidence of disasters. During the 1970s, six times as many people died from 'natural disasters' each year as in the 1960s, and twice as many suffered from such disasters. Droughts and floods, disasters among whose causes are widespread deforestation and overcultivation, increased most in terms of numbers affected.

Such disasters claim most of their victims among the impoverished in poor nations, where subsistence farmers must make their land more liable to droughts and floods by clearing marginal areas, and where the poor make themselves more vulnerable to all disasters by living on steep slopes and unprotected shores — the only lands left for their shanties. Lacking food and foreign exchange reserves, their economically vulnerable governments are ill-equipped to cope with such catastrophes.

GROWTH

In some parts of the world, particularly since the mid-1950s, growth and development have vastly improved living standards and the quality of life. Many of the products and technologies that have gone into this improvement are raw material- and energy-intensive and entail a substantial amount of pollution. The consequent impact on the environment is greater than ever before in human history.

Over the past century, the use of fossil fuels has grown nearly thirtyfold, and industrial production has increased more than fiftyfold. The bulk of this increase, about three-quarters in the case of fossil fuels and a little over four-fifths in the case of industrial production, has taken place *since* 1950.

In recent years, industrial countries have been able to achieve economic growth using less energy and raw materials per unit of output. This, along with the efforts to reduce the emission of pollutants, will help to contain the pressure on the biosphere. But with the increase in population and the rise in incomes, per capita consumption of energy and materials will go up in the developing countries, as it has to if essential needs are to be met. Greater attention to resource efficiency can moderate the increase, but, on balance, environmental problems linked to resource use will intensify in global terms.

SURVIVAL

The scale and complexity of our requirements for natural resources have increased greatly with the rising levels of population and production. Nature is bountiful, but it is also fragile and finely balanced. There are thresholds that cannot be crossed without endangering the basic integrity of the system. Today, we are close to many of these thresholds; we must be very mindful of the risk of endangering the survival of life on Earth. Moreover, the speed with which changes in resource use are taking place gives little time in which to anticipate and prevent unexpected effects.

The 'greenhouse effect,' one such threat to life-support systems, springs directly from increased resource use.

Another threat arises from the depletion of the atmospheric ozone layer by gases released during the production of foam and the use of refrigerants and aerosols.

A variety of air pollutants are killing trees and lakes and damaging buildings and cultural treasures, close to and sometimes thousands of miles from points of emission.

In many cases the practices used at present to dispose of toxic wastes, such as those from the chemical industries, involve unacceptable risks. Radioactive wastes from the nuclear industry remain hazardous for centuries. Many who bear these risks do not benefit in any way from the activities that produce the wastes.

Desertification — the process whereby productive arid and semi-arid land is rendered economically unproductive — and large-scale deforestation are other examples of major threats to the integrity of regional ecosystems.

Many of the risks stemming from our productive activity and the technologies we use cross national boundaries; many are global. Though the activities that give rise to these dangers tend to be concentrated in a few countries, the risks are shared by all, rich and poor, those who benefit from them and those who do not.

Little time is available for corrective action. In some cases, we may already be close to transgressing critical thresholds. While scientists continue to research and debate causes and effects, in many cases we already know enough to warrant action. This is true, locally and regionally, in the cases of such threats as desertification, deforestation, toxic wastes, and acidification; it is true globally for such threats as climate change, ozone depletion, and species loss. The risks increase faster than do our abilities to manage them.

Perhaps the greatest threat to the Earth's environment, to sustainable human progress, and indeed to survival is the possibility of nuclear war, increased daily by the continuing arms race and its spread to outer space. The search for a more viable future can only be meaningful in the context of a more vigorous effort to renounce and eliminate the development of means of annihilation.

THE ECONOMIC CRISIS

The environmental difficulties that confront us are not new, but only recently have we begun to understand their complexity. Previously our main concerns centered on the effects of development on the environment. Today, we need to be equally concerned about the ways in which environmental degradation can dampen or reverse economic development. In one area after another, environmental degradation is eroding the potential for development. This basic connection was brought into sharp focus by the environment and development crises of the 1980s.

The heaviest burden in international economic adjustment has been carried by the world's poorest people. The consequence has been a considerable increase in human distress and the overexploitation of land and natural resources to ensure survival in the short term.

Many international economic problems remain unresolved: developing country indebtedness remains serious; commodity and energy markets are highly unstable; financial flows to developing countries are seriously deficient; protectionism and trade wars are a serious threat. Yet at a time when multilateral institutions, and rules, are more than ever necessary, they have been devalued. And the notion of an international responsibility for development has virtually disappeared. The trend is towards a decline in multilateralism and an assertion of national dominance.

NEW APPROACHES TO ENVIRONMENT AND DEVELOPMENT

Human progress has always depended on our technical ingenuity and a capacity for cooperative action. These qualities have often been used constructively to achieve development and environmental progress: in air and water pollution control, for example, and in increasing the efficiency of material and energy use. Many countries have increased food production and reduced population growth rates. Some technological advances, particularly in medicine, have been widely shared.

But this is not enough. Failures to manage the environment and to sustain development threaten to overwhelm all countries. Environment and development are not separate challenges; they are inexorably linked.

Development cannot subsist upon a deteriorating environmental resource base; the environment cannot be protected when growth leaves out of account the costs of environmental destruction. These problems cannot be treated separately by fragmented institutions and policies. They are linked in a complex system of cause and effect.

First, environmental stresses are linked to one another.

Second, environmental stresses and patterns of economic development are linked to one another.

Third, environmental and economic problems are linked to many social and political factors.

Finally, the systemic features operate not merely within but also between nations. National boundaries have become so porous that traditional distinctions between matters of local, national, and international significance have become blurred. Ecosystems do not respect national boundaries.

Many environment-economy links also operate globally.

Each country may devise national agricultural policies to secure short-term economic and political gains, but no nation alone can devise policies to deal effectively with the financial, economic, and ecological costs of the agricultural and trade policies of other nations.

What is required is a new approach, in which all nations aim at a type of development that integrates production with resource conservation and enhancement, and that links both to the provision for all of an adequate livelihood base and equitable access to resources.

The concept of sustainable development provides a framework for the integration of environment policies and development strategies — the term 'development' being used here in its broadest sense. The word is often taken to refer to the processes of economic and social change in the Third World. But the integration of environment and development is required in all countries, rich and poor. The pursuit of sustainable development requires changes in the domestic and international policies of every nation.

Sustainable development seeks to meet the needs and aspirations of the present without compromising the ability to meet those of the future. Far from requiring the cessation of economic growth, it recognizes that the problems of poverty and underdevelopment cannot be solved unless we have a new era of growth in which developing countries play a large role and reap large benefits.

The pursuit of sustainable development requires a new orientation in international relations. Long-term sustainable growth will require far-reaching changes to produce trade, capital, and technology flows that are more equitable and better synchronized to environmental imperatives.

The mechanics of increased international cooperation required to assure sustainable development will vary from sector to sector and in relation to particular institutions. But it is fundamental that the transition to sustainable development be managed jointly by all nations. The unity of human needs requires a functioning multilateral system that respects the democratic principle of consent and accepts that not only the Earth but also the world is one.

Overall, our report carries a message of hope. But it is hope conditioned upon the establishment of a new era of international cooperation based on the premise that every human being — those here and those who are to come — has the right to life, and to a decent life. We confidently believe that the international community can rise, as it must, to the challenge of securing sustainable human progress.

Chapter 5A

Global and Domestic Facts

DOMESTIC ISSUES

The gap between rich and poor is widening in the United States. The Census Bureau reported in 1989 that the poorest fifth of U.S. families received just 4.6% of total income - the lowest percentage since 1954. The wealthiest fifth accounted for 44% - the highest share ever recorded.

13.1% of the U.S. population lives below the poverty line; in 1988 the poverty line was set at $12,091 for a family of four.

Farmers have a higher poverty rate than the rest of the country. The farmer poverty rate in 1986 was 19.6%

Children constitute the poorest age group in the U.S. 20.5% of all children live in poverty: 1 in 7 whites; 1 in 2 blacks; and 2 in 3 Hispanics.

Almost 20% of U.S. jobs will not support a worker and two dependents.

The fastest growing group among the poor is the working poor. More than 8 million heads of household work full or part-time but earn less than official poverty level.

In 1985 about 20 million Americans, including 12 million children, were hungry at some point each month.

Medicaid, the health insurance program for the poor, covers only 42% of all poor families.

Poverty is an "integrated" problem; over two-thirds of the poor are white and just under one-third are Black, Hispanic, Asian, and American Indian.

Minority people are significantly overrepresented among the poor. In 1986 whites made up 84.8% of the population but had a poverty rate of 11%; Blacks had a poverty rate of 31.1% while constituting 12.1% of the population; Hispanics, who made up only 7.9% of the population, had a poverty rate of 27.3%.

INTERNATIONAL ISSUES

The heaviest burden in international economics is carried by the world's poorest people. Half the world's population lives in low-income developing countries where the average GNP per capita is $270 per year. In many urban areas, real minimum wages have declined by as much as 50%.

880 million adults in the world cannot read or write.

100 million have no shelter whatsoever.

Over 30 developing countries are dependent on a single commodity for 50% of their export earnings. Prices fluctuate, making economic planning difficult. Multinationals control more than 85% of each of the following: coffee, tea, cocoa, tobacco, cotton, and forest products.

More than a quarter-million of the world's small children die each week of easily preventable illness and malnutrition. If clean water were universally available, it is estimated that the world rate of infant mortality could be halved.

In the third world only 3 in 5 workers are fully employed.

90 million workers remain unemployed; another 300 million are underemployed.

For the very poorest, those who are forced to spend three quarters of their incomes on food, cuts in income can mean nothing else but the malnourishment of their children.

Each year 40 million people die from hunger and hunger related diseases.

In very poor countries, children may be ill for 30% to 50% of their young lives.

Each child born in the industrialized world will consume 20 to 40 times as much as a child born in the developing world in his or her lifetime.

The developed countries of the world (26% of population) consume 34% of the world's calories, 38% of its protein, and 53% of its fat; moving beyond food, they consume 85% of its paper, 79% of its steel, 86% of its other metals, and 80% of the world's commercial energy.

Chapter 6

A Balanced Spirituality

Donal Dorr

There is a passage in the book of Micah which is used as the chorus for a very beautiful hymn:

> This is what Yahweh asks of you, only this:
> That you act justly,
> That you love tenderly,
> That you walk humbly with your God. (Micah 6:8)

The three demands made by the Lord in this text provide the basis for a balanced spirituality. Many of the distorted spiritualities one meets today can be explained in terms of an over-emphasis on one or another of these three demands, to the neglect of others. In speaking of a spirituality here I do not mean just a set of theological ideas. I am thinking more of the outlook and attitudes we have; our spirituality is revealed not so much by the theories we propose as by the way we act and react. It is an implicit theology which, if we are reflective and articulate, may eventually become explicit—and then it is very convincing because it represents a truth that is lived.

WALK HUMBLY WITH YOUR GOD

We can begin by looking at the demand that we "walk humbly with God." I take this to refer to my personal relationship with God. Each one of us is called to a deeply personal religious conversion. This may be sudden or gradual; more likely it will come in the form of a combination of slow growth with some rather dramatic breakthroughs. What really matters is not so much the process as the effect—namely, an awareness that God has carved my name on the palm of God's hand, so that even if a woman should forget her baby at the breast, God will not forget me. (Is 49:15-16). This sense of the love and care of God is what changes the notion of providence from an abstract theological theory into a living experience. It is a consciousness that even the hairs of my head are numbered and that not even a sparrow falls to the ground without God's permission (Mt 10:29).

The sense of providence is both the cause and the effect of my conviction that it makes sense to speak of "the plan of God." God is acting in my life to carry out God's will for me; and what God wills is my salvation. The Lord is leading me, shaping me through the events of my daily life, enabling me to overcome obstacles and to grow in the way the Lord wants me, so that I can become fully human, fully healed, and therefore a person who is of the kingdom, as Jesus was.

I want simply to insist that theologians must resist the temptation to explain away either of the key elements of the Christian concept of providence, namely, God's sovereignty and human freedom. It may be difficult for the theologian to find some overall framework in which both elements are given their full weight. But theology is built on faith; it must respect the data of the Christian faith as found both in the Bible and in the living experience of Christians. So, as a theologian, I do not doubt that I am free—at least in some degree; that is part of my experience and of my faith. Neither do I doubt that my free human actions are somehow used as part of God's loving plan; that too is part of my faith—and even, in a sense, of my experience.

The sense of providence may begin with an awareness of God's care for me personally; but it does not end there—for otherwise religious conversion and personal religion would be reduced to a purely private affair between God and myself. I see the hand of God not merely in my own life but also in the lives of my friends. I can be led on to believe that God's plan of salvation is all-embracing—it touches the lives of nations as well as individuals. My trials, my rescue, my being led into a more authentic pattern of living, my whole destiny—all these are fitted by God into the destiny of my people and of all peoples. The Old Testament constantly keeps this perspective before us; for instance, God's care for Judith and for Cyrus is an integral part of the saving plan for God's people (Judith 9:5-14; 13:24-25; Is 45:1-6).

The awareness that I am in the hands of God is a gift, but somebody who is over-anxious or frenetically active is not really able to accept this gift. In order to be open to it, I need a certain peace and tranquillity, as the psychological under-pinning for the sense of providence. This deep peace of mind and heart is nourished by regular extended periods of prayer. In prayer I learn to let the harassment of daily life flow away. Presumably this is what Jesus was doing when, having been besieged by crowds all day, he went off alone to pray in the hills at night (for example, Mt 14:23). Prayer is even more necessary if I want to retain the sense of God's providence when everything goes wrong, when others reject me, and when evil shows its full power. In such situations one follows Jesus into the agony prayer, as he struggles to recognize God's hand in the failure and tragedy that envelop him (Mt 26:36-44).

In the parable about the Pharisee and the tax-collector at prayer in the Temple, Jesus expressed a central feature of what it means to "walk humbly with God." To find oneself converted religiously is to experience a sense of forgiveness. This is not merely pardon for past sin but, above all, the awareness of being loved and accepted in spite of, and even in a sense because of, my weakness, my faithlessness, my lack of single-mindedness, my inability to respond as I would wish (Rom 7:21). With the tax-collector I pray: "O God, be merciful to me a sinner" (Lk 18:13)—knowing that I shall have to make the same prayer tomorrow; for God's acceptance of my prayer does not justify me in such a way that I can tomorrow pray the prayer of the Pharisee.

The sense of providence is so central to religious conversion that it would seem that it must be present, at least in some implicit way, in *any* authentic religion. One of the most distinctive features of the Christian faith, as compared with other religions, is that it gives a very explicit expression to this sense of the love and care of God: Jesus reveals the *Fatherhood* of God even more thoroughly than was done in the Old Testament. (And of course there is a motherly aspect to God's care as well—cf. Ps 131:2; Is 42:14; 49:15; Jer 31:20—as there is to the concern of Jesus who compares himself to a mother hen, Mt 23:37.)

The issue of the explicitness of the Christian sense of providence is not, however, quite as simple as I have suggested so far. There are many fine Christians who have what Karl Rahner would call "a winter experience" of faith. Their sense of God's care seldom reaches the degree of explicitness which I outlined above; and they can speak of God's "plan"—and especially of God's "intervention" in their lives—only with many reservations and hesitations. On the other hand, there are enthusiastic Christians who speak of God as though God were constantly at their disposal, like a "Mr. Fixit." Our Christian instinct may recognize an authenticity in the "winter experience" of faith which contrasts sharply with the glibness and triviality of the other.

I am not saying that the genuine Christian must always remain somewhat agnostic in regard to providence; in fact I have been claiming that the Christian conception of providence is remarkably explicit; but I want now to add a corrective to that position. All the words we use to express our sense of providence—"love," "care," "fatherhood/motherhood," "plan of God," "God's presence and interventions," etc.—all these are used analogously. We are trying to find human words to express aspects of our relationship to a God who remains transcendent, beyond human comprehension. If these words we use are not to distort the full depth of the Christian experience, they have to be balanced out and qualified in some way. This balancing can sometimes be done by using other words. But it is done more effectively by *silence*— by being struck dumb, by being confronted with the inexpressible, the mysterious. The mystery is so deep that it cannot be conveyed in simple, univocal words; yet to use complex and difficult words seems to distort it even further. It is better then to be childlike—to be willing to use the simple words as Jesus did, while retaining the child"s sense of wonder and humility.

I have already given many references to the Old and New Testament to show that the Christian conception of providence is quite explicit. But there is also a solid biblical basis for a certain degree of "agnosticism" about God's plans and about the divine action in our world. For instance, Judith says: "If you cannot sound the depths of the human heart or penetrate even the human mind, how can you fathom the God who made all things, or sound God's mind, or unravel God's purposes?" (Judith 8:14). Again, the climax of the book of Job is reached with Job, having been confronted by the incomprehensible power of God, has to confess: "My words have been frivolous...I have spoken once but I will not speak again. ...I have been holding forth on matters that I cannot understand, on marvels beyond me..." (Jb 40:45; 42:3). Even Jesus, the beloved Son of the God, has to say, "as for that day, only the Father knows it, nobody else—not even the Son" (Mt 24:36). So a spirituality of providence has to be expressed not only in words but also in meaningful silence.

The Christian sense of providence includes a sense of the Lordship of Jesus Christ—in my personal life and in human history as a whole. What does it mean to have Jesus as the Lord of my life? The way in which I understand it, is that I feel called to allow Jesus to be the criterion of my plans and actions: I discern the consonance or discordance between my proposed line of action and the life of Jesus. To accept Jesus as the Lord of my life is to allow my hopes and projects and concerns to be judged on his "Way," his pattern of living as it shows itself to me in the Gospels when I savour them in prayer. As for the Lordship of Jesus in human history: at present I experience this mainly through my commitment to a transformation of the world in accordance with the Kingdom values proclaimed by Jesus—above all in the Sermon on the Mount (Mt ch. 5-7; cf. Lk 6:17-49). At this point the demand to "walk humbly with God" overlaps with the demand to "act justly," which I shall be looking at in the third section of this chapter.

LOVE TENDERLY

The second demand of the Lord as expressed by Micah, the call to "love tenderly," can be taken to refer to a second major area of Christian spirituality, namely, the interpersonal aspect. Here we are concerned with face-to-face relationships with other people—including friendships, family life, community living and even our more casual relationships. There is, of course, a great variety in the way I have to relate to others: at one end of the spectrum are my deepest friendships and at the other end are my contact with those I meet in a passing way. But I am called to love them all—even to love them "tenderly." This means treating everybody with respect and gentleness in a manner appropriate to the kind of relationship.

I have suggested in the previous section that to "walk humbly" with God we need to be *religiously* converted; I want now to add that to "love tenderly" we need to be *morally* converted. The person who is morally converted in a deep degree has been given the gift of being other-centered, genuinely interested in other people. This is something that can be sensed very quickly, even by people who meet this person for the first time. It establishes a *rapport* which can eliminate the need for the cautious small-talk and the reconnoitering and skirmishing that characterizes many relationships.

A crucial element in moral conversion is the willingness to expose oneself, by trusting the other person. It is really a matter of *entrusting* myself to the other, allowing myself to be vulnerable. This is what "openness" means—being willing to take the risk of leaving myself open to rejection or hurt.

Moral conversion, like religious conversion, is a gift, a grace. It cannot just decide to be trusting, open to others. But when the gift is offered I can refuse it, or accept it only grudgingly and partially. Alternatively, I can recognize what a great gift is being offered, welcome it with open arms, and push it as far as possible, trusting "the reasons of the heart" to lead me between the extremes of a "cagey" reserve and an off-putting brashness.

If I am to share myself with others in an openness that is not coy, the precondition is an ability really to *listen*. Some people are naturally good listeners while others are too self-conscious, or too anxious, to be able to listen well. Both the good listeners and those who find it hard to give their undivided attention to others can benefit from some training in what we might call "deep listening." What I have in mind is the kind of short training courses offered by the "Co-counselling International" movement. There we can learn to give to the other person our full "free attention" without allowing our own concerns or distress to interfere with respectful listening.

Really to listen to a person is already to affirm that person in a deep way. It allows the person to "feel heard" and accepted rather than judged. Mostly that is the kind of affirmation that people need and want. But where there is a deep or more intimate relationship it may, on occasion, be appropriate to show our love for the other either by a more explicit expression of affirmation or of sympathy, or by challenging the person respectfully.

The Lord's demand that we "love tenderly" also includes a demand for *fidelity*. Spontaneous openness and patient listening must be offered not just in the first flowering of friendship; our love is to be modelled on the enduring faithful love that God shows us (for example, Jer 31:13). Therefore, moral conversion involves not merely the power to reach out to others but also the power to "stay with" them, to be loyal even in the difficult times. The prophet Hosea shows the limitless extent of this tender love which endures even in the face of the unfaithfulness of the other person (Hos 3:1-2).

There is a close relationship between the ability to "love tenderly" and to the power to "walk humbly," between moral conversion and religious conversion. In order to be able to relate deeply and enduringly to others I need to be in touch with, and able to cope with, the negative parts of my own personality especially my feelings of inadequacy and fear. Religious conversion helps me to accept myself in my weakness. This gives me the kind of sympathy I need to have with others who, willingly or unwillingly, reveal themselves to me in their inadequacies as well as their gifts.

ACT JUSTLY

The third element in a balanced spirituality is expressed in the demand of the Lord that we "act justly." Like the request that we "love tenderly," this is a moral matter. But it merits separate mention because now we are no longer in the sphere of interpersonal, face-to-face relationships but in the area of public life, the political sphere. Justice is to be understood primarily as concerned with how society is organized, how wealth, power, privileges, rights, and responsibilities are distributed to every level—local, national, and global. Commutative justice—the kind of justice that deals with how individuals relate to each other—should be fitted into the wider pattern established by social justice for society as a whole; the older textbook theology wrongly started from commutative justice and thus gave rise to many of the difficulties we had in regard to obligations of social justice.

To "act justly" means much more than paying our debts and not stealing from others. It means, above all, working to build a society that is intrinsically just—a society in which the structures are just. It means, for instance, constructing a society in which minorities, such as homeless people, are not discriminated against either in law or in practice; and a society in which women are not second-class citizens. It means struggling against the bias in our present society, a bias which enables the better-off people to widen the gap between themselves and the poor. It is easy to give examples:

* The children of the wealthy get better education services, leading on to better jobs.
* The value of property in privileged areas rises more rapidly than in poor areas.
* Those who have money to invest in property or in building sites see their investment pay off, while the poor have to pay ever higher rents.
* Even the law of the land often gives more protection to property rights than to the basic rights of the poor; and in deprived areas the police and "the law" can be experienced as oppressive rather than as protectors of the people.

At the international level, the same kind of bias operates—and as a result the poor countries lag further and further behind the wealthy nations.

To struggle to bring justice into society means in practice making "an option for the poor." This is not a matter of being biased against the rich, or discriminating morally against them. It is simply a question of recognizing that, as Leo XIII pointed out in *Rerum Novarum* over ninety years ago, the wealthy are well able to look after their own interests, but the poor need special protection from society and those in authority. But it can be very difficult for people like us to recognize that we are privileged in many ways. It is not easy to break with the vested interests of our own class, our friends and associates, in order to work for effective social justice. Much of the spirituality in which we were brought up discourages us from making such an option.

There are "escapist" elements in the older spirituality. Emphasis was laid on the assurance that people (especially the poor) will be rewarded in heaven if they patiently endure injustice in this life and thus people were encouraged not to challenge social injustice. There are also dualist elements in that older spirituality—suggestions that those who are "holy" or "spiritual" are not deeply involved in earthly affairs, and especially not in political matters. Furthermore, the spirituality in which we were brought up tended to support the given order in society, an order in which there was a great deal of inequality in wealth, power, and status between different categories of people. It suggested that this order was God-given and should not be questioned. It was not a very prophetic spirituality, one that would encourage people to challenge the existing order and seek the kind of radical changes that social justice requires.

Obviously, there is need for a real change of outlook—a change of heart, a conversion—if one is to respond adequately to the call to "act justly." I think it can be useful to speak of this as a "political conversion," corresponding to the two other conversions of which I spoke earlier (i.e. "religious conversion" concerned with my relationship to God, and "moral conversion" concerned with my interpersonal relationships). To be "politically converted" involves two things:

> We need some *understanding* of how our society works—and particularly how it is structured in ways that favour certain groups and give them an unfair advantage over others, even when the privileged ones do not intend to be unjust.

> We need a commitment to *correcting* injustices, not just on an ad hoc basis, but by replacing the unjust structures with ones that are equitable.

The test of genuine conversion at this public or "political" level will be the extent to which we are working to protect the poor and the marginalized. The Bible leaves no room for doubt that in God's eyes to be just is to safeguard and respect the rights of the poor, the oppressed, and the vulnerable (for example, Is 10:1-2; Am 8:4-6; Lev 26:10-17; Mt 15:6; 20:13-16; 25:36-37; Lk 4:18; 16:19-31; 20:47; Jm 2:1-9). But it is not enough for me to feel called by *my* God to be concerned for the poor; I must enable the poor; I must enable the poor themselves to experience God as *their* God, the God who is one their side to protect them against oppression, the God who "puts down the mighty an exalts the lowly, who fills the hungry with good things and sends the rich away empty" (Lk 1:52-53).

If I really accept that God is, above all, the God of the poor, this has major implications for my spirituality. It means I must look for God particularly in the lives of the poor. I must refuse to accept that the actions of "the important people" are what really shape the history and progress of the country, the Church, and the world. Instead, I will set out to see as really significant the events that touch the lives of the poor, for better or worse. The Old Testament showed that what happened to a group of despised Jewish slaves in Egypt was of major importance in the eyes of God (Ex 3:7-8, etc.). The New Testament similarly brings out the point that those who are most important are people who seem to be insignificant (for example, Mt 13:55; I Cor 1:26-28). So the Christian today must attribute particular value to the initiatives taken by those who are poor and despised, however insignificant such actions may seem by the standards of society. This aspect of Christian spirituality calls me to re-define what I mean by "success." It challenges me to change my priorities, my hopes, and my concerns, and to allocate my time and energy according to standards that may seem foolish to others, and even at times to myself.

There is no way in which such a major change of approach can take place without notable changes in my lifestyle, my friends, and my loyalties. To "opt for the poor" it is not enough for me to be providing services for them; I must be in some way *with* them, sharing at least some of their experiences, suffering and hoping with them. Together we may be able to work for a more just and human society, starting from below rather than from above.

If such a "political conversion" is to succeed it will need to be supported by the two other kinds of conversion. I cannot really be "with" poor people, in real solidarity with them, unless I am "morally converted"—able to relate to them on a person-to-person basis. And I need also to be "religiously converted"—convinced of God's saving presence and power, aware that in the long run it is only by God's power that salvation comes; otherwise I would be quite daunted at the apparent hopelessness of the task of working with the poor and marginalized.

BALANCE AND INTEGRATION

Any one of the three kinds of conversion can be complete only if it is linked to the other two. A proper balance and integration of all three is the basis for a truly Christian spirituality; and this is more important than ever in today's world. If I am not *religiously* converted, or if this aspect of my conversion is inadequate, then I am allowing false gods to rule my life—ambition, or greed, or anxiety. If my *moral* conversion is absent or inadequate, then I remain distrustful and closed to others; or else I am unfaithful, unreliable, disloyal. If I am not properly converted in the *political* sphere, then I will assume that religion is just a private or interpersonal affair and so I will condone the structural injustices of society.

Unfortunately, it frequently happens that different people concentrate almost exclusively on one, or at most two, of the three aspects of conversion. Many "good" people wake up to a deep sense of God's providence and this leads them to a prayerful and enthusiastic spirituality; but they may remain quite insensitive in their human relations and may lack all sense of the "political" dimensions of the Christian faith. Other people build their spirituality around openness to others; but they may be lacking in depth because they give little time to prayer and reflection; and they may imagine that the world can be changed without major structural changes in society. Finally, there are some deeply committed Christians who are so intent on changing the social, economic, and political order that they sacrifice their own peace of spirit and their human relationships in a frenzy of quasi-political activity.

Our spirituality must be rooted not in just one or two aspects of conversion but in all three—the "religious," the "moral" and the "political." It is a distortion of Christian faith to neglect any of them or to fail to work for a full integration of the three.

> This is what Yahweh asks of you, only this:
> That you act justly,
> That you love tenderly,
> That you walk humbly with your God. (Micah 6:8)

Part II

Approaches to Education, Worship, and Action

Overview

This section suggests approaches for helping people, young and old, personalize God's call to justice in their own lives. In **Chapter Seven** we return again to the writings of **Jim McGinnis**. For McGinnis educating for peace and justice involves a movement from awareness to concern and action. Following a helpful overview of the cognitive (awareness), affective (concern) and behavioral (action) goals of justice education, McGinnis offers his reflections on start-up issues and approaches that balance the prophetic and pastoral dimensions of the justice call. The chapter closes with suggestions on how to invite people to action. The material presented is basic, but can be applied to many different aspects of ministry with youth and young adults.

Education and action for justice need to make global-local links. As is clear from the essays in Part One, the development of a global perspective is essential for effective justice education. **Chapter Eight**, unlike the other chapters in this book is not an essay, but a comprehensive listing of the goals and objectives of global education. **Graham Pike** and **David Selby** outline five aims which together constitute a global perspective (systems consciousness, perspective consciousness, health of planet awareness, involvement consciousness and preparedness, and process mindedness) and offer an array of knowledge, skill and attitude objectives for incorporating a global perspective in justice eduction.

Chapter Nine looks at several important principles of liturgy and social justice. The authors are convinced that "worship and justice are intimately and intrinsically linked as a theme that runs through the scriptures, that is brought to expression through the Church's history, and that finds contemporary expression in our Sunday morning liturgy." They suggest thirteen principles which summarize the connections between worship and social justice, principles aimed at both linking and enlivening the faith community's experience of worship and justice.

This section closes with a brief essay on service and solidarity by **Albert Nolan**. Nolan highlights four spiritual passages that people go as they grow in their service to the poor. Compassion, the first stage in service to the poor, is most often expressed through direct service and possibly simplification of one's lifestyle. The second stage, structural change, begins with the gradual discovery that poverty is a structural problem. During this stage people pass through into a recognition of the need for politically motivated social change. Humility marks the third stage. Humility recognizes that true change most often is change that takes place from within, that is, the poor themselves best understand their own situation and what is necessary to change. The fourth and final stage centers around the experience of a genuine, realistic solidarity with the poor. Understanding these passages helps us identify where we are personally in our growth in service to the poor and makes it possible to accompany young people in their growth.

The suggestions and approaches featured in this section will help to shape and direct the practical processes offered in the third section of this book.

Chapter 7

Educating for Peace and Justice

James McGinnis

In the past two decades, Christian educators have been challenged in a variety
of ways. One of the most forceful and hopeful of these challenges has been the call
to educate for peace and justice. Roman Catholic educators were addressed by the
Second Vatican Council in words repeated in the 1968 US Catholic Bishops
statement *Human Life in Our Day:*
> Those who are dedicated to the work of education, particularly the young,
> or who mold public opinion, should regard as their most weighty task the
> effort to instruct all in fresh sentiments of peace. (#132)

The task for educators, as laid out 15 years later by these same bishops in the
1983 *Challenge of Peace* pastoral letter, is both ambitious and clear:
> Therefore we urge every diocese and parish to implement balanced and
> objective educational programs to help people at all age levels to
> understand better the issues of war and peace. Development and
> implementation of such programs should receive a high priority during
> the next several years. (#280)
> To teach the ways of peace is not "to weaken the nation's will" but to be
> concerned for the nation's soul. (#305)

This same concern has been echoed in Protestant religious education circles.
For one, the Educational Ministry of the Presbyterian Church USA issued the call
in a reflection paper entitled *The Movement of Faith — The Meaning of Ministry:*
> Authentic Christian life in contemporary society expresses such Biblical
> qualities of faithfulness as: justice for oppressed people, love for near and
> distant neighbors, preservation of basic human rights, concern for the
> integrity of the family, care for the world creation, responsible exercise of
> power, and creative action for peace across every line of hostility. A
> faithful teaching church will help its members learn to act responsibly in
> public life by cooperating with authorities and policies that serve the
> common good, and by standing over against unjust structures and officials.

Education ministry that is responsible to God's future enables people to undertake a pilgrimage of growth in ability to serve others, especially "the meek." (19)

This article takes up the challenge to educate for peace and justice and offers a concrete methodology for implementing education for peace and justice (EPJ). This methodology moves from awareness to concern to action. For each of these three components, a number of principles and implementation suggestions are presented, particularly with regard to the middle component of "concern." The article concludes with some pastoral suggestions. Effective peace educators need to blend the challenging, prophetic dimensions of EPJ with a pastoral concern for the whole person.

A METHODOLOGY
FOR EDUCATING FOR PEACE AND JUSTICE:
THE BASIC CONCEPT

Education for Peace and Justice (sometimes called peace education or global education; here abbreviated EPJ) is both a "what" and a "how." EPJ involves methodology and lifestyle as well as content. In order to communicate effectively the values and skills necessary for the building of peace, these values and skills must be experienced in the process. Peace, then, is not simply a concept to be taught, but a reality to be lived.

Peace is understood here in a positive sense. It means, first, developing alternatives to violence as a means of resolving human conflicts. But peace is more than the absence of war or overt violence. Peace is also the realization of justice. Working for peace is working for the kinds of relationships among persons and groups, and for the kinds of institutions (political, economic, social, education) that promote the well-being or development of all persons. Such well-being includes, first, basic human necessities such as food, clothing, shelter, and skills development. Further, well-being necessitates the growth of persons in dignity, in self-determination, and in solidarity and service with their fellow human beings.

The overall goal in EPJ can be expressed in a way that reveals the basic methodological components of EPJ: from awareness to concern for action. EPJ promotes a process of conscientious decision-making on crucial social issues and thus seeks informed, compassionate, and courageous agents of change. In a Christian context, such persons are agents of the Gospel, responding to God's call and to God's love for them by sharing that love with others, by promoting God's Kingdom of Shalom, of peace and justice. Because of the threatening aspects of peace and justice for most people, youth and adults alike, promoting this process of awareness, concern, and action requires educators to be pastoral as well as prophetic. Finally, in order for learners to experience the values and skills involved in EPJ, they need to seek them modelled in our classrooms and lives. Let's examine each of these methodological elements.

AWARENESS, CONCERN, AND ACTION

A. AWARENESS (COGNITIVE GOALS)

1. ...of their own giftedness. This two-fold awareness is probably the most important building block of EPJ. First, it means promoting a sense of self-esteem in both youth and adults. Without a positive self-concept or self-image, no one takes a stand, "goes public," works for change. Thus, in Gandhi's schools in India, there is 30 minutes every day of public performance (dance, song, poetry, etc.) as a way of encouraging students to stand up in front of others, to overcome their self-consciousness and become public persons. Second, the more we become aware of our giftedness—that who we are and what we have in talents and possessions are really gifts from God assisted by the efforts of thousands of others and not something we went out and earned/created all by ourselves, and the "rugged individualists" would have us believe—the more willing we are likely to be in sharing these talents and goods with others and in giving our lives for others in working for social.

2. ...of peace and justice issues. The key point is not to cram all the justice and peace issues into a single program or course but to help learners focus on a limited number (maybe only one in depth) in a way that enables them to delve into the causes of problems as well as data about the problem and to begin to see connections between their issue(s) and other peace and justice issues.

3. ...of the human consequences involved. What policy-makers as well as ordinary citizens often do not see or consider are the human consequences of their decisions. Conscientious decision-making demands that we become aware of the effects of our decisions on other people. Awareness of the "social costs" as well as the "economic costs" of federal budget cuts or job programs, for instance, is crucial in evaluating such measures. Awareness of the victims of policy decisions is also a part of generating concern (see below). Further, discovering the connections between these issues/policies and our own lives, especially if we are victimized in some way, has a way of stimulating our learning and increasing our willingness and opportunities to respond.

4. ...of manipulation/propaganda. "It's OK, Dad, they only kill the enemy," was a nine-year old's response to a question from his father when he described an airborne ranger film he was shown in class by a military recruiter. An awareness that it is people who are killed, not some impersonal "the enemy," needs to be fostered at an early age. So too an awareness of the manipulation of our wants and needs by advertising. EPJ helps us become more critically aware of the "Gospel—Culture Contrasts" in our society and to develop critical thinking skills in general. To be conscientious decision-makers, youth need to be encouraged to think for themselves, to see and evaluate alternative positions on various issues, to formulate their own positions, and articulate more and more clearly the basic reasons for their positions.

5. ...of why evil or injustice exists. Young people especially struggle with this question. While we cannot fully comprehend this mystery in a theological

context, we affirm with M. Scott Peck in his study of human evil in *People of the Lie*: "Let us remember why so many theologians have said: Evil is the inevitable concomitant of free will, the price we pay for our unique human power of choice. Since ours is the power to choose, we are free to choose wisely or stupidly, to choose well or badly, to choose for evil or for good." (Peck 244) Because he found in his study of the My Lai massacre during the Vietnam War what he calls "gross intellectual laziness and pathological narcissism" (selfishness, desire to be #1) to be the fundamental cause of group evil, he concludes his chapter of My Lai with a vision and appeal for educators:

> Children will, in my dream, be taught that laziness and narcissism are at the very root of all human evil, and why this is so. They will learn that each individual is of sacred importance. They will come to know that the natural tendency of the individual in a group is to forfeit his or her ethical judgment to the leader, and that this tendency should be resisted. And they will finally see it as each individual's responsibility to continually examine himself or herself for laziness and narcissism and then to purify themselves accordingly. They will do this in the knowledge that such personal purification is required not only for the salvation of their individual souls but also for the salvation of their world. (Peck 253)

6. ...of church teaching. Adults and students alike need to have their awareness of social issues placed in the context of their faith—in the context of the Bible and the social teaching of their church (the application of the biblical vision and principles to these social issues), so that they can better understand the respond to these "signs of the time."

7. ...of how social changes takes place. This involves an awareness of how institutions, especially political and economic ones, operate and how to address them most effectively. EPJ includes learning other skills, especially conflict resolution skills. Finally, becoming aware of the wide variety of action possibilities in relation to any issues is important in breaking open our imaginations about what we can do for peace and justice.

B. CONCERN (AFFECTIVE GOALS)

Perhaps the most constant task facing educators is nurturing an inner sense of solidarity or concern, which is the link between awareness and education. EPJ involves attitudinal change, not just content. Thus, as Gandhi realized, the heart as well as the head must be educated. At least four elements are involved in this conversion process, which peace educators need to consider for their own lives as well as for their students. Because of the critical importance of this task/process, I offer a variety of examples of ways to implement and integrate each element into our own lives as well as those of our students.

The following four elements are certainly not the only ones that are involved in this conversion process, but they are the four that consistently emerge when we do "personal histories" with people in our peace and justice workshops and courses. We ask participants to make a list of all those experiences—events, people, books, moments—that they perceive have helped them to be more "concerned," "involved," "working for peace and justice." They share some of these experiences in small groups, after which we then ask them to identify the commonalities among all these experiences. Consistently, they speak of significant experiences of personally encountering both victims of injustice and people whose risk-taking action inspired them. Generally, in religiously based groups, participants identify moments of faith when they felt called by God, often through Scripture and especially as witnessed in the lives of faith-filled prophetic people. Almost universally named are one or more experiences of being nurtured by others, especially by participating in a group of concerned people.

Three of these four elements are also central in the research done by Douglas Huneke, reported in *The Moses of Rovno*, on the characteristics of several hundred people who helped rescue Jews during the Nazi holocaust. Of the nine characteristics Huneke found common to most rescuers, six clearly overlap with three of the above, while his other three characteristics are contained in several of the elements under the "awareness" goal above. Similar to personal encounters with victims of injustice, Huneke's rescuers had significant experiences with suffering and death earlier in their lives and had developed empathetic imagination, i.e., they could really imagine themselves in the situation of those hurting. Because many of them came from homes where hospitality was a high value, they had a variety of experiences with people needing help of some sort.

Similar to personal encounters with risk-taking advocates, Huneke's rescuers were all exposed to compassionate people early in life and identified with a morally articulate parent, parents who would both discuss and model moral behavior. As an example, Huneke describes one rescuer who described his mother as a person who would pose moral dilemmas for him and ask what he would do if he were in that situation.

Similar to being nurtured and challenged in some kind of supportive community, Huneke describes how so many of the rescuers became part of a group, not only for support but for more effective action. If one or two were to be "picked off," they need to know that the work could carry on.

Overlapping with several of the "awareness" elements above are three or four of Huneke's characteristics. His rescuers were also adventuresome, implying a good self-image and awareness of their giftedness. Further, they were socially marginal, i.e., willing to be different, to be questioners rather than conformists which embodies the critical thinking emphasis in awareness element #4. Finally, with empathetic imaginations, the rescuers were people able to see opportunities to help and were emotionally able to help, in contrast with so many who literally don't see. Part of this ability to see is an awareness of the human consequences involved in policies and actions.

With such extensive corroboration from a much more scientific study of compassionate and/or risk-taking behavior, we feel more confident in recommending these four ingredients of "concern" or elements in an on-going conversion process not only for our students but also for ourselves.

1. Experiencing working for peace and justice as a call from Jesus

The more that the call to peace and justice is experienced as a call from Jesus, the more likely a person is to respond. We can increase our ability to hear and respond to this call especially through biblical, contemplative, liturgical prayer and through fasting.

a. Biblical prayer

Fostering a personal relationship with Jesus, especially through prayerful reflection on the Hebrew prophets as the New Testament, is essential. Knowing that Yahweh and Jesus walk with us as we try to follow their call makes us more willing to say "yes." The invitation and commissioning passages in John 15:16-20, Isaiah 6:4-13, Jeremiah 1, and elsewhere should be pondered and shared with our students again and again. We and they need to hear ourselves being addressed. For instance, in the first chapter of Jeremiah:

v5—God knowing each of us so intimately even before we were born

v5—God appointing each of us to be prophets for a portion of God's people

v6—Our own reluctance to accept God's call, using youth or inexperience as an excuse

v7—God chiding us and sending us to specific people to say what God has shared with us through our prayer, study and discussion with others

v17-18—God sending us into action and reminding us to anticipate resistance from all sectors of society

v8,19—God promising to be with us to protect us—"it is Yahweh who speaks"

Prayerful reflection on the Scriptures is essential if we and our students are to discover what it is that God is "commanding us to say"(v.7) when we exercise the prophetic dimension of ministry. Following the example of J. Elliott Corbett in his *Prophets on Main Street*, you and/or your students could select one or parts of one of the prophetic books and rewrite it to speak to contemporary issues paralleling those addressed by particular Hebrew prophets. As a group activity, the class could be divided into smaller groups, each group examining a specific prophet. This might mean asking the individuals in each group to read and jot ideas down first; then meet to brainstorm all possible applications to our own society and world; then have each individual take a particular segment of the prophet to rewrite; and finally have the individuals share their individual written reflections with others in their group and discuss their similarities and/or differences. Perhaps each person could find visuals to illustrate his or her reflection. Each group might make a presentation of their prophet to the whole class. This could be in the form of reading the written reflections, with or without some kind of visual collage illustrating their applications of the prophets to today's realities. An alternative would be some form of dramatic presentation in which the rest of the class might be the people to whom the message is addressed. This step might be especially appropriate during Advent or Lent and might also be presented to a larger assembly of students (and possibly parents).

The more that prayerful reflection on the Scriptures accompanies this activity, the more abundant will be its fruit. Pastorally and strategically, the more our invitation to others to peace and justice is rooted in the word of God or is the word of God, the more likely is that invitation to be heard and responded to positively. (McGinnis, *Religious Dimensions* 59-62) *b. Liturgical prayer*

The liturgical year embodies the life of Jesus and, thus, his social mission. To make this mission explicit in the celebration of the liturgical year is essential in the conversion process. Advent and Christmas speak to us of the coming of Jesus in simplicity, to serve and not to be served, of Christ as the Prince of Peace. (McGinnis and Webber) Lent issues a call to respond to Jesus as he suffers today, as his passion is relived in the hungry, the elderly, the victims of racism and repression. Easter and Pentecost are the source of our hope and courage. (McGinnis, *Religious Dimensions* 192-201)

A number of churches, communities, and smaller groups of families and others have done what some have called "Stations in the City" during Holy Week as a way of reliving and responding to the passion of Christ as lived out in the lives of the suffering of our communities today. Places in the community with which suffering people are associated—jails, shelters, food pantries, soup kitchens, military industries/or installations, welfare offices, federal buildings, closed medical facilities, clinics, abandoned homes, nursing homes, etc.—are identified, visited, prayed at, and whenever possible responded to in the form of direct service (for example, sharing Easter eggs with guests in a local house of hospitality) or social action (for example, delivering tax protest letters to the IRS over cuts in programs for the poor or a prayer vigil and fast at a federal building over US policy in Central America). Incorporating our social concerns into our faith-life makes clearer the social dimensions of our faith, allows them to take deeper roots within us, and nourishes the inner core of solidarity out of which our external actions should flow. This is especially true of the Lord's Supper. As Arlo Duba expresses it,

> The Lord's Supper, together with baptism, expresses the charter, covenant-establishing event of Jesus' death-resurrection, by which we are incorporated into the covenant community. The Lord's Supper is God serving us, and it is our thankful response. In our responsive sacrifice, Calvin said, 'are included all the duties of love.' Radical self-giving should be the outcome . . . Receiving the Lord's Supper and living out the social implications of the Supper are one. Body broken 'for the life of the world'(John 6:51) and blood 'poured out for many'(Mark 14:24) carry cosmic, world-wide implications . . . Life itself must become the dynamic prolongation of the Lord's Supper. (Duba 108-110)

Making the social dimension of the Lord's Supper explicit has abundant possibilities. The hymns and prayers of petition can be broadened to include cultures and peoples of many different parts of our communities, country, and world. The visuals on vestibule bulletin boards, as well as in the sanctuary, can depict the people of God as the whole human family. The passing of peace or the kiss of peace can embrace people far away as well as people up close. The invitation to receive Communion can include an explicit invitation to embrace ("take in") the whole body of Christ. Occasionally, the gifts brought to the altar can include an "offering of letters"—letters of concern addressed to political representatives on behalf of the suffering members of the body of Christ and solicited the week before.

c. Contemplative Prayer

At the heart of compassion is contemplation. "Suffering with" or "passion with"—is defined by Matthew Fox as "our kinship with the universe and the universe's Maker; it is the action we take because of that kinship." (Fox 23) This kinship is rooted in prayerful solidarity with God and all of God's creation. It is that inner oneness that Gandhi understood and lived as the essence of nonviolence—"the power that manifests itself in us when we become aware of the oneness of life." Gandhi is referring not just to an intellectual awareness here, but to a biblical understanding of "knowledge." This "inner oneness with" is what is meant when Jeremiah wrote that we have to take up the cases of the needy and the poor in order to know God. "Is not this what it means to know me— it is Yahweh who speaks"(Jeremiah 22:16). To nurture this oneness, this power of nonviolence or love, and compassionate action, we and our students need regular moments for contemplation, need to be still, open, and reverent before creation and our Creator, to "make our home in Jesus as Jesus makes his home in us"(John 15:4).

d. Fasting

Fasting has a significant role to play in deepening our relationship to God as well as deepening our commitment to peace and justice, our willingness to sacrifice and take risks for peace and justice and our sense of solidarity with others. Fast days should be special days of prayer, not just in periods set aside for prayerful reflection on the Scriptures but primarily in tiny moments throughout the day. In fasting from food, there are often many moments of wanting to eat during the day. These moments become opportunities and invitations to prayer—to speak with Jesus, to be more fully aware of his presence, to beg him for peace, to be reminded that God's will for the world truly is shalom. When our fast days are regular—at least weekly—this sense of prayerfulness seems to carry over to other days as well. Some combine their fast days with silence, more consciously to focus on the presence of God.

The overwhelming sense of evil manifested in the arms race and suffering in Central America, Ethiopia, and elsewhere brings us to our knees, figuratively and literally. This sense of evil can drive us on to work harder for peace and justice, but it should also drive us back to God. After we have done what we can—writing Congress, giving talks, writing books or articles, mobilizing local groups, setting up "urgent action networks," vigilant and demonstrating, resisting war taxes, etc.—we depend on you. Raise up evermore courageous instruments of your peace. Work your miracles through others. Touch the hearts of decision-makers. Give courage to those victimized by the evils we are resisting. Give us greater courage, hope, and insight into your will and your role.

Jim Wallis in the November 1983 issue of *Sojourners* magazine, reflects on the "cost of discipleship" and challenges us with Jesus' questions about whether we have "counted the cost" of following him (see Luke 14:25-33). Are we really willing to suffer or are we just "hanging around" the Gospel? We are not sure how really willing we are to suffer for peace and justice, but we know that the tiny acts of self-denial involved in fasting can be a preparation for greater demands made by sacrificial love. Most of us do not jump from 0 to 10 in one leap. We move one step at a time. The pruning process (John 15:1-7) that God has in mind for each of us, calling us to be ever more willing to let go and follow Jesus, involves many moments of self-denial. Fasting can be an important part of this process, preparing us for the greater demands of sacrificial love.

A tiny "no" of self-denial can also be a tiny "yes" of solidarity. We can experience many moments of solidarity on fast days, as we bring to mind the lives of those victimized by the evils we are resisting: friends in Nicaragua, other victims of injustice we have met or read about, those persecuted for their convictions, peace-makers working hard for change. It might be especially helpful to write one such person each day we fast, to communicate that sense of solidarity and thus encourage them to remain faithful and strong. The more we bring to consciousness and prayer the lives of persons for whom or with whom we are resisting, the more deeply drawn into resistance and fidelity we are likely to find ourselves.

The U.S. Catholic bishops recommend that fasting "be accompanied by works of charity and service toward our neighbor." Fast days are opportunities for fuller presence to those around us, if we do not allow our work schedule to dominate our day. Special little acts of service—doing an extra task for someone we live with, a phone call to a hurting friend or relative, time for a co-worker at the office—make the solidarity of fasting more genuine. Those closest to us should also be the beneficiaries of our fasting.

To be more serious about our solidarity projects and to sustain our prophetic efforts for justice and peace, we need to be engaged at the deepest levels of our being. Service and simplifying our lifestyle as well as prayer and fasting all have a way of opening us up at these levels, making it possible for God to work more fully in our lives and the world through us. (Fox 236-237; McGinnis, *Solidarity* 153-156)

2. Being touched by the advocates for justice

People working hard for justice provide us with both inspiration and imagination. The witness of people who are giving themselves generously, often at some risk, can help young and old overcome our fears of being questioned, laughed at, ignored, or worse. The witness of people whose motivation is not financial gain and who find challenge and joy in working for change offers an important counter-model to the materialism all around us. Such people demonstrate the truth of God's Word: that it is in giving our life away that we find life. The activities of these advocates for justice, especially if we have a chance to ask them questions and listen to their stories, can give all of us ideas about what we can do.

Specific possibilities for incorporating this element into our own as well as our student's lives are enormous and fall into several categories. Most effective are direct personal encounters with such people. Going to their talks, or visiting their centers or work-places, or arranging a presentation in our church, school, or even home are possibilities. Offering hospitality to a refugee, a farm working organizer or speaker passing through your community can provide a wonderful experience for household members of all ages. Participating in peace and justice groups or in group actions where we are in regular contact and sharing with more risk-taking persons is even more helpful than occasional one-shot encounters.

Less personal but nonetheless effective encounters include reading and viewing opportunities. Magazines like *Maryknoll, The Other Side* and *Sojourners* regularly feature prophetic individuals, some well-known and others no so, whose faith and courage can inspire us. Biographies and autobiographies of contemporary prophets, *Gandhi, Dorothy Day, Martin Luther King,* and *Archbishop Romero,* are even more inspirational. (McGinnis, *Religious Dimensions* 8-29) Films like *Gandhi, Roses in December* or *Choices of the Heart* (about Jean Donovan and the other three women martyrs in El Salvador), *Silkwood* and *Norma Rae,* also have the added power of visual impact. Young people have become concerned about African hunger and racism in South Africa at least partially because of the involvement of their rock star heroes, for example, "We are the World" and "Sun City."

3. Being touched by the victims of injustice

For people who are not victims of injustice, such exposure has similar benefits, especially in terms of inspiration. Statistics about hungry people or the victims of racism often do not touch our hearts and move us to action. However, the experience of a hungry person or victim of racism often does. There is an urgency about injustice that we do not experience generally unless we encounter the victims of that injustice.

Further, encountering the victims of injustice, especially in their struggle against that injustice, can break down another counter-productive attitude. Most nonpoor and nonvictims think of the poor as needy and deficient. The economically poor are not seen as gifted nor as often capable of helping themselves. Experience can dispel this stereotype. Meeting the victims of injustice in their giftedness can open us to learn from them. And we have much to learn from them, particularly about injustice and about action for justice.

As with the previous element, implementation possibilities are numerous. Local soup kitchens, houses of hospitality and shelters, food pantries, jails, nursing homes, wherever people are suffering, provide immediate opportunities and often offer the chance for longer term relationships to develop. Letter-writing presents another level of relationship. Corresponding with a prisoner (*Sojourners* and *The Other Side* magazines regularly include the names of prisoners wanting to correspond with fellow Christians) or becoming part of a "pairing project with a person, group, or mission" in the Third World can concretize realities in a way to move us to solidarity action on their behalf. (McGinnis, *Solidarity*)

Contact with victims of injustice through their handicrafts presents yet another possibility. Supporting the self-help efforts of poor artisans in Third World countries by buying and/or distributing their handicrafts at gift-giving times has several benefits. These purchases—through such outlets as Jubilee Crafts (300 W. Apsley, Philadelphia, PA 19114), Self-Help Crafts, Mennonite SERV—provide economic benefits to the artisans who receive the bulk of the purchase price. Second, they can connect our lives with the artisans through the descriptions of the artisans and the situation of their country that Jubilee Crafts provides with many of their handicrafts. The accounts of the struggles of Santiago Alonzo and his family, a former political prisoner in the Philippines who makes bone pendants inscribed with sayings like "those who would give light must endure burning," and the stories of the Chilean women whose husbands have "disappeared" and whose wall hangings are a beautifully simple statement of their hope and commitment to life are very moving. These can be shared with the recipients of our gifts.

Each time we would put on one of Santiago's pendants could be a moment of prayerful solidarity—not only for Santiago and others like him but also for ourselves to become more willing to "endure burning" so that we can "give light."

4. Being supported in community

Working for peace and justice clearly involves some risk. The support of others helps us overcome our fears. Coming together regularly with several others for prayer and reflection on our resistance to injustice can be beneficial in several other ways. Such sharing can broaden the insights that we arrive at in private reflection. Other persons sharing both our internal and external struggles can support us in difficult times, and challenge and inspire us to take the next, more risky, steps. Such sharing groups can also increase our level of awareness of issues and expand the outreach and thus the effectiveness of our solidarity actions, as well as help us persevere in this study and action, in our fasting and prayer, in our service and efforts at simplifying our lifestyles. Finally, working with others often provides the necessary ingredient of fun or enjoyment. Young people especially need to experience social action as fulfilling on a number of levels, if they are to integrate it into their own lives. Having other children along makes a real difference in many cases.

Some people have implemented this element by meeting monthly to share their reflections on the current issues of *Sojourners* magazine. Others use a Scripture passage and focus on what that passage says to them about the level of "faith and resistance" efforts they see as appropriate at this point in their life. In working with student Christian service projects, many educators stress the importance of small groups (rather than individuals working alone) working together on the same project and meeting regularly to share their feelings, reflections, and even pray about their actions/projects.

C. ACTION (BEHAVIORAL GOALS)

Genuine concern expresses itself in action. Compassion is action, as Matthew Fox stresses throughout his excellent book, *A Spirituality Named Compassion*. Conscientious decision-making implies courageous action in implementing our decisions. This action component of EPJ is broadly defined. No one type of action is recommended for everyone. Individuals are at many different points, and what is appropriate for one person is not necessarily appropriate for another. The range of action suggestions in EPJ includes:

1. *Actions of direct service as well as social or structural change.* Direct service
   actions (the "works of mercy") provide several benefits. As noted above,
   encountering suffering people touches our hearts. Also, these actions often have
   immediate results and can give a sense of "doing something" or that "short term
   success" so important for people just starting out, especially young people. On
   the other hand, the "works of justice"—structural change—are often more
   difficult because they are less immediate in their results, require a longer-term
   commitment, and often involve more conflictual or confrontational elements.
   But unless we are willing to address the practices, policies, and institutions that
   create the victims in the first place, all of our direct aid to victims may be
   rendered relatively meaningless. Effective love of neighbor seems to require
   that we walk with both of the feet of Christian social action.
2. *Actions that focus on local issues as well as global issues, on both the local and
   the global dimensions of the same issue.* It is a luxury, as it were, to limit our
   attention to overseas problems when there are so many in our own communities.
   Local issues generally permit much more concrete and personal actions,
   coalitioning possibilities, opportunities for longer term relationships. But the
   Christian vision is also global—the whole "body of Christ" or "family of God."
   How to effectively embrace people far away as well as close up is important for
   young people and adults to learn. Food and hunger issues have a special
   potential for enabling us to respond on both the local and global dimensions of
   social action.
3. *Actions that can be done within the home or school as well as in the community
   and larger world.* Social action needs to be experienced as a regular part of life
   if it is to take deep root in our lives. The more it is integrated into home life, the
   more regular it can become. And sometimes such actions are "safer" or gentler
   first steps for "beginners." Actions like political letter-writing can be whole
   household activities. Valentine greetings for prisoners and lonely members of
   our own congregations can be added to those for relatives and classmates.
   Baking goodies as a whole family for Christmas gifts or for raising money for
   social change groups is fun, as well as helpful. Providing hospitality from meals
   at holiday time for lonely people to temporary shelter for a teen or a victim of
   domestic violence—brings not only social action but victims themselves into
   the home. Because peace and justice issues often threaten people, it is important
   to work with them carefully. The challenging, prophetic dimensions of EPJ need
   to be balanced with some gentle, pastoral approaches, if we are to be effective
   peace educators. The following suggestions and strategies are ways that have
   proven effective over the years, both with children and adults.

WHAT ISSUES TO START WITH

1. *Start with issues that speak to participants' felt needs and advertise them in a
   way that links with these needs.* For families, this might mean focusing first on
   conflict resolution within the home, how to help children cope with materialism
   and peer pressure, TV violence. Adults looking for alternatives to the rat-race

and consumerism of gift-giving times can be introduced to economic justice issues through alternative gift-giving; for example, buying Third World handicrafts. For children, interpersonal conflict resolution, the media, and consumerism are often good places to begin.

2. *Start with issues that victimize the participants and then proceed to ways in which the same forces/institutions victimize others,* for example, a film like *Seeing Through Commercials* on how children are manipulated by children's commercials is a good prelude to an issue like infant formula where the victims of advertising are the poor. Similarly, as a prelude to a study of racial stereotyping, have students identify ways in which adults stereotype them. More empathy is generated this way.

3. *Start with a limited number of issues and encourage participants to delve into one issue in some depth while keeping up with the others covered in the course or program.* In adult education programs, consider dividing an 8-week program into two 4-week parts and at the end of part one ask how many would like to do part two.

4. *Whenever possible, allow participants to help determine which issues are studied* (especially in a "part two" of a series or the last part of a course) or choose a specific issue focus for their research or project during the course. We can more effectively invite others to be concerned about our justice and peace issues if we are open to responding to the ones with which they are most concerned. Ultimately, it is important and more effective to mobilize people for action around their issues than around ours.

HOW TO TEACH EPJ
IN (RELATIVELY) NON-THREATENING WAYS

1. *Take people where they are.* In addition to what was said above about focusing on issues that are pertinent to participants, we need to be explicit at the beginning that it is OK to disagree that the "truth" of any issue is not something that any one person has completely and that we all need to contribute our portion of the truth of an issue in a spirit of openness to and respect for one another. Having participants express (in an essay, collage, etc.) their own vision of peace and justice or understanding of a given issue at the beginning of a study and then again at the end of the study is a creative way of demonstrating growth as well as affirming their persons.

2. *Share personal histories.* Another way of taking people where they are is at the beginning of a course or program to ask each participant to identify those experiences in their life that have led them to where they are with regard to peace and justice, i.e., those events or persons that have touched or influenced them in some way to sensitize them to these concerns. Sharing these personal histories—even if it means describing just one of these experiences—with others is important for both personal affirmation and community building.

3. *For people of faith, share the biblical/faith basis early on and insist that outside resource persons share the faith basis for their actions when they make*

presentations. Also encourage such persons to share their personal stories and experiences to personalize their presentation.

4. *Often it is helpful to communicate more threatening content through audiovisuals, readings, outside speakers, rather than always in our own presentations, so that when participants want to disagree with the content they can focus on that "third thing" and not solely on us.* This way we are in a better position to help them work through the issue and be less defensive ourselves. Audio Visuals that have a "lighter touch" are often helpful in this regard.

5. *Anticipate some of the participants' objections and speak to these concerns in the course of presentations.*

6. *Use "expert" resources, persons with a lot of credibility.*

HOW TO INVITE PEOPLE TO ACTION

1. *Start by having participants identify what they are already doing.* First, it affirms them for who they are rather than starting by pointing out all the actions they are not doing and thus generating needless guilt and defensiveness. Second, participants are often more open to accepting new possibilities when they come (in group sharing) from other participants rather than from the leader whom they expect to be doing those actions.

2. *Acknowledge our own "brokenness" by using examples of failures early on, so that participants can identify with our struggles.* Honesty adds credibility.

3. *Acknowledge our awareness of the obstacles in their lives that make social action difficult and then help them generate strategies to overcome these obstacles.* It is especially helpful here to have participants working in smaller groups with others in similar situations and/or facing similar obstacles.

4. *Invite participants to campaigns/actions that offer a range of action possibilities, since people are at many different places and need to move one step at a time.* Similarly, invite participants to campaigns/groups already underway, so that they experience a sense of community, support, and increased effectiveness. Especially for youth, these action possibilities have to be within their capability to deal with emotionally as well as intellectually.

5. *Encourage participants to invite others to join them in actions.* Set up a support system for participants for implementing their action decision (for example, choosing a partner with whom to work or check in and perhaps to pray with.)

6. *Integrate social action with joy.* Without joy, heavy issues and serious study and struggle will probably not be very appealing to either youth or adults. Besides working together with friends, making social action more joyful means finding creative actions. It means celebrating little victories or coupling a difficult service activity with a fun event.

7. *Stress quality rather than quantity.* A longer-term relationship with a person, group, campaign is much more valuable than flitting from issue to issue. And always stress taking one step at a time and that the multitude of action possibilities generated in a course is not meant to overwhelm participants but to

break open their imaginations as to what can be done. In general, help people feel good about what they can do rather than guilty about what they cannot do.

A CONCERN FOR THE WHOLE PERSON

Whether we are teaching children in a classroom or an adult education program, the more that the participants experience our concern for them as persons, the more open they generally are to learning with/from us and the more difficult it is for them to write off our prophetic challenges. If they know we are genuinely concerned about their well-being, if we take an interest in their daily lives, then our prophetic words will be listened to differently.

MODELLING OUR VALUES

Again, EPJ is both a "what" and "how." Participants learn best when the process is consistent with the content and when the content is fleshed out in the life of the teacher.

a. In our Classrooms

The process of EPJ must itself be peaceful and just. If peace means cooperation and non-violence, if justice includes dignity, self-determination, and interdependence or solidarity, then EPJ demands a mutual or cooperative model of education. A process whereby both teacher's desires and the young people's desires are incorporated into decisions needs to be established. Mutual decision-making, using the insights and skills gained in nonviolent conflict resolution, can extend to what is to be learned, to how the student's performance is evaluated, to discipline, and to decisions about time and space in the classroom. The development of cooperative, rather than, competitive ways of learning, relating, and playing is a giant step toward the realization and experience of peace in the school.

b. In our Lives

While we are very willing to share our brokenness, our failures, youth also need to see in us our fidelity to God's call. The more we try to live what we teach, the more credible and effective we are as teachers. We cannot be involved in every cause or action, but we need to be involved in at least one and be willing to share this involvement—humbly and without laying guilt trips—with our young people. And they need to see our involvement rooted in our faith, in an ever deepening spiritually.

WORKS CITED

Duba, Arlo D. "Theological Dimensions of the Lord's Supper," *Worship in the Community of Faith*. Ed. Harold M. Daniels. Louisville: The Joint Office of Worship of the PCUSA, 1982.

Fox , O.P., Matthew. "Towards a Meaning of Compassion." *A Spirituality Named Compassion*. Minneapolis: Winston Press, 1979.

Huneke, Douglas. *The Moses of Rovno*. New York: Dodd, Mead & Co., 1985.

McGinnis, James. *Educating for Peace and Justice: Religious Dimensions*. St. Louis: Institute for Peace and Justice, 1985.

McGinnis, James. *Solidarity with the People of Nicaragua*. Maryknoll: Orbis Books, 1985.

McGinnis, James & Kathleen and Mary Webber. "Advent Activities for Families." Ellenwood, GA: Alternatives.

Peck, M. Scott, *People of the Lie*. New York: Simon & Schuster, 1983.

Chapter 8

Educating for Global Awareness

Graham Pike and David Selby

THE FIVE AIMS OF GLOBAL EDUCATION

SYSTEMS CONSCIOUSNESS

Students should:

* *acquire the ability to think in a systems mode.*

Simple dualities such as cause/effect, problem/solution, observer/observed, value/fact, reason/emotion, local/global are put aside. In their place, students are encouraged to see phenomena and events as bound up in complex, interactive and multi-layered webs in which relationship is everything. So-called "effects" loop back and trigger more "effects" that impact elsewhere in the system. Observers in part determine what is observed. Solutions are, at best, helpful adjustments within the system.

* *acquire an understanding of the systemic nature of the world.*

Firstly, in a spatial dimension; on a range of scales intra-personal to global. Secondly, in the temporal dimension, i.e. the interacting nature of past, present, and future. Thirdly, in the issues dimension, i.e. the interlocking nature of global issues.

* *acquire an holistic conception of their capacities and potential.*

Our true potential can only be realized when the bodily, emotional, intellectual, and spiritual dimensions of personhood are seen as equal and complementary dimensions. The characters and well-being of person and planet are inescapably locked together. Under this heading, students should be given the scope to exercise and develop their potential and, hence, achieve higher levels of personal autonomy and empowerment.

PERSPECTIVE CONSCIOUSNESS

Students should:

* *recognize that they have a worldview that is not universally shared.*

Students are helped to realize that they have their own particular perspective, that they interpret reality from within a particular framework of thought and perception and that there are difficulties and dangers attached to using that framework of reference as a yardstick for interpreting and judging the lifestyles, patterns of behavior, values, and worldview of others. They are also encouraged to see how perspective is shaped by factors such as age, class, creed, culture, ethnicity, gender, geographical context, ideology, language, nationality, and race.
* develop receptivity to other perspectives.

Such receptivity can be profoundly liberating. It can help students challenge previously unexamined assumptions, feed the imagination, and promote divergent and lateral thinking; it can lead to a radical reassessment of the nature of both problems and solutions.

HEALTH OF PLANET AWARENESS

Students should:
* acquire an awareness and understanding of the global condition and of global developments and trends.

Through study and discussion students should learn of global conditions, trends, and developments, for example, wealth distribution, population growth, types of development, the environmental impact of human activity, international tensions, setbacks, and success stories in the safeguarding of human rights. They should become equally familiar with the range of, often conflicting, arguments surrounding those conditions, trends, and developments.
* develop an informed understanding of the concepts of justice, human rights and responsibilities and be able to apply that understanding to the global condition and to global developments and trends.
* develop a future orientation in their reflection upon the health of the planet.

Whilst present conditions, developments, and trends need to be set within their historical context, it is equally important that students are encouraged to reflect upon the mid and long-term consequences of what is happening in the world today and upon possible, probable, and preferred futures.

INVOLVEMENT CONSCIOUSNESS AND PREPAREDNESS

Students should:
* become aware that the choices they make and the actions they take individually and collectively have repercussions for the global present and the global future.

Choices made and actions taken at any point in the intra-personal to global scale can have contemporaneous impact on all other points on the scale. Likewise, present choices and actions can carry implications for the future well-being of humankind and the environment. Failure to choose and act can have as many repercussions as conscious choice and action.
* develop the social and political action skills necessary for becoming effective participants in democratic decision-making at a variety of levels, grassroots to global.

Students should explore avenues and techniques for participation in school and society. They should practice participation and, thus, develop discernment and judgement in making choices and in their participation in social and political processes.

PROCESS MINDEDNESS

Students should:

* *learn that learning and personal development are continuous journeys with no fixed or final destination.*

Decisions and judgements we reach are, by their nature, impermanent; stills taken from a life-long moving picture. New information, new perspectives, new paradigms will help us see things in new ways.

* *learn that new ways of seeing the world are revitalizing but risky.*

New paradigm vision is double-edged; it enables us to see lots of things in new ways but it may mean that other things are not seen as clearly. The systemic paradigm is not a panacea; it now offers a coherent and challenging framework for present and future thought and action. We need to recognize that it will, in turn, be overtaken.

GLOBAL EDUCATION OBJECTIVES

What, then, are the knowledge, skills, and attitudinal objectives of global education which, if met, will satisfy the five broad aims outlined above? The following list of objectives is by no means comprehensive, but it attempts to illustrate the breadth of learning required for life in the next century. For convenience and ease of reference, the objectives are categorized under generic sub-headings and listed in sequential form. It should of course be recognized that, in keeping with the holistic and systemic approach of global education, the categories should not be regarded as definitive or exclusive and the capacity for interrelatedness and interdependence within and between them is limitless.

KNOWLEDGE OBJECTIVES

1. PERSONAL

(a) *Self-awareness*: students should acquire an understanding of their own physical, intellectual, emotional, and spiritual capacities and potential, their strengths, weaknesses and principal areas for development.

(b) *Own perspective*: students should understand that their own perspective is not universally shared and become aware of how their perspective is shaped.

(c) *How others see us*: students should learn about their own culture, lifestyles, and identities through studying how other peoples view them.

2. SYSTEMS

(a) *Systems theory*: students should develop an understanding of the nature of systems and how they operate, evolve, and change.

(b) *World systems*: students should know about the workings of some principal world systems, for example, trading systems, ecological systems, political systems.

(c) *Interdependence*: students should understand the concept of interdependence and how people, places, events, and issues are linked through interdependent relationships.

(d) *Commonality*: students should become aware of the commonality of needs, behavior, talents, and aspirations shared by humankind.

3. DEVELOPMENT

(a) *Forms of development*: students should understand the concept of development and some principal forms of development (including capitalist, socialist, and alternative) in operation in their own and other societies.

(b) *Trading relationships*: students should know about the principal commodities traded between countries, the places and processes of growing/extraction, manufacturing and retailing of those commodities, and the relative positions of power and wealth between countries, regions, and companies in a trading relationship.

(c) *Aid*: students should understand the historical background to development aid, its forms and processes, and the principal, economic, social, and cultural arguments surrounding its use.

(d) *Colonialism*: students should understand the concepts and processes of colonialism, neocolonialism, and imperialism, and their historical and contemporary influences in the world.

(e) *Role of women*: students should know about the role of women and their contribution to the development process in a range of societies.

(f) *Population*: students should know about the current demographic trends and developments in the world and the principal arguments surrounding population issues.

(g) *Health and nutrition*: students should know about the causes and effects of major diseases in the world and understand the importance of a balanced diet and safe water supplies to health. They should also know about developments in primary health care.

(h) *Education and literacy*: students should know about current educational trends and developments in a range of societies and understand the significance of literacy to development.

4. ENVIRONMENT

(a) *Destruction of ecosystems*: students should know about the causes and effects of the destruction of, or threat to, principal local and global ecosystems and a range of alternative solutions put forward for their protection.

(b) *Natural resources*: students should know about the location, extraction processes, and usage of the world's natural resources and understand the causes and effects of the depletion of non-renewable resources.

(c) *Conservation*: students should understand the principles of conservation and know about conservation projects from local to global levels.

(d) *Pollution*: students should understand the causes and effects of pollution — of ground, sea, and air — locally and globally and know about the principal measures which are or could be taken to combat it.

(e) *Land use and reform*: students should know about the current usage of available land and the principal developments and arguments concerning land use reform and land reclamation.

(f) *Built environments*: students should understand the environment problems within, and resulting from, major urban centers and know about a range of alternative solutions proposed.

5. PEACE AND CONFLICT

(a) *Negative and positive peace*: students should understand the concepts of negative peace and positive peace and should be conversant with examples of each condition at a range of levels, local to global.

(b) *Interpersonal peace*: students should understand some of the major causes of conflict at an interpersonal level, at school, home, or in the community, and know a range of appropriate conflict management techniques.

(c) *Inter-group peace*: students should understand some of the major causes of conflict between different groups in society and know about the strategies in operation to restore peace or avoid conflict.

(d) *International peace*: students should understand some of the major causes of conflict between nations and know about historical and current attempts to establish peace.

(e) *Armaments*: students should know about the major suppliers and purchasers of armaments (conventional and nuclear) and the economic, political, and social ramifications of the arms race. They should also know about past and present movements towards disarmament and understand the principal arguments in the debate concerning nuclear disarmament.

(f) *Terrorism/freedom fighting*: students should understand the reasons for and the implications of terrorist or freedom fighting activities and know about the historical development and aims of some of the major active movements.

(g) *Non-violent protest*: students should know about the aims and influences of historical and contemporary non-violent protest movements and their leaders, in their own and other societies. Students should also know what opportunities for non-violent protest are open to them.

6. RIGHTS AND RESPONSIBILITIES

(a) *Human rights and responsibilities*: students should know about the *Universal Declaration of Human Rights*, its strengths and weaknesses, and understand the implications of this document for themselves and for humankind in general.

(b) *Moral and legal rights and responsibilities*: students should understand the concepts of moral rights and legal rights, and their relation to human rights, and be aware of their own moral and legal rights and responsibilities.

(c) *Liberty-oriented and security-oriented rights*: students should understand the distinction between liberty-oriented rights (concerned with individual liberties) and security-oriented rights (concerned with material and physical well-being), and that the prioritization of these rights varies according to ideology and perspective.

(d) *Freedom from, freedom to*: students should understand the concepts of "freedom from" and "freedom to" and know about some of the major incidents in the world in which personal freedoms were violated.

(e) *Prejudice and discrimination*: students should understand the nature and workings of prejudice, in themselves and others, and how such prejudices can lead to personal and social discrimination by means of age, class, creed, ethnicity, gender, ideology, language, nationality, or race. They should also know about measures to combat discrimination at personal, societal, and global levels.

(f) *Oppression*: students should know about the oppression of groups, in their own and other societies, for reasons of their age, class, creed, ethnicity, gender, ideology, language, nationality, or race. They should have an understanding of the personal attitudes and social structures which nurture oppression, the part they as individuals play in this process and the contribution each can make towards its diminution.

(g) *Self-determination*: students should have an understanding of the right to self-determination for individuals and social groups, and should know about cases in which this right is violated.

(h) *Animal rights*: students should understand the various arguments concerning the rights of animals and should know about cases in which animals are subjected to cruelty or mistreatment.

7. ALTERNATIVE VISIONS

(a) *Futures*: students should be aware that there are a range of alternative futures open to humankind and they should know what contribution they can make to the realization of their personally preferred futures.

(b) *Sustainable life-styles*: students should know about the arguments and practices concerning the limiting of economic growth and how their own life-styles can contribute to or negate a process of sustainable development for the planet.

(c) *Human and planetary health*: students should understand the holistic concept of health as being the fusion of the bodily, emotional, intellectual, and spiritual dimensions of a person living in harmonious relationship with the planet. They should also know about personal, social, and global action to restore and maintain human and planetary health.

SKILLS OBJECTIVES

1. INFORMATION MANAGEMENT

(a) *Receiving and expressing information*: students should have competence in receiving and expressing information through observing, reading, writing, listening, talking, questioning, graphical, and other non-verbal communication processes.

(b) *Organizing and processing information*: students should have competence in classifying, defining, analyzing, synthesizing, and sequencing information, relating and contrasting one idea or experience to another, and deductive and inductive reasoning.

(c) *Evaluating information*: students should have competence in determining the quality, appropriateness, or priority of information, in distinguishing between evidence and opinion, and in recognizing bias and perspective.

(d) *Storing and retrieving information*: students should have competence in memorizing information, including facts, concepts, physical movements and processes, in recalling and utilizing stored information, and in storing, and retrieving information from manual or computerized information systems.

(e) *Systems analysis*: students should be able to use systems analysis techniques so as to perceive the interrelationships and interdependencies within and between systems.

2. PERSONAL GROWTH

(a) *Centering*: students should be able to utilize a range of skills, such as relaxation, correct breathing, and imagery, so as to integrate mind and body, i.e., to become centered.

(b) *Physical well-being*: students should be able to maintain their physical well-being by means of a balanced diet, sufficient exercise, and an appropriate life-style.

(c) *Manual*: students should have competence in a wide range of manual skills, including domestic, horticultural, and technical skills, so as to facilitate personal and planetary development.

(d) *Creative potential*: students should be able to identify and develop their own areas of potential and have competence in expressing themselves creatively.

(e) *Values, beliefs, and perspectives*: students should be able to identify and clarify their own values and belief systems, and be able to modify personal values and beliefs to accommodate appropriate new perspectives and ideas.

(f) *Shock avoidance*: students should be able to cope with stress and be prepared to manage and gain from major shocks, setbacks, and transitions in personal and professional life.

(g) *Time management*: students should be able to manage their time effectively through planning, prioritization, and time-saving techniques.

3. INTERPERSONAL

(a) *Assertiveness*: students should be able to clearly state desires, feelings, and preferences without infringing the rights of others.

(b) *Empowerment*: students should be able to express feelings about themselves and others constructively and be able to both give and receive help, encouragement, and feedback.

(c) *Trust building*: students should be able to build and maintain trust through openness and sharing in their personal relationships, whether at home, school, or in the community.

(d) *Co-operation*: students should be able to work and play co-operatively, ensuring the effective participation of all members of a group in the achievement of a common goal.

(e) *Negotiation*: students should be able to make contracts, compromise, and reach mutually satisfactory agreements or conclusions.

(f) *Conflict management*: students should be able to handle controversy and resolve conflict in such a way as to maximize the creative force of conflict. They should also be competent in using conflict avoidance techniques where appropriate.

4. DISCERNMENT

(a) *Decision-making*: students should be able to make informed decisions in all spheres of their lives on the basis of sound information gathering, organizing and evaluating, intuition.

(b) *Ethical judgment*: students should be able to select and use criteria to determine the moral rightness and wrongness of an idea or a course of action.

(c) *Aesthetic appreciation*: students should be able to judge, appreciate, and express qualities of beauty in the creative arts and in natural or built environments.

5. IMAGING

(a) *Creative thinking*: students should be able to make lateral moves outside their established frameworks of thought so as to generate fresh insights and perspectives.

(b) *Problem-solving*: students should be able to solve problems in all spheres of their lives through a combination of effective information management, creative thinking, and intuition.

(c) *Perception of relationships*: students should be able to perceive and identify patterns, commonalities, and relationships between phenomena.

(d) *Holistic perception*: students should be able to transcend their own personal and cultural experience so as to see a particular situation, idea, or event as a part of a whole.

(e) *Empathy*: students should be able to use their own experience and imagination so as to understand the attitudes, feelings, and actions of others.

(f) *Visualization*: students should be able to reawaken and develop their powers of imaging and visualization so as to help realize their full creative potential.

(g) *Forecasting*: students should be able to make realistic predictions about personal and global futures and the consequences of proposed actions, based on a reasoned analysis of past and present trends.

ATTITUDES OBJECTIVES

1. POSITIVE SELF IMAGE

(a) *Belief in own potential*: students should have a sense of their own worth and a belief in their own physical, intellectual, emotional, and spiritual potential.

(b) *Genuineness*: students should have the capacity to identify, own, and transmit their thoughts, feelings, and emotions.

(c) *Curiosity*: students should want to find out more about themselves and their interdependent relationship with other people and the planet.

2. APPRECIATION OF OTHERS

(a) *Diversity*: students should be willing to find the beliefs and practices of other cultural and social groups of value and interest, and be prepared to learn from them.

(b) *Commonality*: students should appreciate the essential worth of others and the commonality of needs, rights, aspirations, behavior, and talents which binds humankind.

(c) *New perspectives*: students should have a receptivity to perspectives different from their own and be prepared to modify their own ideas and beliefs where appropriate.

3. RESPECT FOR JUSTICE AND RIGHTS

(a) *Defence of rights*: students should have a commitment to defending their own rights and the rights of others and a correlative commitment to carrying out responsibilities.

(b) *Concern for justice*: students should be prepared to show solidarity with victims of injustice in their own and other societies.

(c) *Commitment to equality*: students should have a commitment to principles of equality as the basis on which relationships between individuals, groups, and societies should be organized.

4. TOLERANCE OF UNCERTAINTY

(a) *Ambiguity*: students should be prepared to tolerate ambiguity in their lives, be willing to explore alternative paths before reaching decisions or conclusions, and be prepared to struggle with problems for which there are no single, simple, specific, or final solutions.

(b) *Insecurity*: students should be prepared to accommodate movements of self-doubt and temporary feelings of insecurity in their personal relationships and in their lives.

(c) *Conflict and change*: students should perceive conflict and change as inevitable and natural and be prepared to respond through appropriate modifications of their values, beliefs, and life-styles.

5. CAPACITY FOR CREATIVITY

(a) *Risk-taking*: students should be willing to explore new patterns of interaction and to take calculated risks in all spheres of life.

(b) *Paradigm shift*: students should be prepared to take the creative mental leaps necessary to perceive alternative visions and versions of reality.

(c) *Imagery and intuition*: students should be prepared to utilize and value their natural capacities for intuition and imagistic thinking.

6. WORLD-MINDEDNESS

(a) *Respect for life*: students should have a respect for all living things and their place and function in the overall planetary ecosystem.

(b) *Altruism*: students should appreciate that in an interdependent world system, consideration of the overall good of humankind and the planet should influence their decisions and actions.

Chapter 9

Principles of Liturgy and Social Justice

J. Frank Henderson, Kathleen Quinn, and Stephen Larson

What has worship to do with social justice? Plenty! In Paul's first letter to the Corinthians, we read a critique of worship practice that does not heed *internal* justice within the community:

> But in the following instructions I do not commend you. . . . For, in the first place, when you assemble as a church, I hear that there are divisions among you. . . for in eating, each one goes ahead with his own meal, and one is hungry and another is drunk. ...Do you despise the church of God and humiliate those who have nothing? ...For any one who eats and drinks without discerning the body eats and drinks judgment upon himself. (1 Cor. 11:17-22, 29)

A critique of worship that is too introspective, devoid of concern for justice in daily lives beyond the walls of the sanctuary, that is, devoid of concern for *external* justice, is forcefully declared by Amos:

> I hate, I despise your feasts,
> and I take no delight into your solemn assemblies.
> Even though you offer me
> your burnt offerings and cereal offerings,
> I will not accept them,
> and the peace offerings of your fatted beasts
> I will not look upon.
> Take away from me the noise of your songs;
> to the melody of your harps I will not listen.
> But let justice roll down like waters,
> and righteousness like an everflowing stream.
> (Amos 5:21-24)

Paul and Amos are but two examples who remind us that from stone altar to temple, from synagogue to house church, from basilica to cathedral, from camp meeting to base community, worship and social justice are intimately and intrinsically linked as a theme that runs through the Scriptures, that is brought to expression throughout the church's history, and that finds contemporary expression in our Sunday morning liturgy.

GENERAL PRINCIPLES OF LITURGY AND SOCIAL JUSTICE

WHEN WE WORSHIP WE PROCLAIM THAT ONLY GOD IS GOD

To proclaim God as God is to expose, reveal, and challenge the many false gods and idols that vie for our loyalty or attention or which make claims for our allegiance. Such idols include a military system which calls us to put our ultimate trust in weapons; money, which seeks to become our prime concern; status, which wishes to be our principal pursuit; grades, if they are our main motivation for learning, or... You can add to the list. Such idols are every bit as real as the molten gods condemned by Isaiah, or the golden calf built in the wilderness.

In worship we proclaim that all other relationships, whether to nation or ruler, class or race, economic or social status, must be secondary to our relationship with God. This principle is summarized in the first commandment: "I am the Lord your God, who brought you out of the land of Egypt, out of the house of bondage. You shall have no other gods before me." In worship our idolatries are confronted and exposed as we remember and celebrate our covenant relationship with the one true God.

To confront and expose our idolatries, however, is not a once-for-all event. It requires an ongoing recentering of ourselves around God's word. The Third Reich in Germany may serve as an example. As the state increased in power, it took on the symbols and trappings of a religion. In that context, the Confessing Church in Germany called upon itself, as well as the state, to recenter itself around theGospel of Jesus Christ. A similar example may be observed in South Africa today. Elements of the church, in issuing *The Kairos Document*, have called the church and state away from an idolatry and toward a prophetic reunderstanding of God's word. Idolatries are always around, seeking to seduce us. Our liturgy exposes those idolatries and proclaims only God as God.

One form of idolatry, from which Christians have not always escaped, is to image God too narrowly. In particular, we often express a limited and limiting notion of God through the use of images, names, and pronouns that are largely if not exclusively masculine in nature. Today, we are beginning to realize that though no human speech is adequate to express the mystery and nature of God, we should make every effort to use language that reflects the many facets of God revealed in Scripture and in the experience of the people of God.

WE PROCLAIM IN OUR LITURGY THAT GOD IS THE CREATOR

When we worship the creator, we declare ourselves to be God's creatures, a part of God's creation. Our awareness and use of God's creation should therefore be respectful and conserving; our relationship within the creation should be harmonious. The account of creation in Genesis reminds humankind that we are placed within the created order as stewards, not exploiters.

The four ancient elements of the universe—earth, air, fire and water—are present within our worship. Elements of creation are thus integral to our worship experience: water, fire ashes, bread, wine, incense, beeswax, wood, stone, wool, linen, and most especially, human beings. The list could go on and on. These elements of creation are used by God and by the worship assembly to communicate God's, the creator's, presence. Such affirmation of the creation within worship underscores God's continuing blessing of creation; God's resounding "It is good!" echoes through the ages. Such an affirmation of the created order should encourage the worship assembly to make authentic use of the creation in worship: real flowers, not plastic; genuine and rich fabric, not synthetic materials; fire, not flickering light bulbs.

IN OUR LITURGY WE COMMEMORATE AND CELEBRATE THE DEATH AND RESURRECTION OF JESUS CHRIST

The assembly gathers for worship on the day of the Lord's resurrection. The entire church year builds from Advent, Christmas, and Epiphany through Lent toward the annual remembrance of Christ's death and resurrection. The fifty days of Easter derive from that annual remembrance and move us toward the gift of the Spirit at Pentecost. In weekly cycles commemorating Christ's resurrection we move through a church year centered upon the death and new life of Christ.

Christ's exodus from death to new life is a victory over death, a liberation from slavery to sin. It is a liberation in which we share because of our baptism into Christ's death and resurrection. As God's action in the exodus was a liberation from slavery, so in God's action of raising Christ from death to life there is a liberation from all kinds of deadly slavery. Baptized into this covenantal relationship, we pledge ourselves to seek the liberation of others from all kinds of slavery and death. Our baptismal covenant links us in a vertical relationship with God and within a horizontal relationship embracing the whole human family.

IN WORSHIP WE CELEBRATE THE INCARNATION AND CONTINUED PRESENCE OF JESUS CHRIST

To tell the stories of Jesus' life and ministry is to remember his incarnation into a specific time and place and also communicate social justice themes. Jesus was born in an occupied land, was homeless at birth, a refugee early in his life. He was from among the poor of the land. Yet, Jesus the Christ has promised to be with us always. In his presence today, Jesus himself relates to, and thus joins us to, people of our own time who are poor and outcast. Jesus lived and moved among the marginalized: the bleeding woman who reached out to him from the dusty street, Zacchaeus in the tree, the adulterous woman, tax collectors, a Samaritan woman seeking water. Jesus lives and moves among the marginalized still. We are called to share in these relationships and the consequent responsibilities. Is it any wonder that the Roman Catholic Latin American bishops' conferences at Medellin in 1968, and Puebla in 1979, pleaded for the church to have a preferential option for the poor?

IN OUR LITURGY WE INVOKE THE PRESENCE AND ACTION OF THE TRANSFORMING HOLY SPIRIT

Jesus gifted the church with the Spirit. In our worship we pray to God through Jesus Christ, in the Holy Spirit. This Spirit has called and gathered us into relationship with God and with one another. The sanctifying grace of the Holy Spirit is thus not primarily a privatistic, pietistic, other-worldly influence, but rather transforms the gifts given us to continue the ministry of Jesus Christ in the world today. It is the Spirit that calls us toward a unity among all women and men within the body of Christ.

Many see the work of the Holy Spirit in the process of liturgical renewal and the integration of liturgy and social justice. One example of the Spirit's sanctifying presence may be found in Mexico where a cathedral and a people were transformed. The cathedral in Cuernavaca was an ornate structure. As a parish, it was among the first to be touched by the wave of liturgical renewal in the Roman Catholic Church. It may be hard to imagine an elaborate cathedral and liturgical renewal as elements of a revolutionary transformation. Yet, these were the means by which the bishop of Cuernavaca was able to "hear the cry of the poor" in his diocese. With the assistance of the monks at a nearby Benedictine Abbey, the bishop initiated changes in the decor of the cathedral. Golden images were removed. As the walls were being stripped of their finery, ancient murals of the indigenous people were uncovered. The distance between the people and the presider was lessened, the altar and presider were turned so as to face the people. As other liturgical changes took place, more poor people began to feel that this, too, was their church. Bishop Mendez-Arceo began to meet and listen to these people, their hardships, and their hopes. As he listened, he as well as the cathedral was transformed. He and many priests and Sisters began to rethink their roles. Strong leaders emerged from among the people. They gathered in small groups to pray, listen to the word, reflect—and to act. This brought the people, the bishop, and church workers into many situations of conflict with those who were quite content for poor people to remain voiceless and powerless.

IN OUR LITURGY, WE PROCLAIM AND MODEL THE KINGDOM, OR REIGN OF GOD

That is, we "play," rehearse, and experience a foretaste of the reign of God within the worshiping assembly. Thereby we are both challenged and enabled to proclaim and model this reign in our weekday living. Divisions that are known in society are—or *should* be—banished within our worship assembly. Racism, sexism, ageism, ideologies, and political dogma are challenged by God's reign. We are called to put them aside in our worship and accept a new identity, as equal members in the body of Christ. By virtue of our baptism, we are neither Jew nor Greek, slave nor free, male nor female, black nor white, but all one in Christ. In the world beyond our worship there is hunger; but inside the worshiping assembly all are fed equally from God's gracious table as a sign of how life might be ordered. In the world beyond our worship there is war and hostility; but inside the worshiping assembly all share the peace of the Lord as a sign of how life might be lived. In the world beyond our worship there is hostility and suspicion toward the stranger; but inside the worshiping community the stranger is hospitably welcomed. In the world beyond our worship death reigns with seeming impunity; but inside the liturgical gathering, death is overcome and we celebrate life in spite of death.

IN WORSHIP WE RITUALLY EXPRESS OUR LONGINGS FOR AN ALTERNATIVE FUTURE

Our longing to be whole, forgiving, and to belong is brought to our worship and to occasions to remember or reaffirm our baptismal covenant. Our longing for God's *shalom*, for peace and justice, for an end to war and oppression, for all the world to be fed, is brought to expression in our prayers, addressed to God, but affirmed by the whole assembly with its "Amen." Our longing to be a part of community is brought to the fellowship of the assembly. Our longing to extend the church's mission, to serve those in any need, is brought to the offerings where we offer ourselves, our time and talents, our bread, wine, and money, as symbols of who we are.

But those longings are not left within the sanctuary. Those very longings which come to ritual expression in liturgy become an agenda, a mandate for our daily lives. In the ritual expression, these longings shape us, form our identity, make us who we are as people of God. We bear that identity into all the world as instruments of God's peace, as "little Christs" called and sent not only to proclaim God's reign, but to live it.

OUR LITURGY SUSTAINS AND NOURISHES US IN OUR MINISTRIES AS DISCIPLES OF JESUS CHRIST

Our practice of the "lifestyle of the kingdom" on Sunday prepares us to live these attributes of the reign of God in our everyday, weekday lives, in our work, and within our relationships. In gathering together around word, baptism, and Eucharist, we recenter ourselves and remind ourselves who and whose we are. We bring to our worship the wounds and sorrows encountered during the week and find comfort, healing, forgiveness, and consolation in God's word. We also find the vision and strength to return to the world to live as Christ's disciples, as instruments of God's peace. Our worship is thus an occasion and source of hope, encouragement, and joy, shared among the people of God.

As an example, consider a community of women in Calcutta. Gathered around a modern saint, these Sisters of Mother Teresa together seek to embody the presence of Christ amidst a scene of almost unimaginable poverty, hunger, sorrow, and death. Their ministry includes orphanages for abandoned children, houses of refuge for hungry people, and hospices for the dying. It is the ministry of some Sisters among them to begin the day by gathering the infants born and abandoned on the streets during the night. Some of the infants are rescued and placed in orphanages. Other babies are simply held by warm, loving arms until they die. This community of Sisters begins each and every day of such ministry with Scripture, prayer, and the Eucharist. Their worship sustains, nurtures, and continues to make possible their ministry and witness.

THE WORSHIPING ASSEMBLY TRANSCENDS OUR INDIVIDUALITY AND EMPHASIZES OUR CORPORATE IDENTITY

The church is defined as the baptized *assembly* gathered around word and sacrament. The emphasis is upon the gathered community. In our worship, the assembly acts. We make corporate confession, articulating the implicit nature of common sin, the systemic nature of evil, the collective responsibility of our actions and of our indifference. We move on with words of assurance that there is occasion for *new* beginnings, for the possibility of corporate conversion and change. The gathered assembly is a weekly reminder that in Christ we are one. Barriers of society are dismantled and washed away at baptism. The norms of society are displaced by the ethics of the kingdom when the assembly gathers.

Next Sunday when you gather with others for worship, look around you with care and compassion upon your sisters and brothers in Christ. But look with a critical eye as well. What do you see? Is there in fact a true gathering of God's people? Or are they mostly all alike; of the same race, of similar economic standing, healthy and whole? Where are the disabled, the retarded? Where are the "street people?" Is your corporate identity a true reflection of the diversity of God's human family or is it a ghetto?

WORSHIP CELEBRATES WOMEN AND MEN IN COMMUNITY

The Scriptures speak of there being neither male nor female in the body of Christ. Yet, for centuries there has been a flagrant distinction made between men and women in the community of the church. This principle of worship and social justice thus accuses and judges us, for women (and children) are in practice more often than not *unequal*. An awareness of this principle will lead worshiping communities to affirm the full participation of women in worship, to a sensitivity for the need of language that is inclusive of all, and to care in balancing the roles of women and men (and older children) in liturgical ministries.

A growing edge for many church people today is the concern for using words and images which include and embody all of the members of the worshiping community and their experiences. It is vital that people hear and see that they are part of this community. The pain of exclusion or invisibility can disillusion those who experience it and leave the entire community the poorer. It is a hopeful sign that denominational bodies have undertaken formal studies of the role of women in the church and the question of inclusive language. There have been some helpful changes, but there are still many challenges to be studied and addressed.

OUR LITURGY AFFIRMS AND INTERACTS WITH ITS CULTURAL SETTING

Worship is linked to its scriptural roots in the life and ministry of Jesus of Nazareth. But each generation and each local church is challenged to faithfully relate that scriptural origin to its own context, and to make worship faithfully indigenous in its cultural setting. Inevitably, this raises difficult questions. For example, at the World Council of Churches General Assembly in 1983, some delegates from the South Pacific islands asked whether coconuts and rice wine could be used as the elements in their Eucharist, since wheat bread and grape wine were alien to their cultural context. What is the faithful response to such a question?

To be aware of one's cultural setting involves one in an examination of the totality of worship: texts, architecture, vestments, music, instruments, and so on. Consider the example of northern Canada. If you had been present at a Bible class in northern Labrador in the early part of this century, you would have heard a missionary teaching about Christ as the "harp seal pup of God" instead of the "lamb of God." The native people of that area had never seen a sheep, and Dr. Wilfred Grenfell felt that the harp seal pup more adequately bore the biblical connotations for these people. Or, if you had been present at the Palm Sunday worship for a community of Dene in Fort Simpson in 1982, you would have held a pine bough in your hand during the procession instead of a palm branch. You would have observed that the presiding minister's vestments were adorned with moose hair and porcupine quills. You would have felt the drums pulsing with your own heart beat as you listened to the Dene sing in their own chanting, wailing song.

The heart cries out in prayer, song, and images shaped by one's culture, race, and experience. Some congregations are unicultural while others are multicultural. Some are unilingual while others use a multitude of languages in their worship. Whatever your congregational reality, it is helpful to be aware of the role which culture plays in liturgical expression. Facilitating cross-cultural understanding through the prism of liturgy can be a community-building experience.

If yours is a multicultural congregation, you might consider ways to celebrate different cultures that are authentic and integral to the liturgy, and not merely token or inappropriate. This could be through song, prayer, liturgical dance of procession. Banners, altar cloths, vessels for the Eucharist, or art forms such as carvings, sculptures, or stations of the cross could be used. Invite people who are new citizens, whether by choice or through exile, to participate in the visible ministries exercised during the liturgy. For example, in one large, urban parish, each cultural grouping represented within the congregation has been asked to plan a special Sunday liturgy. Afterward, people are invited to taste ethnic foods, enjoy dance, music, and other art forms in order to learn about the country and experiences of the group.

AT THE SAME TIME, WORSHIP CRITIQUES ITS CULTURAL SETTING

This principle is related to those described above that proclaim God as God in exposing idols and that rehears the values and lifestyles of God's reign. As no culture is perfectly consistent with the Gospel, there are idols and values in every culture that worship needs to expose and challenge. In addition, while being sensitive to the different ethnic cultures represented in any of our congregations, it is also crucial to be aware of a larger, more dominant context within which many of the other cultures exist. Various names have been used to describe ours: consumer culture and western culture are two.

Current bumper stickers, only partly in jest, declare: "This car stops at all garage sales" or that human beings are "Born to shop." Critically examined, these statements lay bare the idolatry of this consumer culture.

What values give birth to such a statement? Without exploring in depth here, we can see that the ways in which Jesus interacted with people affirms a higher calling than being "born to shop." As well, the reign of God promises more than the winning of a lottery. Some elements of the church glibly proclaim that you can accept Jesus into your heart and then expect to have follow wealth, happiness, fame, and fortune. The liturgy of the church says otherwise. In our worship, we are called to insure that the values and symbols of the consumer kingdom do not shrewdly and deceitfully displace the values and symbols of the reign of God.

IN WORSHIP WE EXPRESS AN AWARENESS OF HISTORICAL AND GLOBAL REALITIES

That is to say, we worship in a given time and space, and like Jesus' time ours is laden with social justice realities. Historically, we worship in the era of Auschwitz and Hiroshima, twin holocausts that have indelibly scarred us and raised implications for us in how we worship. The ancient Greeks had two words for time: *chronos* was the normal, chronological unfolding of history; *kairos* described the sacred, holy moments of history. We worship as people of God sensitive to and aware of the "kairos" moments within the "chronos" of our lives. In other words, we worship with a keen sense of memory but also with the anticipation of God's reign. This keen sense of memory is attentive to "the underside of history," the history of the victims which has usually been overlooked by the victors who write the official histories. In our worship we celebrate already the presence of God's reign even as we await its final consummation. Our global awareness in worship begins in our local setting and extends outward through city, province, nation, continent, and planet. Issues and events are addressed by God's word, are incorporated into our prayers, and are shaped into our lives and our longings.

A good example of worship with such awareness may be observed, perhaps surprisingly, at monasteries. Virgil Michel and Thomas Merton and their monastic communities could be mentioned, but consider rather Taize, a small, ecumenical monastic community located in the beautiful, pastoral countryside of southern France. High above the green fields of Burgundy, intersecting contrails of Mirage jet fighters dispute the notion that Taize is remote and isolated. Since 1940, an ecumenical community of Brothers has gathered and grown near the small village of Taize. During World War II, Taize was a haven for Jews escaping the death camps of the Third Reich. Now it is a place of pilgrimage for young people from all over the world. Three times a day the Brothers and their guests gather in the Church of Reconciliation for Scripture reading, song, silence, and prayer. Praise and thanksgiving, intercession and lament give shape and content to their communal prayer. At the same time in other parts of the world, "cell groups" of three Taize Brothers gather thrice daily for prayer. Their locales are not as idyllic as Taize, for they seek out the poorest places on earth to name as home: Hell's

Kitchen in Manhattan, Haiti, and Calcutta are among them. But whether in Burgundy or Haiti, their prayer is shaped and informed by an awareness of the poverty, oppression, sorrow, and tragedy of humanity's inhumanity. Their prayer and their lives of ministry are turned toward the hope and shalom of God's reign.

These principles summarize some of the connections between worship and social justice that can assist our pastoral practice.

WORKS CITED

The Kairos Document. Braamfontein 2017, South Africa, 1985. (Available from the Center of Concern, 3700 13th Street, NE, Washington, D.C. 20017.)

Chapter 10

Service and Solidarity

Albert Nolan, O.P.

In this essay, I want to talk about what service of the poor means, how it should develop, and the spiritual development we can go through in our service to the poor in the many different ways in which we try to perform it. There is a real development that goes through stages in very much the same way as the stages of prayer. For example, some of us will know quite a bit about the stages of humility, steps of humility which St. Bernard talks about. Or the stages of love and charity that we read about in spiritual books. I am suggesting that in our commitment to the poor there is a parallel spiritual experience that also goes through different stages. Crisis, dark nights, and light . . . and it is that which I will present in this essay.

FIRST STAGE: COMPASSION

The first stage then, as I understand it, of this commitment to the poor is characterized by compassion. We have all been moved personally by what we have seen or heard of the sufferings of the poor. That is only a starting point and it needs to develop and to grow. Two things help this growth and development of compassion. The first is what we have now come to call exposure. The more we are exposed to the sufferings of the poor, the deeper and more lasting does our compassion become. Some agencies these days organize exposure programs and send people off to a Third World country to enable them to see something of the hardships and grinding poverty. There is nothing to replace the immediate contact with pain and hunger. Seeing people in the cold and rain after their houses have been bulldozed. Or experiencing the intolerable smell in a slum. Or seeing what children look like when they are suffering from malnutrition. Information is also exposure. We know and we want others to know that more than half the world is poor and that something like 800 million people in the world do not have enough to eat and in one way or another are starving. For many people the only experience of life from the day they are born until the day they die is the experience of being hungry. All sorts of information can help us become more compassionate, more concerned. Providing of course we allow it to happen. That we don't put obstacles in the way by becoming more callous, or saying, "It's not my business," or "I'm in no position to do anything about it." We as Christians have a way of allowing our compassion to develop, indeed, we have a way of nourishing this compassionate feeling, because we can see compassion as a virtue. Indeed, we can see it as a divine attribute, so that when I feel compassionate I am sharing God's compassion, I am sharing what God feels about the world today. Also, my Christianity, my faith, enables me to deepen my compassion by seeking the face of Christ in those who are suffering, remembering that whatever we do to the least of his brothers and sisters we do to him. All these things help, and this developing compassion leads on to action, action of two kinds that we may to some extent be involved in.

The first of these is what we generally call relief work, the collecting and the distributing of food, of money, of blankets, of clothes, or sophisticated ways of doing that to help the poor. And the second action that leads immediately from our compassion would probably be a simplification of our lifestyle, trying to do without luxuries, trying to save money to give to the poor, doing without unnecessary material goods and so forth. There's nothing extraordinary about that; it's part of a long Christian tradition: compassion, alms giving, voluntary poverty.

My point is that this is the first stage. And what seems to be extremely important is that we go on from there.

SECOND STAGE: STRUCTURAL CHANGE

Now the second stage begins with the gradual discovery that poverty is a structural problem. That is, poverty in the world today is not simply misfortune, bad luck, inevitable, due to laziness or ignorance or just a lack of development. Poverty, in the world today, is a direct result of political and economic structures. It is the result of political and economic policies. In other words, the poverty that we have in the world today is not accidental, it has been created. It has been, I almost want to say, manufactured by particular policies and systems. In other words poverty in the world today is a matter of justice and injustice, and the poor people of the world are people who are suffering a terrible injustice. They are the oppressed and the poor of the world. Not that I want immediately to blame individuals. Certainly the greed of the rich is the reason why there are the sufferings of the poor, but what I am trying to say is that it is a structural problem. We are all involved in this; we're victims, we're pawns, whatever you like, but we're all part of it. It is a structural problem.

This characterizes what I am calling the second stage of our spiritual development. It immediately leads to indignation or, more bluntly, anger. It leads to anger against the rich, against politicians, against governments for their lack of compassion, for their policies that cause poverty and suffering. Now anger is something that we, as Christians, are not very comfortable with. It makes us feel a little guilty when we discover that we are angry. But there is a most important sense in which anger is the other side of the coin of compassion. If we cannot be angry then we cannot really be compassionate either. If my heart goes out to the people who are suffering, then I must be angry with those who make them suffer.

The problem, of course, for us Christians is that there can even be a crisis at this stage. What about forgiveness, or loving one's enemies? Anger doesn't mean hatred to begin with. I can be angry with a person whom I love; a mother can be angry with a child because the child nearly burned the house down. And mustn't we be angry with the child because of love and concern? So sometimes I must be angry. Sometimes I must share God's anger. The Bible is full of God's anger, which we tend to find embarrassing at times, rather than helpful to our spiritual lives. My suggestion that we need to share God's anger means not hatred, but rather, as we say so often, not a hatred of the sinner but a hatred of the sin. What I want to suggest here is that the more we all understand the structural problem as a structural problem, the more we are able to forgive the individuals involved. It's extremely important for us in South Africa, for example, to recognize that the wickedness, the extreme wickedness of what is happening is not something that we can blame the president for, as if he were by himself a particularly wicked individual. We blame the system, and if he were to disappear, someone else would take his place and the system would go on. It is not a question of hating or blaming or being angry with individuals as such, but of tremendous indignation against a system that creates so much suffering and so much poverty. My suggestion is that the more we have that anger, the closer we are to God. And if we cannot have that anger, not only about South Africa but about any system or any policy that creates suffering, we don't feel about it as God feels about it and our compassion is wishy-washy.

During the second stage, our actions will be somewhat different, or we may add to what we were dong before. Because as soon as we realize that the problem of the poverty in the world is a structural problem, a political problem, then we want to work for social change. Relief work deals with the symptoms rather than the causes. Relief work is somewhat like curative medicine, and the work for social change is somewhat like preventive medicine. We want to change the structures, the systems that create the poverty, not only to relieve people when they are suffering form that poverty. Both are necessary but at this stage you begin to recognize the need for social change. And this may be through a tremendous amount of activity on our part, action for social change, trying to fight the system and to change governments maybe, getting involved in politics, campaigns of one sort or another. For some people, it leads to paralysis. What can I do against the system? I can't do anything to effect structural change. What can one possibly do in Britain about the structures in the world and policies that create poverty? Some people feel totally paralyzed by it, while others become very active. This then is what I would describe as the second stage. A struggle goes on within a person at this stage.

THIRD STAGE: HUMILITY

We come now to the third stage. It's difficult to know what to call this third stage. Basically, it develops with the discovery that the poor must and will save themselves, and that they don't really need you or me. Spiritually, it's the stage where one comes to grips with humility in one's service to the poor. Before we reach this stage, we are inclined to think that we can, or must, solve the problems of the poor. We, Europeans, aid agency people, conscientized middle-class people, the church maybe, leaders, either alone or perhaps together with others, have got to solve all these problems. Governments or people who are educated must solve these problems of the poor. We see the poor as what we often call the needy; we must go out and rescue them because they are helpless. There may even be some idea of getting them to cooperate with us. There may be some idea of teaching them to help themselves. But it's always we who are going to teach them to help themselves. There is a tendency to treat the poor as poor, helpless creatures. Now I am suggesting that at this third stage the shock comes, perhaps gradually, as we begin to realize that the poor know better than we do what to do and how to do it. That they are perfectly capable of solving structural problems, or political problems. In fact they are more capable of doing it than you and I are. It is a gradual discovery that social change can only come from the poor, from the working class, from the Third World. Basically I must learn from them. They know better than I what is needed and they, and only they, can in fact, save me. I need something that only they can give me. It is not that I have things that only I can give them.

This can amount, in spiritual terms, to a crisis. It can also amount to a very deep conversion. I myself came first to pastoral work after a doctorate in theology from Rome. I thought I had the answers, only to discover gradually I really knew nothing and that the people who were uneducated, who seemed to be simple, ordinary poor people, to whom I would have to speak very simply, they knew better than I, for example, what needed to be changed in South Africa and how it needed to be changed. I had to come to terms with that.

We discover that the poor are God's chosen instruments and not me. The poor themselves are the people that God wants to use and is going to use in Christ to save all of us from the crazy madness of the world in which so many people can be starving in the midst of so much wealth. This can become an experience of God acting and of God's presence in the poor, not merely as an object of compassion, not merely seeing the face of Christ in their sufferings, but discovering in the poor, God saving me, God saving us, God acting and speaking to us today.

The hazard in this third stage is romanticism. Romanticizing the poor, the working class, the Third World. As soon as we've made this discovery, we tend to put the poor on a pedestal: the poor, the Third World, the working classes perhaps. We can get ourselves into a position where, if somebody is poor and says something, then it is infallibly true. Or, if somebody comes from the Third World, we must all listen simply because they come from the Third World. And if they do something, it must be right. That's romanticism, and it's nonsense. On the other hand, it is a kind of romantic nonsense that somehow we all seem to need at one stage. As long as we recognize what we're doing, I don't think it's necessarily very bad. But it can become a problem at the end of this third stage. We are likely to reach a crisis, a crisis of disillusionment and disappointment because the people of the Third World, or the poor have not lived up to the heroic picture we had of them. We have misunderstood something. We have misunderstood the structural problem. It doesn't mean to say that poor people in themselves and by themselves are any different as human beings from anyone else.

FOURTH STAGE: SOLIDARITY

That brings me to the fourth and last stage. That stage, I am suggesting, centers around the experience of solidarity, real solidarity with the poor and the oppressed. And I think the real beginning of this stage of our spiritual development is the disappointment that we experience when we discover that the poor are not what we thought romantically they were. I am not saying that we do not have a great deal to learn from the poor. I maintain that. I am not saying that they are not God's chosen instruments. They are. All of that remains true. But they are human beings; they make mistakes, are sometimes selfish, sometimes lacking in commitment and dedication, sometimes waste money, are sometimes irresponsible. They are sometimes influenced by the middle class and have middle-class aspirations, and sometimes believe the propaganda and perhaps don't have the right political line. Maybe they are not all that politicized. Nevertheless I can and must learn from them. Nevertheless only the poor and the oppressed can really bring social change. It is simply a matter of moving from romanticism about the poor to honest and genuine realism, because that's the only way that we can move into this fourth stage. I'm talking about the stage of real solidarity.

Real solidarity begins when it is no longer a matter of we and they. Up to now I've described everything in terms of we and they because this is how we generally experience it. Even when we romanticize the poor, make tremendous heroes of them, put them on a pedestal, we continue to alienate them from ourselves—there is a huge gap between us and them. Real solidarity begins when we discover that we all have faults and weaknesses. They may be different faults and weaknesses according to our different social backgrounds and our different social conditions and we may have very different roles to play, but we have all chosen to be on the same side against oppression. Whether we're in Europe or South Africa, whether we're black or white, whether we were brought up in a middle class or working class, we can be on the same side against oppression, well aware of our differences. We can work together and struggle together against our common enemy, and unjust policies and systems, without ever treating one another as inferior or superior, but having a mutual respect for one another while recognizing the limits of our own social conditioning. This experience, and it is an experience of solidarity with God's own cause of justice, can become spiritually an experience of solidarity with God in Jesus Christ. It is a way of coming to terms with ourselves in relationship to other people, with our illusions, our feeling of superiority, with our guilty, our romanticism, which then opens us up to God, to others, to God's cause of justice and freedom. This is a very high ideal and it would be an illusion to imagine that we could reach it without a long personal struggle that will take us through several stages—dark nights, crisis, struggles, shocks, challenges.

The four stages I have described then are not rigid so that you have to go through exactly one stage after another. It does get mixed up. But I have presented this model in the hope that our attitude to the poor may always remain open to further development. The one really bad thing that can happen to any of us is that we get stuck somewhere along the way. We are then no longer able to appreciate others who have gone farther. Because we don't realize that it's a process, we also don't appreciate and understand those who are still beginning. We need to understand that we and the church are all going through a process, spiritual development, a growth and a struggle. We're in it together and need to help and support one another in it. We in South Africa and the church in general, are going through this process. Let us help it, encourage it, struggle with it in ourselves, because today it is the only way we are going to come closer to God and be saved.

Part III

Practical Application

Overview

This section highlights practical strategies and approaches for enlivening the service dimension of parish and school ministry with youth. The pastoral circle process outlined in **Chapter Eleven** offers a singular approach to education and action for social change. This four stage process helps people to claim justice issues as their own; to analyze the structures that support injustice; to reflect on scripture and the living tradition of the faith community as they speak to the reality of injustice; and finally, to move out to change the systems and conditions which sustain injustice. An understanding of the past causes, present reality and future consequences of injustice leads inevitably in this process to concerted action for social change.

There are, of course, other approaches to service and social change, and other ways of relating education and social involvement. Two approaches to education and action for justice are explored in **Chapter Twelve**. The first, based on Thomas Groome's work in **Shared Christian Praxis**, provides a strong educational framework for a Christian response to social concerns. This process both flows from and returns naturally to the everyday lived experience of the Christian. It lends itself to a variety of faith responses: local and global, individual and group, direct service and social change, further study and shifting expressions of one's spirituality. The second, based on the Justice and Peace Education Council's work in the **Infusion Methodology**, provides a process for integrating justice concepts into every component of your ministry with youth. The infusion process involves four simple steps: 1) Looking at the original aim of the lesson or program; 2) Observing the suggested learning activity or program component; 3) Choosing a related justice and peace concept; and 4) Expanding the learning activity or program activity to include the new infused concept.

Chapter Thirteen offers practical suggestions for designing dynamic service and action programs for youth. The need for a balance between programs of direct service and social change is stressed and an eight step process offered for organizing parish and school based programs. Education and reflection play an important role in any program of service or social change and are particularly important in programs with youth. Effective service programs help young people responding to immediate needs. Equally, if not more importantly, they should introduce young people to a way of being of service to others, a process of caring that they can adapt and adopt as their own.

Skillfully mixing these different approaches into your ministry with youth will make for a fuller program — and should make for a fuller life for the young people with whom you work and for all the people they, in turn, reach out and touch.

Chapter 11

The Pastoral Circle:
A Guide to Analysis and Action
on Justice Issues

Thomas Bright and John Roberto

INTRODUCTION

A frequent temptation in service and justice programming with youth is to jump right from an experience of justice, especially one which touches young people personally, to action. Young people want, and need, to do something. While this approach may be of some help in responding charitably to pressing needs, it is less helpful as a response to structural injustice.

Structural injustice is not beyond the understanding of young people. In fact, it is a very real experience for many. Prejudice, discrimination, poverty, and need know no age limits. The challenge to those who work with youth is not to help them understand an abstraction called injustice, but rather to help them believe that they can do something about the very real social problems that touch their lives.

What leads young people, or any people for that matter, to action for justice? Several elements suggest themselves. First, they need to be connected — they need to be personally impacted by the issue, or at least feel how it effects others. Second, they need to understand the issue well enough to believe that their response will make a difference. Third, they need a sense of direction and hope, a sense that as large as a problem may be, it can be whittled down to size when people of faith work on it together.

The process of analysis and action described in this article involves young people in action for social change. It involves them too in analysis and reflection, a process aimed not just at immediate action, but at helping them understand the world in which they live and what they can do to make it a better place for all.

The Pastoral Circle process described here is adapted from the work of Peter Henriot and Joseph Holland. The adaptations to their excellent process have been made in the hope of making their process more usable with youth and young adult groups.

The Pastoral Circle

(Adapted)

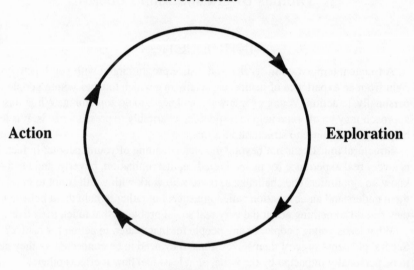

Involvement

Action

Exploration

Reflection

THE PROCESS DESCRIBED

STEP ONE: INVOLVEMENT

The first step in the process — and the basis for any action — is *Involvement*. Through *Involvement* we connect with social issues and make them our own. *Exploration, Reflection,* and *Action* flow naturally from the lived experience of individuals and communities. Because we live not just independently, but as members of families, neighborhoods, school and work groups, towns and nations, *Involvement* moves us beyond personal experience to reflect on the experience of the wider community. Because we are members of a church community, we experience and explore social issues from the perspective of Catholic social teaching. We try to feel and understand how social issues touch the lives of the poor. Getting in touch with what people are feeling, what they are undergoing, and how they are responding to the situations they find themselves in — these are some of the experiences that constitute *Involvement*.

The entry point for analyzing and acting on an issue may be:
  * an event — an experience of injustice
  * an issue — hunger, poverty, environment, the arms race
  * a set of problems — economic deterioration of a neighborhood, pollution
  * a question — why does poverty persist in the richest country in the world?

Involvement, in some cases, may begin naturally with the experience of the group. What justice issues are part of the lived experience of the young people with whom you work? If these are the issues you are dealing with, *Involvement* provides the young people in your group with the opportunity to express their feelings and thoughts about their experience. It gives them the opportunity to ask how this same injustice is experienced by others.

Involvement, in other cases, may not spring from personal experience. You will need to provide an opportunity which helps young people to creatively connect with the issue to be explored. You can simulate the experience of injustice, helping youth "feel" the issue being analyzed, or expose them to what is happening in the local community, helping them to "hear" and "think" from a broader perspective.

Once they are connected with an issue, people are ready to move to *Exploration*, to ask the "why" questions from an *Involved* perspective.

STEP TWO: EXPLORATION

The *Involvement* of individuals and communities in situations of injustice must be understood in the richness of all their relationships. *Exploration* is a means of widening our reflection on our experience to search out the relationships between values, events, structures, systems, ideologies. *Exploration* helps makes sense of our *Involvements* by putting them into a broader picture and drawing connections between them. It goes beyond our immediate experience to probe the historical roots and future implications of events and issues and systems. The task of

Exploration, the second step in the Pastoral Circle, is to examine causes, probe consequences, and delineate linkages rooted in the structural realities which condition our experience and limit or expand our freedom of choice.

For the Christian, *Exploration* will become a *habit of thought* which comes to expand our approach to all of our experiences. It will stretch us to move:

> from the *personal* to the *societal*
> We will look beyond the immediate hunger of the poor family to ask what there is about our economic system which enables it to produce abundant food yet not feed all its people.

> from the *anecdotal* to the *analytical*
> We will look beyond the single unemployed worker to runaway factories and the interrelated choices and policies which create the mismatch between her/his skills and the available jobs.

> from the *ahistorical* to the *historical*
> We will go beyond saying "our immigrant ancestors made their way out of poverty, why can't THEY?" to looking at the differences between the 19th century with its needs for legions of unskilled workers to the 20th in which over two-thirds of the labor force is providing services, many of which require relatively high levels of skill.

> from the *local* to the *global*
> We look not only to the needs of the refugees moving into our area, but also to the realities of war and economic exploitation which force people to leave their homelands.

> from *guilt* to *responsibility*
> We will see the linkages between our privileged position in the world and the hardships of our brothers and sisters and we will join with them and others in action toward a just society.

We will become persons who habitually ask *WHY* in the face of human suffering and injustice. We will always look for causes, relationships, structural realities in order to understand the plan for effective action for change.

The scope of *Exploration*, the resources needed, and the length of the process will vary from issue to issue. If *Involvement* (the entry point) is an event with which youth are very familiar, not much data gathering from external sources will be needed. We will not require a resource person to assist with *Exploration*. However, if we are trying to understand a complex social issue, or the way a whole system functions we may need a longer time period and some external resource persons to assist.

STEP THREE: REFLECTION

The third step is *Reflection* upon the issue that people are involved in and that they have explored, in light of the Scriptures, Church social teachings, the resources of our Tradition, and the lived faith of the Church community.

Faith is not just an intellectual process, but a lifestyle as well. This step involves people in exploring what faith *says* about particular social issues. It involves them likewise in exploring what the faith community is *doing* about social issues and what *motivates* its response. *Reflection* should call forth not just an intellectual assent to faith, but a commitment to incorporate it within one's life. The witness of committed individuals can go a long way toward making *Reflection* real. The Word of God brought to bear upon the situation challenges old ways of thinking and responding by raising new questions, suggesting new insights, and opening people up to new action possibilities.

STEP FOUR: ACTION

Since the purpose of *Exploration* and *Reflection* is decision and action, the fourth step, *Action*, is crucial. Complex social issues seldom lend themselves to simple solutions. Social problems can seem overwhelming. But their very complexity makes it possible to approach action for change from many different angles. If *Reflection* helps people to feel part of a wider faith community committed to justice, then the *Action* step helps them to identify the particular role they can play in weakening and eventually destroying injustice. *Action*, whether individual or group, is always seen within a community context. It can be locally or globally focused, short term or long term. It can be expressed in a variety of ways. But if it is grounded in *Involvement, Exploration,* and *Reflection* it will be effective. At the same time that it brings about small changes in social problems, *Action* can produce major changes in the lives of those involved.

A response of action to a particular injustice brings about new *Involvements* which call for further *Exploration, Reflection,* and *Action* — each time building on and extending previous insights and experience. The process is more like a "spiral" than a "circle" — leading individuals and communities deeper into action for justice.

THE PROCESS APPLIED

STEP ONE: INVOLVEMENT

A. Select a Justice Issue

The starting point for *Involvement* in justice is always the experience of the local community. People are more likely to stay involved and to work hard for change if an issue impacts them personally. As people grow familiar with the Pastoral Circle and experience the interconnectedness of social problems, it becomes easier to move them on to other issues. The following strategies can be used in selecting an issue:

* Brainstorm with a leadership core the issues that confront those you work with on a regular basis. Lead questions might be: In what ways do the young people in your group see themselves as victims of injustice? What justice issues can they identify within their family, school, or work settings?

What issues touch their neighborhood or parish, their town or country?
What issues seem most pressing on the international or global level?
* Develop a *Hit List of Injustice Topics* using local newspapers. Vote for the problem you would most like to see wiped out.
* Check out what's playing in local theaters or on MTV. Have the group select an "in" issue from the movies and videos directed their way.

B. Develop an Involvement Activity

The variety of strategies we can employ to help young people get *involved* in justice is limited only by the extent of our creativity and access to resource materials. *Involvement* lends itself to a broad range of experiential learning activities. Among the possible *Involvement* options are the following: surveys of justice issues, true-false quiz, word association games, simulation games, video or film (that portrays a person's story or exposes an issue), guest speaker (telling a person's story or exposure to an issue), case study, role play, skits, journaling, mock newscast, guided imagery, reviewing written articles (newspaper/magazine), field trip, interviews, personal sharing, creating a video or photo essay, creative art, use of literature/drama, music with slides and discussion, taking a stand or claiming a viewpoint (forced choice continuum or four-corners activity), analogy questions, photos, cartoons, maps, creating a map.

C. Focus Discussion

The *Involvement* activity selected should engage young people's heads and hearts. They should be encouraged to share their touch with the issue — what they personally know about it, feel about it, and are doing about it. Moving beyond their individual experience, they should ask the same questions from a community perspective: As family members, workers, students, parishioners, citizens how does this situation impact us? What are we doing to bring about understanding or change?

STEP TWO: EXPLORATION

Exploration helps people understand the elements that give birth to or sustain injustice. It explores the assumptions that allow injustice to go unchecked and the social structures that too often work against social change, consciously or not. A *formal* approach to exploring a social issue would include the following elements.

A. Clarify the Focus

Identify the purpose of *Exploration* through a clear statement of the issue that the group has decided to explore.

B. Gather the Data

Learn more about the issue by researching answers to the following questions:

1. What is the history of this social situation? How long has the problem been with us? How has it changed through the years? Who benefits from the present situation? Who suffers?

2. What influence does economics have on this issue? *Economic structures* like a bank or business determine how society organizes resources and their production, distribution, and consumption.
   Ask: Who controls the resources involved (natural and human resources, manufactured goods and money)? Who benefits economically from this situation? Who suffers? Who pays? Who gets?

3. What influence does politics have on this issue? *Political structures* determine how society organizes power and what degree of participation people have in decisions which effect their lives.
   Ask: Who has the critical decision-making power in this situation? How does the deciding get done? Who benefits? Who suffers?

4. What values are at work, or absent in this situation (like patriotism, independence, inclusion, human dignity, acceptance of cultural differences)? *Cultural structures* determine how society organizes meaning and its "way of life."
   Ask: Who benefits from these values? Who suffers? What influences what people believe in?

5. What influence do social groups and organizations have on this issue (like family, neighborhood, education, communications, media)? *Social structures* determine how society organizes relationships — how people group themselves to relate to one another (ethnic group, class group, age group, sex group).
   Ask: Who is left out? Who is included? What is the basis of the exclusion? inclusion?

C. Analysis and Synthesis

Look at what you have learned. What seem to be the *causes*? What *linkage* is there between the social, economic, political, and cultural structures — either positive or negative? This should result in two concise statements of the reality as understood at this point.

* One statement will identify the causes and linkages in the problem area.
* A second statement will point out the resources available and the positive factors on which to build.

Knowing the causes and linkage is the first step in identifying both the problems to be addressed and the strengths on which change can build.

The process suggested above is a formal one. It is a standard research approach, an academic approach to information gathering that many young people are able to handle. But it is not the only valid approach. Other, creative approaches to *Exploration* can be used to reach the same results — to help young people understand the history, players, connections, and real-life consequences involved in social justice issues.

The following ideas can be used in conjunction with the questions above and may smooth your journey of *Exploration*. (For example, you may show a video or film which explores the issue and invite young people to analyze what they have seen using the questions above.) Suggested ideas for *Exploration*: simulation game, Socratic method—dialogue, debate, political/social cartoons, research project, written reflection, use TV game show format to present information (like *Jeopardy*), interviews, word association, ranking/listings, True-False quiz, multiple choice quiz, speaker, simulate *Nightline* or *20/20* or *60 Minutes* format, forum, create video or photo essay, video or film, sculpturing, diagramming, research and teach what you find to others, map/atlas, fact-finding tour, point—counterpoint debate (using a panel or a video), letter to leaders/politicians (where do they stand on issues).

STEP THREE: REFLECTION

A. Identify the Religious Values

Identify the religious values and traditions that seem to be at stake in the issue you have explored. What things in your experience and education lead you to say, "Things shouldn't be this way!"

B. Explore the Scriptural Basis

Explore the Hebrew and Christian Scriptures to see where and when the values you have identified have come into play. How has God's word of justice been revealed in the history of the Hebrew people? How was this issue approached by the teachers, prophets, or psalmists of the Hebrew Scriptures? What did Jesus say or do when confronted by the same or similar instances of injustice? What can be learned from the life of the early Christian community as it tried to fashion a new community around Jesus' teachings and lifestyle?

C. Examine Church History and Tradition

The Church's understanding of God's justice continues to grow and develop through time. When, in the course of its long history, has the church community been faced with this same challenge to justice? What principles or approaches are set forth in the Church's Social Teaching, either Vatican documents or pastoral letters developed by national bishops' conferences? In many cases it will be appropriate to give close attention to the recent writings of the American bishops, for example their pastoral letters on peace, economy, racism, and international relations.

D. Experience the Church in Action

Like Jesus, the Christian community speaks not just through what it says, but by how it embodies its words in action. See what the Church is doing to respond to the short or long term problems created by injustice. Listen as Christians share *why* they are doing the work they are.

Be as creative in your approaches to *Reflection* as you were in your approaches to *Involvement* and *Exploration*. Try *Reflection* activities like the following: storytelling, music and slides, Scripture search and reflection on selected passages, re-create the Scripture reading through role-playing, audio-visual presentation, use of literature/drama, Scripture pictionary, audio tapes, word association, journaling and sharing, role play a bishop's committee writing a pastoral letter on a justice issue, explore the church in other cultures, creative arts, writing prayers, preparing a liturgy or prayer service, testimonials from involved people, church history nuggets, preparing a penance service on social sin, writing a creed, writing or reading poetry, creating a video or photo essay, survey of social teachings, comparing pastoral letters from around world to United States pastorals, cartooning, creating symbols.

STEP FOUR: ACTION

Action helps people identify and organize their response to injustice. Action strategies may vary in level of response (personal, interpersonal, structural) geographical focus (local or global) and duration (short or long term). But all action should promote transformation, that is, should help change the systems and structures that make it possible for injustice to flourish. *Action* programming includes the following steps:

A. Select an Appropriate Action Response

1. Brainstorm possible actions appropriate to the situation as it has been analyzed.
2. Eliminate any actions which seem impossible for the group or unlikely to be effective.
3. List the pros and cons of each of the plausible options.
4. Use a consensus process to select the course of action to be taken by your group.

There are many possible approaches to action. Consider the following:

Personal: lifestyle changes, examine consumer patterns, further education, fasting, prayer, career goals (long, short), planning/choices, educating others, participating in an immersion experiences, taking a personal action, taking responsibility for change in the family, keeping informed (reading newspaper and magazines), watching use of language (stereotypes), tithing.

Interpersonal (Service): working with local service agencies (church groups, civic groups, service agencies, issue groups), family activities, adopt a _____, twinning, fundraising for relief work, collecting /distributing _____, workcamps (local, global, national), peer to peer actions.

Structural (Action for Social Change): attending political hearings/councils, lobbying and letter writing, creating a youth chapter/joining existing social change organizations (local, national, international), boycott and using money for social change, influencing policy programming (student council), supporting change organizations (money or volunteer time), organizing around local issues/advocacy (campus), orchestrating media events/ newspapers (awareness campaigns), stewardship of investment (stocks, money), consciousness raising and advocacy, voting/education.

B. Develop a Strategy
1. Describe the component pieces of your action response.
2. Identify key resource materials and persons that will be helpful in planning and implementing your action response. Check out other groups involved with this same justice issue. Explore options for networking and cooperative action.
3. Develop a realistic timeline for your action plan, assigning tasks and setting up procedures for accountability.
4. Re-examine the whole strategy to see that all the essential elements have been included.

C. Implement
After appropriate preparation and training, implement your plan of action.

D. Evaluate
1. Assess the action response and the process that led up to it. Explore its impact on individuals and on your group as a whole.
2. Offer options for sustained involvement with this issue or with other expressions of the Christian call to justice.

(A detailed treatment of Christian Service and Action for Social Change is found in Chapter Thirteen.)

BIBLIOGRAPHY

Hofbauer, G.N.S.H., Rita, Dorothy Kinsella, O.S.F., and Amata Miller, I.H.M. *Making Social Analysis Useful.* Silver Spring: Leadership Conference of Women Religious, 1983. (8808 Cameron Street, Silver Spring, MD 20910)

Holland, Joe and Peter Henriot. *Social Analysis — Linking Faith and Justice.* Maryknoll: Orbis Books, 1983.

Carey, R.D.C., Loretta and Kathleen Kanet, R.S.H.M. *Structural Analysis. The Leaven Movement.* Dubuque: Brown-Roa Publishers.

Chapter 12

Education for Justice

Thomas Bright and John Roberto

This chapter is a guide to designing justice education programs. It presents several key ingredients for justice education and then describes two methodologies you can use. The first description applies the Shared Christian Praxis methodology of Thomas Groome to designing a learning experience on a justice issue. The second describes how to utilize the Infusion Method for incorporating justice and global concepts into an entire curriculum. The emphasis in this chapter is on practical application of what was presented in Sections One and Two of this book.

INGREDIENTS OF JUSTICE EDUCATION

1. **ALL** CHRISTIAN RELIGIOUS EDUCATION, REGARDLESS OF CONTEXT OR CURRICULUM, MUST EDUCATE FOR JUSTICE.

Education for justice cannot be merely one isolated theme among many others in the curriculum of religious education/catechesis. Justice is not a separate topic, and education for justice cannot be treated, as is often the case, as merely one elective among many in our curriculum. We place a tremendous burden on justice teachers when their course is the only area of the curriculum in which young people experience the message of justice and peace. In light of the theological and scriptural foundation that we developed in the first section of this book, it should be clear that the message of justice and peace must permeate that entire religious education/catechetical curriculum. At the Synod of 1971, bishops from throughout the world stated that justice is a constitutive element of the proclamation of the Gospel.

> Action on behalf of justice and participation in the transformation of the world fully appear to us as a constitutive dimension of the preaching of the Gospel, or, in other words, of the Church's mission for the redemption of the human race and its liberation from every oppressive situation.
> (*Justice in the World*)

This means our entire religious education/catechetical curriculum effort must incorporate the message of justice. Thomas Groome offers a starting point for this task.

> The curriculum question can be posed as follows: What stories, traditions, values, myths, practices, and so on will we make accessible to learners in the present and how and to what end will we make them available? Like other educators, religious educators can choose a version of our Story and Vision that will serve to legitimate and maintain the present as it is, or we can choose a version that will recreate our present toward what it ought to be but is not yet. (Groome 75-76)

How will we make the justice story central to our curriculum and teaching? Here are several examples. There are many ways to teach the *Hebrew Scriptures*, but the approach to the Hebrew Scriptures that is chosen often neglects the centrality of social justice in the life and teachings of Israel. Young people need to examine the rich tradition of justice teachings, the vision of Kingdom or Reign of God, and the message of the Prophets. In the study of the *Christian Scriptures* is there an emphasis on social justice teachings like poverty and wealth, simplicity of lifestyle, love of neighbor, and service to those need? Are we ready to teach the difficult message found in Luke's Sermon on the Plain (Chapter 6)? In the study of *Jesus*, is the centrality of justice in Jesus' proclamation of the Kingdom or Reign of God emphasized? Is Jesus' compassion for the poor/outcast and his challenge to those who oppress them included in a course on Jesus? Do young people understand that in becoming disciples of Jesus much will be required of them — loving without boundaries, forgiving seventy times seven, being compassionate toward outcasts, loving one's enemies, giving without counting the cost, serving the least of our brothers and sisters? When we teach *morality,* is only the personal dimensions of sin explored or are the place of social sin in our lives and world and the social responsibilities we have as Christians also explored? Is the *Church* presented as a people with a mission which includes service in the socio-political order according to the vision and values of the Reign of God? Are *Catholic Social Teachings* incorporated into all of our courses (see concepts in Chapter 4A)?

2. TO EDUCATE FOR JUSTICE, RELIGIOUS EDUCATION/CATECHESIS MUST EDUCATE JUSTLY.

Young people cannot be passive recipients of justice content or, worse, be coerced to accept *our* conclusion on a particular justice issue. The process or methodology of educating for justice must itself be *just*, that is, it must respect the freedom of the learner to make his or her own decisions regarding the content and action of the educational program. This educational approach empowers young people to think critically, assess information, reflect on the meaning, make decisions, and act on them. If the process is experiential and leads to action, young people can gain a feeling of solidarity with others, especially those in need, and overcome their sense of powerlessness.

It is important to model justice concepts like dignity, participation, cooperation, peace, and empowerment, in the approach taken to developing and implementing a program of justice education. Young people should have the opportunity to participate in a process of mutual decision making regarding the content. Where possible, they could share responsibility and have the opportunity to explore their own ideas and to develop personal initiative. The group can become a microcosm of the larger society. Young people can help shape the type of school or parish environment they would like to learn and grow in at the same time they begin to imagine and shape the type of *world* they would like to live in. The participatory process can help teens to overcome their apathy and feeling of powerlessness before the forces and institutions which shape their lives. If young people cannot participate and promote reasonable change in their parish or school setting, how will they be able to convince themselves that they can alter society?

3. EDUCATION FOR JUSTICE INCORPORATES A GLOBAL—LOCAL LINK.

We live in one interdependent world, where we all share things in common with our fellow human beings — economically, culturally, politically, environmentally, socially. Each justice issue has its local and global manifestations. Linking the global reality to local and personal experience is an essential element of justice education. Such linking can happen throughout the learning experience: in the experience of injustice, in the analysis of the issues, in the reflection on the Scriptures and Catholic Social Teachings, in actions of service and social change.

There are many approaches to discovering the links between our own lives and those of our peoples in other parts of the world. For example,

1) Discover links to your own community. What cultural, economic, historical, political, and religious links does your community have with the Third World?

2) Relate the Third World reality to the daily experiences of the young people from your parish or school. What feelings, goals, interests, desires do they share in common with youth in the Third World?

3) Present the reality in the form of a story of real life narrative. Most people have a natural curiosity about the lives of others so this should strike a special chord of interest in those you work with.

4) Use a "marketbasket" approach. Rare is the person who does not want to know more about their own food or their own belongings. Look at the everyday things around us — an automobile, a chocolate bar — for ties to the Third World.

(*Teaching Toward Global Understanding* [4])

4. EDUCATION FOR JUSTICE PROMOTES THREE GOALS: *AWARENESS* (COGNITIVE GOALS), *CONCERN* (AFFECTIVE GOALS), AND *ACTION* (BEHAVIORAL GOALS).

In Chapter Seven, Jim McGinnis developed three goals for peace and justice education: Awareness, Concern, and Action. Education for justice must promote an *awareness* of a person's own giftedness, of justice issues, of the human consequences involved in personal and public decisions, of manipulation and propaganda, of why

ce exists, of the scriptural and church teachings, and of how social
place. Education for justice must also nurture an inner sense of
solidarity or concern (conversion), that is the link between awareness and action. The
heart as well as the head must be educated. McGinnis identifies four elements that are
involved in this conversion process: 1) experiencing working for justice as a call from
Jesus — deepening the young person's relationship with Jesus through reflection on
Jesus' concern for justice; 2) being touched by advocates for justice — locally and
globally; 3) being touched by the victims of injustice — locally and globally; 4)
being supported in community through healthy peer relations which create a sense of
belonging and identification with others in a communal setting that influences the
social values of young people. Education for justice also promotes *action* for justice.
These actions include direct service to those in need, actions of social or structural
change. Action for justice focuses on local issues as well as global issues and on both
the local and the global dimensions of the same issue.

DESIGNING JUSTICE EDUCATION USING SHARED CHRISTIAN PRAXIS

The Shared Christian Praxis methodology developed by Thomas Groome
(*Christian Religious Education*) is an excellent approach to justice education —
embodying the key ingredients outlined above. Like the Pastoral Circle, Shared
Christian Praxis is an action-reflection methodology, grounded in the experience
and social setting of the individual or community. Shared Christian Praxis includes
six elements, beginning with the life experience of the person, engaging him or her
in critical reflection on that experience, relating that experience to the Story and
Vision of our Faith (the Scriptures and Tradition), and concluding by reflecting on
the meaning of the learning and the implications of this learning for his or her life.

While Shared Christian Praxis parallels the Pastoral Circle process described in
Chapter Eleven, it must be remembered that Shared Christian Praxis is a *learning
methodology* that *may* lead to individual or group action for social change, but
could also result in direct service, a commitment to further study, or a shift in
attitudes. The Pastoral Circle is an *organizing methodology* that is directed to
group action for social change. Here are the parallels between the two processes:

Shared Christian Praxis	Pastoral Circle
Focusing Activity	Involvement
Movement One: Experiencing Life	Involvement
Movement Two: Reflecting Together	Exploration
Movement Three: Discovering the Faith Story	Reflection
Movement Four: Owning the Faith	——
Movement Five: Responding in Faith	Action

In designing and conducting Shared Christian Praxis justice learning
experiences, it is essential to integrate the four steps of the Pastoral Circle into the
appropriate movements. In a sense, the Pastoral Circle provides strategies for each
step of Shared Christian Praxis.

FOCUSING ACTIVITY

The purpose of the Focusing Activity is to bring the attention of the group to bear on the theme or issue of the lesson so that they can begin to identify it in their own life, their family, culture, society, church. The Focusing Activity is meant to grab the attention of young people through an experiential learning activity. It tries to help young people look at their own activity (beliefs, values, attitudes, understanding, feelings, and doing) around the theme of the lesson.

Some learning experiences need very short focusing activities because the topic is easy to draw out from their life experience and concerns (topics like sexuality, personal growth, relationships, moral dilemmas). For young people who are *or* have experienced the injustice being explored, the Focusing Activity helps them to get in touch with the experience. At other times there is a need to draw young people creatively into the topic because it may, on the surface, seem removed from their current life experience and concerns (topics like Scripture, prayer and worship, justice and peace). In many situations, teachers/leaders will need to create a focusing activity on justice themes to compensate for the lack of experience in the lives of the young people on the particular issue being explored. Experiential activities which help young people affectively enter into the issue are essential at this stage of the learning process.

The focusing activity can be programmed in a number of ways: group activity, story, poem, rock music and videos, a project, scripture reading, role playing, field trip, movie/video, simulation game, creative art, case study, demonstration, reflection questionnaire. (For further ideas see *Involvement* ideas in Chapter Eleven.)

MOVEMENT ONE: EXPERIENCING LIFE

Having focused the group on the theme or issue of the lesson, Movement One invites the young people to express their feelings and thoughts concerning their experience. Young people are encouraged to express what they already know about the theme/issue, or how they feel about it, or how they understand it, or how they now live it, or what they believe about it. Movement One enables them to express their own life activity (knowing, action, feeling) and that of their community, ethnic culture, youth culture, popular culture or society on the theme/issue of the learning experience.

Inviting the group to express their life experience on the topic of the learning experience can be accomplished in a variety of ways: presentations, reflection questionnaires, drama/role playing, making and describing something, symbolizing or miming. Helping young people express their present action needs to done in a non-threatening way. It is important to make it clear that they should feel free to share or simply to participate by listening. Be sure to leave time for silence.

As young people move through the lesson, Movement One becomes the reference point against which they can compare what they are learning and what impact it will have on their lives.

MOVEMENT TWO: REFLECTING TOGETHER

The purpose of Movement Two is to allow the group an opportunity to reflect together on the justice theme or issue of this lesson. This will sometimes be intuitive as well as analytical — engaging reason, memory, and imagination. In exploring justice themes or issues, Movement Two uses the analysis process found in the *Exploration* step of the Pastoral Circle (see Chapter Eleven). This process engages the young people in analyzing the history of the situation, the major structures which influence the situation (economic, political, social, and cultural), the key values operative in this structure, and the future direction of the situation. By conducting an analysis of the situation, the young people will be able to name the two or three "root" elements most responsible for the current situation.

The teacher or leader will need to provide the group with the resources and information on the problem or issue so that the young people will be able to explore the issue. Through the use of media, guest speakers, printed resources, simulation games, and the participants' own experience of the issue, the teacher can assist the exploration process. (For further ideas see *Exploration* ideas in Chapter Eleven.) In conducting Movement Two it is often helpful to communicate more threatening content through audiovisuals, readings, and outside speakers — "experts" with a lot of credibility. It is also helpful to anticipate some of the participants' objections and speak to these concerns in the course of the presentation.

It is important *not* to name the causes of the injustice for the young people, handing them a completed analysis of the issue. Teachers/leaders guide young people to think critically on the structural influences causing the injustice, to identify the causes, and to make decisions about what it will take to alleviate the injustice. Even if presentations are utilized, young people can be prepared to ask the right questions and to debate or discuss what they have seen and heard.

MOVEMENT THREE: DISCOVERING THE FAITH STORY

Movement Three presents the *Story* and *Vision* of the Catholic Christian community in response to the justice theme or issue. The *Story* is a metaphor for the whole faith identity of the Christian community. Here young people encounter the Story of faith that comes to us from Scripture, Tradition, the teachings of the Church, and the faith-life of Christian people throughout the ages and in our present time. The *Vision* is a metaphor for what the Story promises to and demands of our lives. It is God's Vision of God's Reign (the Kingdom of God). We engage people in exploring how we are called to faithfully live God's Vision, individually and as a community — at the personal, interpersonal, and social/political levels of human existence.

From a Christian faith perspective, it is within the *Story* and *Vision* that we interpret, make sense out of, and respond to our own stories and vision, and to the challenge of injustice in our world. In Christian faith, our own stories must be interpreted within the Christian Story — in dialogue with it. Our own visions must be critiqued and lived within the Christian Vision — in dialogue with that Vision.

Socially, the norms of peace and justice provide a base from which youth and adults can criticize and evaluate political and economic systems, foreign and domestic policy, as well as the alternatives generated by the young people themselves.

In a justice session the resources of the Scriptures and Catholic Social Teachings, especially the most recent encyclicals from the popes and the pastoral letters of the U.S. bishops provide a rich tradition to draw on in educating for justice. In addition, the Christian men and women who embody in their lives and work the call to justice provide rich role models for others.

Sharing the *Story* and *Vision* is accomplished through a variety of means: presentations, guided study (of the Scriptures), media, reading, discussion, research, field trip, group project, demonstration, or panel presentation. Teacher *and* learner are involved in sharing the *Story* and exploring the *Vision*. Learners need to be actively involved in Movement Three, overcoming the tendency for passive reception of the *Story* and *Vision*. (For further ideas see *Reflection* ideas in Chapter Eleven.)

It is important to keep in mind the following points in designing Movement Three:

1) The *Story* shared reflects the most informed understanding the community (magisterium, scholars, faithful) has at this time
2) The *Vision* proposed and the *Story* shared promote the values of God's Reign in people's lives — peace, justice, equality, love, freedom, life, and wholeness
3) The *Story* and *Vision* engage the participants — touching the focus, stories, visions of their lives as expressed in the Focusing Activity and Movements One and Two.

MOVEMENT FOUR: OWNING THE FAITH

Movement Four provides the group with an opportunity to compare their own life experience and faith with the *Story* and *Vision* of the Catholic Christian community. Through this dialogue young people can test out their experience and their experience can be informed by the Christian *Story* and *Vision*. The *Story* will confront, challenge, affirm, and/or expand the faith of each person. The purpose of Movement Four is to enable the young people to take the *Story* and *Vision* back to their own life situations, to appropriate its meaning for their lives, to make it their own. It attempts to promote a moment of "aha" when the participants come to know the *Story* as their own, in the context of their lives. There will be as many responses to this dialogue as there are people. It is vitally important, at this step, to allow them the freedom to come to their own answers and conclusions. With this freedom people can be guided to see the "why" of the Christian *Story* and *Vision*.

Movement Four can be accomplished in a variety of ways: reflection questionnaire comparing Movement One and Two responses with the Movement Three story; creative expression of one's learning by writing, creating a role play or a dramatization or a case study, creating an audio-visual presentation (video, slide show), creating a symbol, poster, TV or radio commercial; group activity/discussion; imagination activities where people envision how they can live the learnings from the session.

In justice lessons, it is important to help young people envision or imagine what it would be like if the world were transformed by the *Story* and *Vision*. Questions like the following could be explored: If the *Story* and *Vision* were applied to this injustice what would happen? What would it look like? What would the consequences be for the people experiencing the injustice, for the structures which promote the injustice, for you? for our society? What has to happen to make these changes? How would you do it? It is important to engage young people in imaging a better world. This leads the way to Movement Five.

MOVEMENT FIVE: RESPONDING IN FAITH

The purpose of Movement Five is to help bring the group to a lived faith response, helping people translate their learning into a lived faith response. Once again, applying the learning must be a free response. Some will be changed by the learning experience and motivated to concrete action, while others will need time to ponder its meanings and implications, and still others will not be affected. The teacher/leader creates an environment which invites a faith response, a decision for living more faithfully as a Christian, but respects the right of young people to choose their own response, even if it is not the response that had been hoped for.

In justice lessons, it is especially important to help young people respond at all three levels of their lives. Young people need to probe the implications of their learning for all three levels. They need to be engaged in developing concrete plans for the coming week (personally, interpersonally, socially); in developing individual or group action projects which involve them in living their faith (service and social change actions in their faith community, school, family, community/society/world); in prayer experiences which celebrate or draw people into reflection on their response; in journaling activities where they can reflect on how they are living their faith. The teacher or leader will need to make available specific ideas for service and social change actions (like programs and action organizations) in which young people can be involved and help young people freely choose a course of action. (See Chapter Thirteen for a process to design service and social change projects.)

INCORPORATING JUSTICE CONCEPTS THROUGH THE INFUSION METHOD

The Infusion Method is an excellent tool for insuring that *all* educational programs, regardless of context or curriculum, educate for justice and global awareness. The social teaching of the Catholic Church contains concepts which can form the framework of a new worldview (see Chapter Four). These concepts frequently run counter to concepts generally accepted in our society. Collaboration replaces competition; interdependence replaces individualism; empowerment replaces dependency; multicultural understanding replaces racial and ethnic division. Such concepts can be introduced to children at an early age and reinforced through educational programs. They are best taught indirectly, through learning activities. This is what the Infusion Method aims to do. It is a method which can be used in any subject at any level of elementary and secondary schools.

It is also flexible enough to be integrated within a variety of youth program settings: social, catechetical, service, and worship. It is a way of enriching existing programs and approaches, of breathing fresh life and significance into them.

The Infusion methodology involves the following steps:

1. **Look** at the aim of the lesson or program activity as originally envisioned.
2. **Observe** the suggested learning activities or program components.
3. **Choose** a related justice and peace concept from the list.
4. **Expand** one of the learning activities or program components to include the new infused concept.

Here are several examples of the Infusion Method in practice:

Example #1: "Considering Career Options" (A Minicourse)

1. Original Aim: To help young people explore possible career options in light of their individual talents and gifts.
2. Suggested Learning Activity or Program Component: Panel presentation by local community members representing a variety of careers and professions.
3. Related Justice and Peace Concept: Stewardship
4. Expanded Learning Activity/Program Component: Apart from sharing the career basics (like skills needed, schooling or training, typical day on the job, income potential) ask panel members to share how their jobs assist them in or prevent them from using their talents to make the world a more just and healthy environment for all people.

Example #2: A Dance

1. Original Aim: Building Community, Celebrating Life
2. Suggested Learning Activity or Program Component: Music
3. Related Justice and Peace Concept: Multicultural Understanding
4. Expanded Learning Activity/Program Component: Work with the DJ to see that the music played represents a broad national and cultural mix — not a difficult task given the internationalization of youth music and culture. On a large map in the refreshment area post the names or pictures of the groups featured next to their state or country of origin.

Example #3: A Youth Penance Service

1. Original Aim: To help young people reflect on how sin impacts their relationship with God and with one another.
2. Suggested Learning Activity/Program Component: Scripture readings and examination of conscience
3. Related Justice and Peace Concept: Simpler Lifestyle
4. Expanded Learning Activity/Program Component: Include James 2:14-17 among the readings for the service (faith without action is dead; the poor need our assistance as well as our prayers). Employ a guided meditation as an examination of conscience; suggest ways in which people, individually and nationally, can separate faith and action to the detriment of the poor. Have the group share ways in which they can simplify their lifestyle in order to meet others needs.

In ways as simple as these, youth ministers, teachers, and catechists can expand young people's understanding of basic justice concepts, further global awareness, and encourage social responsibility. *Infusion is not an extra burden* — it is a challenge to the leader's creativity. It implies adding something which gives new life or significance to what is being shared with youth. It enables everyone to take an active role in justice education. It is a way of responding to the Gospel command to love one another by showing that love is intended to permeate all of life, not just Sunday worship or religious education.

Some may think that infusion is a method they have been using all along, that it is nothing new. However, perhaps what they were doing might better be termed *spontaneous inclusion*, rather than infusion. The two methods differ in these ways:

Infusion Method
    a. Integrates the learning within the framework of the program event or the activity section of the lesson.
    b. Presumes deliberate planning of activity; learning is intentional.
    c. Approaches justice and peace education through concepts.

Spontaneous Inclusion
    a. Usually only verbalized by the teacher or adult leader.
    b. More likely to result in over-emphasis of some points, neglect of others.
    c. Usually deals with issues.

The Infusion Method uses a conceptual approach in order to provide young people with the Christian attitudes, values, and skills of analysis and critical thinking which they will need in confronting issues. It does not provide a pre-packaged solution to issues, but rather relies on a gradual building up of the young people's ability to analyze and respond on their own.

WORKS CITED

Groome, Thomas. *Christian Religious Education*. San Francisco: Harper & Row, 1981.

Groome, Thomas. "Religious Education for Justice by Educating Justly." *Education for Peace and Justice*. Ed. Padraic O'Hare. San Francisco: Harper and Row, 1983.

Justice and Peace Education Council. *Dimensions of Justice and Peace in Religious Education*. Washington, D.C.: NCEA, 1989.

Teaching Toward Global Understanding. Global Education Office. Baltimore: Catholic Relief Services, 1986.

Chapter 13

Service and Action for Justice

Thomas Bright and John Roberto

No component or program in youth ministry is more maligned or misused than service. Too often service projects serve in the unrewarding role of a parish requirement for the sacrament of Confirmation or a school requirement for graduation or course grade. Service becomes another "must" in the lives of youth. Many service projects are so poorly planned that they do more harm than good to youth and the people they are trying to help. How many parishes and schools, for example, regularly "inflict" unprepared youth, on a "captive audience" of elderly in the name of service? Lack of creativity in identifying viable service projects, forced youth participation, and inadequate planning combine with the absence of adequate education, reflection, and training for service to create poor programs. It is hard to believe this is what Jesus had in mind when he spoke about serving the needs of others.

When service programming is well done the results can be life-changing. We have seen and worked with programs that are well designed. Young people experience a bonding and identification with the people they serve. They come to understand the social causes of the injustice experienced by these people and communities. They realize how meaningful a life of service to others can be. They discover what Christian discipleship really means. Unfortunately, what should be a powerful and life-changing experience for youth has become largely irrelevant and oppressive. We share a hunch that the last service involvement for the majority of young people takes place is in their high school years. It does not have to be this way!

There is another way to think about Christian service. In this chapter we will suggest key ingredients for developing an effective Christian service component for your ministry with youth, provide a framework for envisioning service and social change approaches, and offer a practical process for organizing your service—social change programming. They are not the last word, but they can help alleviate many of the problems discussed above.

I. SEVEN INGREDIENTS
OF SERVICE—ACTION PROGRAMMING

Incorporating the following seven ingredients into your planning will make for a more effective and well-rounded service/action program.

#1 — CHRISTIAN SERVICE INCLUDES DIRECT SERVICE AND SOCIAL CHANGE.

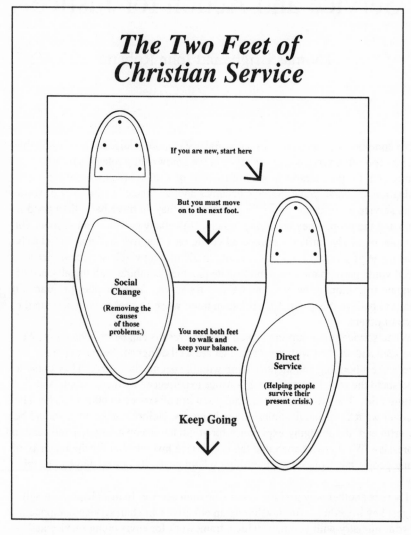

The Two Feet of
Christian Service

If you are new, start here

But you must move
on to the next foot.

Social
Change

(Removing the
causes
of those
problems.)

You need both feet
to walk and
keep your balance.

Direct
Service

(Helping people
survive their
present crisis.)

Keep Going

Christian service involves more than direct service. The majority of youth ministry programs emphasize direct service to help people survive their present crisis or need. Direct service rarely addresses the root causes of the problems. The strength of direct service is the face-to-face, interpersonal nature of the action. Working at a soup kitchen or food center, visiting the elderly or sick, and tutoring children are common examples of direct service. This is not enough though. Direct service needs to be coupled with social change — actions aimed at removing the causes of the problems that direct service is addressing. Social change analyzes the social causes of the problem and develops a response that addresses the injustice. Legislative advocacy, community organizing, and working with organizations that are changing the structures that promote injustice are examples of social change actions. Too often we overlook social change actions because we consider them too demanding for young people. Instead, we need to combine direct service and social change in the same action project. For example, young people who are working at the homeless shelter and soup kitchen could also be involved with the local coalition for the homeless which is working to create housing, employment, and just policies for the homeless. In this way young people will experience the benefits of working directly with the homeless *and* learn to change the system which keeps people homeless.

Examples of Direct Service

- Stocking Parish or Community Food Pantries or Clothing Closets
- Delivering Thanksgiving or Christmas Baskets to the Poor
- Volunteering in a Soup Kitchen or Homeless Shelter
- Responding to the Needs of Local Shut-Ins
- Walk-, Rock- or Starv-athons Fundraisers for Those in Need
- Volunteer Dispatchers or Drivers for a Safe Rides Program
- Participating in a Big Brother/Big Sister Program
- Assuming Responsibility for Regular Clean-up of a Local Park

Examples of Social Change

- Political Action Aimed at Expanding Affordable Housing for the Poor
- Developing a Community Voter Awareness Program to Explore
- Candidates Views on Issues Impacting the Poor
- Organizing a High School Voter Registration Drive
- Establishing a Parish or School Al-a-Teen or S.A.D.D. Program
- Volunteering With or Financially Supporting Organizations that Work to Alleviate the Causes of Social Problems: for example, Children's Defense Fund, Oxfam, Greenpeace, Pax Christi, Amnesty International

#2 — CHRISTIAN SERVICE IS BOTH LOCAL AND GLOBAL.

Not only should our service programming embrace direct service and action for social change, but we need to bring a global perspective to our actions. The most common problem with this ingredient is that people always ask how can you serve people who are so distant. You can not directly. But by working through organizations which have a global focus, like Catholic Relief Services and Church World

Service (CROP), young people in your community can learn about people of another culture and country, as well as be in service to them. Most local service projects and justice issues have a global counterpart, for example, homelessness locally, refugees globally. Hunger, poverty, racism all have local and global dimensions.

#3 — CHRISTIAN SERVICE FLOWS FROM OR LEADS TO EDUCATION FOR JUSTICE AND INCLUDES ONGOING REFLECTION.

Christian service cannot be done in a vacuum. We need to develop an educational component in which young people can a) reflect on their service/action experiences, b) analyze the root causes of the injustice, c) relate their experiences to their Christian faith. Reflection is important because young people need to debrief their experience and discover what they are learning about themselves, about those they are serving, about injustice, and about Christian service. Social analysis is critical because this is where young people will learn the history and discover the structural causes (economic, political, social, and cultural) of the problem. Social analysis leads to better informed action. Relating the Scriptures and the Church's Social Teachings to the experience of service helps young people see that they are serving others because of their faith in Jesus Christ.

#4 — CHRISTIAN SERVICE PROGRAMMING INCLUDES SPECIFIC TRAINING FOR EACH ACTION PROJECT.

For many service/action projects young people need specific skills training, for example, skills for working with the elderly or the handicapped, organizing legislative advocacy or a hunger walk. This specific training is often provided by the service placement. Be sure to check out opportunities for specific training.

#5 — PLANNING FOR CHRISTIAN SERVICE UTILIZES EXISTING ACTION PROGRAMS AND ORGANIZATIONS, ENGAGING YOUTH, THEMSELVES, IN RESEARCHING AND IDENTIFYING THE SOCIAL JUSTICE NEEDS OF THE LOCAL COMMUNITY, NATION, AND WORLD.

Involve youth and adults in researching opportunities for both Direct Service and Social Change actions. Check out community, state, regional, church, and national organizations and agencies. You will find that many organizations and agencies have existing service projects that you can utilize. There is no need to create service opportunities that already exist.

#6 - EFFECTIVE CHRISTIAN SERVICE PROGRAMMING IS VOLUNTARY, OFFERING YOUTH A VARIETY OF CHOICES.

If Christian service is interesting, challenging, and exciting there is no need to mandate or force anyone to participate. Young people will want to serve. We will need to provide choices, so that they can select the project and when, where, and how they will serve. We must work with their schedules and commitments and not force them into our convenient schedule.

#7 - EFFECTIVE CHRISTIAN SERVICE PROGRAMMING MATCHES THE
GIFTS AND TALENTS OF YOUTH WITH THE REQUIREMENTS OF
SPECIFIC PROJECTS OR ACTIONS.

When you do your research, develop a report or profile on each project: a) list
and describe the placement/project, b) identify a contact person(s), c) describe
skill/knowledge requirements and time commitment. This will become the basis
for your orientation program and the choices the young people will make.

II. A FRAMEWORK FOR ENVISIONING SERVICE
AND SOCIAL CHANGE

The following framework provides a way of understanding four different
approaches to social involvement. Together these four models provide a
complementary response to situations of need and injustice. Social involvement is
not exhausted by any one approach. Although *service* is the most common *starting
point* for social involvement it should not be the end point as well. Service
activities should be related to, and whenever possible, lead toward the
complementary responses of advocacy, development, and empowerment.

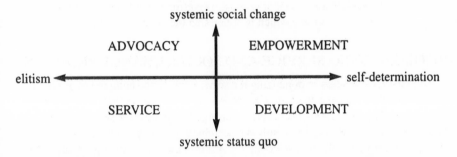

Horizontal Axis

The further *left* you move on the horizontal axis, the more the action (ministry)
is that of someone (group) doing something *for* others or *on behalf* of others
(elitism). The motivation is *altruistic*.

Service is something done for other, or provided for others.

Advocacy is something done by someone (group) on behalf of another's
(group's) neglected or violated rights and dignity.

The further *right* you move on the horizontal axis, the more the action is that of a
person or group *doing for itself* (self-determination). The motivation is *self-interest*.

Development is that which occurs when a person or group relies on its
own resources and strengths — seeking an end to its dependency on
others (self-help, self-reliance, alternative institutions).

Empowerment is that which occurs when a person or group asserts its own
power/control over its own destiny — successfully liberating themselves
from the control exercised over them.

Vertical Axis

The lower you move on the vertical axis, the more the action does not alter the *status quo* of the system. The action may alleviate the *symptom*, but it does not address the *cause*.

Service, although a necessary compassionate response, does not result in changing the system, policy, or public attitude that cause or perpetuated the problem.

Development, although offering a person or group some immediate resources for its own survival, does not alter the system, policy, or public attitude that caused or perpetuated the problem. If, development initiatives (food coops) become significantly widespread, they hold potential for altering the system.

The higher you move on the vertical axis, the more the action results in systemic change. *Advocacy* and *Empowerment* are clearly strategies to address the *causes* of problems — seeking a change in the system, policy, or attitude.

Advocacy is the support a person/group gives another in seeking the systemic change needed to redress its neglected or violated rights and dignity.

Empowerment is a person's or groups' own efforts to change the system, policy, or public attitude which is oppressing the person or group.

III. ORGANIZING SERVICE AND SOCIAL CHANGE PROJECTS

To assist local leaders in organizing the service and action component of youth and young adult ministry, the following process has been developed. It includes many of the key ingredients listed earlier for organizing effective service-social action programs: a) it involves youth in researching, planning, and engaging in service; b) it involves them in selecting the service or social action opportunity that best matches their gifts and talents, and time availability; c) it utilizes existing service and social action opportunities and resources; and d) it builds in educational elements: foundations of justice and exploration of justice issues, and specific training for service and social action.

STEP 1 - SELECT APPROPRIATE SERVICE OPPORTUNITIES

A. Research Service and Social Action Options

Engage youth and adults in researching opportunities for both Direct Service and Social Change. Check out community, state, regional, church and national organizations and agencies. Oftentimes you will find that these groups have existing service projects that you can utilize. There is no need to create programs from scratch or duplicate service or social action opportunities that already exist.

B. Evaluate the Available Options

Given the age, interests, and prior service experience of the young people in your parish or school program, some program options may seem more appropriate than others. Some may fit easily into the flow of your program or academic year while others prove a tighter squeeze. Members of your school or parish community may already be involved in some programs, making peer leadership possible or serving to link the service involvement of youth with that of the wider community. Some service projects may demand or lend themselves to repeat involvement while others are one time experiences. Evaluate all options using criteria developed to fit your unique situation.

STEP 2 - COMPILE A LIST OF CHOSEN OPPORTUNITIES

List and describe each of the placements/projects selected by and for your group. Identify the contact person(s) for each opportunity. Be sure to include skill and knowledge requirements and time commitment. Develop a job description for each project that lets interested young people know what is expected of them in preparing for their involvement, in implementing the project and by way of follow-up.

STEP 3 - DEVELOP AN EDUCATIONAL COMPONENT

If your service/social action involvement flows out of an educational program on justice and peace then you may already have analyzed the issue or concern and presented the Christian response using scriptural and theological sources.

If the service/social action component of your youth or young adult ministry is separate from an educational program (for example, Confirmation requirement), then you will need to provide a basic educational component which helps those you are working with to understand Christian service as a faith-response to inequity or injustice. People, young and old, should understand not just what the problems are, but why they exist. Awareness and analysis are integral elements of effective service/social action programs.

STEP 4 - DEVELOP A TRAINING COMPONENT FOR EACH OPPORTUNITY

For most projects young people will need some specific background or skills training. Start with what the young people already know, feel, or have experienced. Provide new information to erase misconceptions. Provide, too, site-specific skills that will help young people be more comfortable and effective in the service setting, for example, suggestions on how to work with the elderly or handicapped, conversation starters or topics to avoid, practical skills for tutoring or painting a wall, methods for effective lobbying around the issue of homelessness, etc. Make the training real. Do not just share what you would like them to know about the project; give them a glimpse as well of what they will concretely see, hear, touch, and smell. The more prepared they are, the better experience it will be for all concerned. This specific training can often be provided by the organization you will be working with or by local community members already involved in the project. Know your local resources; use training programs that are already in place.

STEP 5 - PRESENT THE SERVICE OPPORTUNITIES TO YOUTH

If the service/social action is a separate component, conduct a "Service Project Orientation Session." Give the young people descriptions and requirements for each opportunity. Emphasize that you are presenting a variety of options so that they may select an opportunity that matches their interests, talents, and time availability. If possible, have representatives present from the organizations and agencies you are working with, or experienced local volunteers, to provide a creative overview of each service option and respond to questions. Have application forms available so that the youth can select their top choices.

STEP 6 - SCREENING, PLACEMENT, SPECIFIC TRAINING

Review the selections made by your youth. Make sure there is enough interest in each project to carry it off well. Knowing your group as you do, check to see that the selections made by individuals meet the requirements of the service organization and are compatible with their personalities, for example, a young person who faints at the sight of blood should not help with the bloodmobile even if all his or her friends will be working there. Balance the ability and commitment of those who have signed up for a specific service project with the very real needs and expectations of the site. Provide an orientation for each service project and any specific pre-service training that will prove helpful. Again, use your local resources and agency contacts. Make sure that everyone understands the project schedule and knows who to turn to for direction or support.

STEP 7 - SERVICE INVOLVEMENT

If people are properly prepared and supported, and if there is regular contact with the service site, the involvement phase of Christian service may prove the easiest.

If the service project is a one-time experience for your group, the involvement of already-experienced community members (peer or other) in the project makes it easy for interested first-timers to continue their involvement.

If the project is an extended one, or if you are coordinating the overall service/social action program and cannot be available for every session, keep in regular contact with the site supervisor or coordinator. Check on the comfort levels of all involved; if a site really is not working for an individual, talk it through and, if necessary change it. Better a temporarily unsettling change of site than a permanent distaste for Christian service.

Make sure that hope and joy are built into every project, either on-site or on the way home. Tough experiences grow easier when they are shared and there is a chance to talk, laugh, and learn together.

STEP 8 - REFLECTION AND EVALUATION

A. Shared Reflection

Throughout the service/social action project there should be opportunities for those involved to reflect on what they are experiencing and learning from the project. Share experiences on several levels: what was seen, heard, touched, or smelled; what is thought and felt; what people have learned about themselves, about those they are working with, and about the situation they are serving in. Such reflection may suggest topics for later consideration or added training that is needed right away.

B. Theological Reflection and Prayer

The service project should lead participants to reflect once again on why they are involved in Christian service. It should lead too to prayer: thanksgiving for unique personalities and abilities, new experiences and relationships; prayer of petition for newly discovered needs; praise for God's presence and assistance. New growth and learning lead naturally to prayer.

C. Evaluation

At the end of the service involvement, engage the youth involved in a systematic evaluation of their experience. Listen to their suggestions for change and improvement, curtailment or expansion of the projects with which they have been involved. Connect their service experience with the educational sessions leading up to the project. Reflect again on the linkage with Scripture and Church teaching, justice awareness, and social analysis. Often their suggestions provide a natural reentry point for additional educational or service ventures.

More important than the "success" of the individual service project is the comfort and sense of ownership felt by the youth who are involved. If young people are at ease with service, and pick up an approach to serving others that they claim as their own, the final result will be a lifestyle of service for others - a result far more valuable than the total hours committed to any single service program or cause.

Appendix One

Justice Assessment Tool

The following profile is designed to assist you in determining areas for improvement of your efforts in justice education, action, and infusion. This tool is meant only to provide you with an overview of what is currently happening backhome. It is a guide to assist you in planning. Adapt it to fit your needs. Not all sections may be helpful to you. Some answers you give may be repeated in other sections. The assessment tool is structured in an abbreviated format. You will need to add space for your answers when you reproduce this form.

A> Education for Justice

This section assesses deliberate, systematic efforts to educate for justice, for example courses or units/themes within a religious education curriculum that address justice and/or peace issues. What specific course(s) are offered on social justice and/or peace? What specific unit(s) are offered on social justice and/or peace as part of a larger course? Please identify the topics or themes addressed (for example justice issues like poverty, hunger, racism; or justice concepts like human dignity, human rights, stewardship). [For a list of justice concepts see the list in Chapter 4A.]

1. Younger Adolescent Ministry (Junior High)
   a. Catechesis/Religious Education:
      Course/Unit(s): _____
      Topics covered: _____

   b. Ministry programs/activities that expose youth to justice issues or broaden their multicultural/global experiences:
      _____

2. Older Adolescent Ministry (Senior High)
   a. Catechesis/Religious Education:

Course/Unit(s): _____
Topics covered: _____
b. Ministry programs/activities that expose youth to justice issues or broaden their multicultural/global experiences:

_____

3. Sacramental Preparation Programs (Confirmation, Adolescent RCIA)

_____

4. Special Justice Education Events (Parish or School)
Please list any special educational events on justice (for example, World Food Day, World Day of Peace)
a._____

B> Service and Social Change Projects

1. Please list the current service/social change projects for youth.
a. _____

2. Do the current projects engage people in:
a) **Service** — working directly to help people survive their present
situation (working with the handicapped, collecting and
distributing food, tutoring children, etc.)   YES NO
If Yes, what % of your projects are service-oriented:_____.

b) **Social Change** — working to remove the cause of social
problems (for example, political action/advocacy, organizing a
hunger walk, community organizing).   YES NO
If Yes, what % of your projects are social change-
oriented:_____.

c) Is there a conscious connection between the projects offered
youth and those presently being done by adult members of the
community?   YES NO

d) Is any of your service/social change program mandatory?   YES NO
If Yes, do you require a certain number of hours?   YES NO
If Yes, how many ___
Do the participants have a choice of which project they will be
involved in?   YES NO

3. Are the participants involved in researching service projects
and/or planning the actual service involvement?   YES NO

4. a) Is there a description of the projects including: a contact
person(s) for each opportunity, skill/knowledge requirements,
and time commitment?   YES NO
If Yes, what % of your projects have descriptions:_____.

b) Do you have job descriptions for each project so that the people will know what is expected of them?   YES NO
If Yes, what % of your projects have job descriptions:_____.

5. a) Are your service/social change programs connected to a course or flow out of an educational program on justice and peace?   YES NO
If yes, how?

b) If your service/social change program is separate from any educational programming how do you provide an educational component which helps the youth understand Christian service as a faith-response and the nature of the injustice or suffering that are trying to address?
Please describe:

6. Does your program provide youth with an orientation and specific skills training related to the project they will be involved in? (For example, how to work with the elderly or the handicapped, how to tutor a child, how to organize a hunger work, how to effectively lobby on an issue.)   YES NO
If Yes, how?

7. Does your program conduct a format presentation of service/social action projects to youth? How?

8. a) Do the participants complete application forms for their projects?   YES NO
If Yes, what % of your projects use applications: _____.

b) Are the applications screened before placements are made?   YES NO
If Yes, what % of your projects screen applicants: _____.

9. a) How do you monitor the participants' involvement in service/action?

b) How does the ministry assist young people in reflecting/debriefing their involvement and what they are learning?

c) At the end of the service involvement, how are the participants helped to systematically reflect on their experience?
How are the learnings from their service involvement connected to social analysis and theological reflection on their issue/injustice?
How are their new experiences/learnings integrated in prayer and worship?

10. Are the projects designed to be repeatable by interested youth?
Are additional resources or contact persons made known to
youth, making further involvement easier?

C> Infusion into All Aspects of the Curriculum and Ministry Programs

*To analyze how your ministry infuses justice and peace into courses/programs
please conduct a dual evaluation: 1. an assessment of how the justice concepts in
Chapter 4 are infused into the programs, and 2. an overall analysis of the
scriptural/theological content of the courses/programs to determine to what extent
social justice and peace is included in the content.*

1. Infusion into the Entire Ministry or Curriculum

*Analyze which programs or courses infuse the justice and peace concepts listed
at the end of Chapter Four into their activities or lesson plans. (For a youth
ministry or campus ministry, think about all the components of a comprehensive
ministry with youth like Evangelization, Community Life, Guidance and Healing,
Prayer and Worship, Advocacy, Enablement. (Catechesis/Religious Education will
be addressed in section 2.)*

Program/Activity: _____
Concepts infused: _____
Program/Activity: _____

2. Infusion of Justice into Scriptural/Theological Content of Programming

*Please assess the approach taken to teaching these theological topics in your
overall educational program. First, determine the extent to which the scriptural
and theological foundations and themes of justice and peace are included in the
course content. Second, identify how a course may infuse the justice and peace
concepts at the end of Chapter 4. (Examples of scriptural/theological content are
provided. Don't be limited to the examples.)*

a) Old Testament

Theological (for example, emphasis on social justice teachings, Prophets,
Kingdom/Reign of God)
Infused Concepts

b) New Testament

Theological (for example, emphasis on social justice teachings: poverty and
wealth, simplicity of lifestyle, love of neighbor, service to those in need,
Kingdom/Reign of God, Jesus' compassion for the poor) _____

Infused Concepts _____

c) **Jesus**
Theological (for example, emphasis on social justice teachings: poverty and wealth, simplicity of lifestyle, love of neighbor, service to those in need, Kingdom/Reign of God, compassion for the poor/outcast) _____

Infused Concepts _____

d) **Morality**
Theological (for example, social sin, social morality, social responsibility) _____

Infused Concepts _____

e) Course/Program: _____
Theological _____
Infused Concepts _____

SUMMARY REFLECTIONS
Please identify what you perceive as the growth needs (areas for improvement) in each section of the assessment tool.

A> Education for Justice
1. Younger Adolescent Ministry (Junior High)
   Catechesis/Religious Education:
   Parish or School Activities/Programs:

2. Older Adolescent Ministry (Senior High)
   Catechesis/Religious Education:
   Parish or School Activities/Programs:

B> Service and Social Change Projects

C> Infusion into All Aspects of the Curriculum and Ministry Programs

Appendix Two

Justice Resource Guide

SECTION I: FOUNDATIONAL JUSTICE READINGS

Section I is a listing of foundational resources specially selected for teachers/leaders in ministry with youth to familiarize them with the scriptural, theological, and social understandings and concepts essential for assisting youth and young adults to develop a social consciousness and spirituality. These understandings and concepts are the foundational building blocks of justice education and action programming.

A. CHURCH TEACHINGS & COMMENTARIES

Baum, Gregory and Robert Ellsberg, editors. *The Logic of Solidarity — Commentaries on Pope John Paul II's Encyclical "On Social Concern."* Maryknoll: Orbis, 1989.

Benestad, J. Brian and Francis J. Butler, editors. *Quest for Justice — A Compendium of Statements of the United States Catholic Bishops on the Political and Social Order 1966-1980.* Washington, D.C.: USCC Publications, 1981.

Brown, Robert McAfee and Sydney Thomson Brown, editors. *A Cry for Justice — The Churches and Synagogues Speak.* New York: Paulist, 1989.

Dorr, Donal. *Option for the Poor — One Hundred Years of Vatican Social Teaching.* Maryknoll: Orbis, 1983.

Gremillion, Joseph. *The Gospel of Peace and Justice.* Maryknoll: Orbis, 1976.

Henriot, Peter, Michael Schultheis, and Ed DeBerri. *Our Best Kept Secret.* Revised Edition. Maryknoll: Orbis, 1987.

Hays, Helen. *Study Guide on The Challenge of Peace.* Erie: Pax Christi USA, 1983.

Hug, S.J., James. *For All The People — Summary of Economic Justice for All Pastoral Letter.* Washington, D.C.: USCC Publications, 1987.

Kownacki, Mary Lou, editor. *Reflection Guide on The Challenge of Peace.* Erie: Pax Christi USA, 1983.

Murnion, Philip, editor. *Catholics and Nuclear War — A Commentary on The Challenge of Peace.* New York: Crossroads, 1983.

NCCB. *Statement on Relieving Third World Debt.* USCC Administrative Board Statement issued on September 27, 1989.

NCCB. *Economic Justice for All.* Washington, D.C.: USCC Publishing, 1986. (*Catholic Update* condensed format available from St. Anthony Messenger, 1615 Republic St., Cincinnati, OH 45210.)

NCCB. *Building Economic Justice — The Bishop's Pastoral Letter and Tools for Action.* Washington, D.C.: USCC, 1986.

NCCB. *To the Ends of the Earth.* Washington, D.C.: USCC Publishing, 1986. (*Catholic Update* condensed format available from St. Anthony Messenger, 1615 Republic St., Cincinnati, OH 45210.)

(A summary, a study edition, a teacher and discussion leader manual, and a video presentation of *To the Ends of the Earth* has been published by The Propagation of the Faith, 366 Fifth Avenue, New York, NY 10017-9990.)

NCCB. *The Challenge of Peace.* Washington, D.C.: USCC Publishing, 1983. (*Catholic Update* condensed format available from St. Anthony Messenger, 1615 Republic St., Cincinnati, OH 45210.)

NCCB. *Brothers and Sisters to Us.* Washington, D.C.: USCC Publishing, 1979. (*Catholic Update* condensed format available from St. Anthony Messenger, 1615 Republic St., Cincinnati, OH 45210.)

The Pastorals on Sundays — March 4, 1990 - February 10, 1991. Passages selected by Jacqueline S. Graham. Chicago: Liturgy Training Publications, 1990. (Published annually) (A week-by-week resource from the pastoral letters of the Bishops of Rome, Second Vatican Council, and the U.S. Bishops' Conference.

Pawlikowski O.S.M., John and Donald Senior C.P., editors. *Biblical and Theological Reflections on The Challenge of Peace.* Wilmington: Michael Glazier, Inc., 1984.

Pawlikowski O.S.M., John and Donald Senior C.P., editors. *Economic Justice: CTU's Pastoral Commentary on the Bishop's Letter on the Economy.* Washington, D.C.: The Pastoral Press, 1988.

Pope John Paul II. *The Social Concern of the Church.* Washington, D.C.: USCC Publishing Office, 1989. [Two Summaries are available: *NCR Supplement* (800-333-7373) and Woodstock Theological Center's Summary (202-687-3532)]

Pontifical Commission *Iustitia et Pax. The Church and Racism.* Washington, D.C.: USCC, 1988.

Shannon, Thomas. *What are They Saying about Peace and War?* New York: Paulist, 1983.

Sheridan S.J., E.F. *Do Justice! — The Social Teaching of the Canadian Catholic Bishops.* Toronto: Jesuit Centre for Social Faith and Justice, 1987. (947 Queen St. East, Toronto, Ont. M4M 1J9)

Social Justice Encyclical Chart. NETWORK. Washington, D.C.: Network, 1989. ($2.00) (Includes: "Denouncing—Announcing: The Prophetic Tradition Continues," "On the Side of the Poor," "Exploring the Call to Solidarity:

Sollicitudo Rei Socialis," study chart on human rights, and overview of the encyclicals.

Walsh, Michael and Brian Davies. *Proclaiming Justice and Peace*. Mystic, CT: Twenty-Third, 1984.

Audio-Video Resources

Between the Times: The Catholic Bishops and the U.S. Economy. Washington, D.C.: Campaign for Human Development. 45 minutes. Study guide included. Purchase: $49.95.

> The themes of the pastoral which call us to conversion are portrayed in an inspiring and new way through song, music, storytelling, and humorous analogy in this videotape performance of the Chicago-based performing arts group.

Send! Receive! Set Free! Columban Mission Education. St. Columbans, NE 68056 (402) 291-1920.

> A presentation on the U.S. Bishop's pastoral statement on mission, *To the Ends of the Earth*. Includes a 20 minute video, commentary, and discussion guide. Free rental.

B. SCRIPTURAL & THEOLOGICAL FOUNDATIONS

Baum, Gregory. *Compassion and Solidarity*. Toronto: CBC Enterprises, 1987; and New York: Paulist, 1990.

Brueggemann, Walter, Sharon Parks and Thomas Groome. *To Act Justly, Love Tenderly, Walk Humbly*. New York: Paulist, 1986.

Crosby, Michael. *Spirituality of the Beatitudes — Matthew's Challenge for First World Christians*. Maryknoll: Orbis, 1981.

Dear S.J., John. *Disarming the Heart*. New York: Paulist, 1987.

Donders, Joseph G. *The Global Believer*. Mystic: Twenty-Third Publications, 1986.

Dorr, Donal. *Spirituality and Justice*. Maryknoll: Orbis, 1985.

Dorr, Donal. *Integral Spirituality — Resources for Community, Peace, Justice, and the Earth*. Maryknoll: Orbis, 1990.

Grassi, Joseph. *Broken Bread and Broken Bodies — The Lord's Supper and World Hunger*. Maryknoll: Orbis, 1985.

Grosz, Edward. *Liturgy and Social Justice: Celebrating Rites—Proclaiming Rights*. Collegeville: Liturgical, 1989.

Gutierrez, Gustavo. *We Drink from Our Own Wells — The Spiritual Journey of a People*. Maryknoll: Orbis, 1984.

Haring, Bernard. *The Healing Power of Peace and Nonviolence*. New York: Paulist, 1986.

Haughey, John, editor. *The Faith That Does Justice*. New York: Paulist, 1977.

Henderson, J. Frank, Kathleen Quinn, and Stephen Larson. *Liturgy, Justice, and the Reign of God — Integrating Vision and Practice*. New York: Paulist, 1989.

Hug S.J., James and Rose Marie Scherschel. *Social Revelation*. Washington, D.C.: Center of Concern, 1987.

Jegen B.V.M., Carol Frances. *Jesus the Peace-Maker*. Kansas City: Sheed and Ward, 1986.

Jegen S.N.D., Mary Evelyn. *How You Can be A Peacemaker*. Liguori: Liguori, 1985.

Kavanaugh, John. *Following Christ in a Consumer Society*. Maryknoll: Orbis, 1981.

McGinnis, James. *Journey into Compassion — A Spirituality for the Long Haul*. St. Louis: Institute for Peace and Justice and Meyer-Stone Books, 1989.

Meehan, Francis X. *A Contemporary Social Spirituality*. Maryknoll: Orbis, 1982.

Nelson-Pallmeyer, Jack. *The Politics of Compassion*. Maryknoll: Orbis, 1986.

Nolan O.P., Albert. *Jesus Before Christianity*. Maryknoll: Orbis, 1978.

Searle, Mark. *Liturgy and Social Justice*. Collegeville: Liturgical, 1980.

Sider, Ronald J. *Cry Justice — The Bible Speaks on Hunger and Poverty*. New York: Paulist, 1980.

Sider, Ronald J. *Rich Christians in an Age of Hunger: A Biblical Study*. Downers Grove: Intervarsity, 1977.

Sobrino, Jon. *Spirituality of Liberation — Toward Political Holiness*. Maryknoll: Orbis, 1985.

Wallis, Jim. *The Call To Conversion*. San Francisco: Harper and Row, 1981.

C. SOCIAL ANALYSIS

The following resources provide analyses of a variety of pressing social problems facing the United States and the world. Some resources focus on providing factual material (graphs, charts, maps, statistics) about social problems, others offer a complete analysis of the issue with recommendations for action.

A Vision for America's Future — An Agenda for the 1990's: A Children's Defense Budget. Children's Defense Fund. Washington, D.C.: Children's Defense Fund.

Brown, Lester, et al. *State of the World 1990 — A Worldwatch Institute Report on Progress Toward a Sustainable Society*. New York: Norton & Company. (Published annually)

Byron, William J, editor. *The Causes of World Hunger*. New York: Paulist, 1982.

The Campaign to End Hunger and Homelessness — The Realities, The Myths, The Strategies. Food Monitor. (A Publication of World Hunger Year) No. 43, Fall 1987.

Exploring the Linkages — Third World Policies, Third World Development, & U.S. Agriculture. Washington, D.C.: Trade and Development Program, 1989. (802 Rhode Island Ave., Washington, DC 20018) [Includes Study Kit and a 14-minute video.]

From Debt to Development: Alternatives to the International Debt Crisis. Washington, D.C.: Institute for Policy Studies, 1985. (1601 Connecticut Ave, NW, 20009)

George, Susan. *A Fate Worse than Debt*. New York: Grove, 1988.

Hofbauer G.N.S.H., Rita, Dorothy Kinsella O.S.F., and Amata Miller I.H.M. *Making Social Analysis Useful*. Silver Spring: Leadership Conference of

Women Religious, 1983. (8808 Cameron Street, Silver Spring, MD 20910)

Holland, Joe and Peter Henriot. *Social Analysis — Linking Faith and Justice*. Maryknoll: Orbis, 1983.

  A description of the foundations and process of the Pastoral Circle. *The Pastoral Circle: Expanding our Horizons* (Video). Presenter: Peter Henriot. (Available with study guide and a copy of *Social Analysis — Linking Faith and Justice* for $50 from the Center for Youth Ministry Development, P.O. Box 699, Naugatuck, CT 06770)

Kidron, Michael and Ronald Segal. *The New State of the World Atlas*. New York: Simon and Schuster, 1987. [Includes maps, graphs, and statistics.]

Lappe, Frances Moore and Joseph Collins. *World Hunger: Twelve Myths*. New York: Grove, 1986.

Morgan, Elizabeth with Van Weigel and Eric DeBaufre. *Global Poverty and Personal Responsibility*. New York: Paulist, 1989.

Mische, Gerald and Patricia. *Toward a Human World Order*. New York: Paulist, 1977. (Four-Filmstrip Program available from Franciscan Communications, Los Angeles, CA)

McGinnis, James. *Bread and Justice*. New York: Paulist, 1979.

A New Vision of Development — The International Campaign Against World Hunger, Poverty, and Injustice. Food Monitor. (A Publication of World Hunger Year) No. 44, Spring/Summer 1987.

Our Common Future. The World Commission on Environment and Development. New York: Oxford UP, 1987.

Potter, George Ann. *Dialogue on Debt: Alternative Analysis and Solutions*. Washington, D.C.: Center of Concern, 1988.

Poverty in America. New Catholic World. Vol. 231, No. 1383, May/June 1988.

Rose, Stephen. *The American Profile Poster — Who Owns What, Who Makes How Much, Who Works Where, & Who Lives with Whom*. New York: Pantheon Books, 1986.

The State of the World's Children 1990. UNICEF. New York: Oxford UP, 1990. (Available through: UNICEF, UNICEF House, 3 U.N. Plaza, New York, NY 10017.) [Annual report]

Simon, Arthur. *Bread for the World*. New York: Paulist, 1984.

Sivard, Ruth Leger. *World Military and Social Expenditures*. Washington, D.C.: World Priorities. (Published annually) (Box 25140, Washington, DC 20007)

The World Bank Atlas. Washington, D.C.: The World Bank. (Published annually) (1818 H. Street, NW, Washington, DC 20433) [Includes graphs, maps, and statistics.]

World Development Report. The World Bank. New York: Oxford UP. (Published annually)

II. EDUCATIONAL & CURRICULUM RESOURCES

*Section II is a listing of educational and curriculum resources specially
selected to assist teachers/leaders in designing and conducting justice learning
programs with younger and older adolescents, and young adults. Part A is a
listing of books on educational approaches/methodologies for teaching justice and
peace. Part B is a bibliography of curriculum materials, organized by
publisher/organization that you can use directly with youth or in designing and
conducting your own justice learning programs.*

A. EDUCATIONAL APPROACHES & METHODOLOGIES

Evans, Alice Frazer, Robert A. Evans, and William Bean Kennedy. *Pedagogies
for the Non-Poor*. Maryknoll: Orbis, 1987.
> This book presents a variety of educational models — rooted in Paulo
> Freire's pedagogy for the poor — that would help to transform the non-poor.

GATT-Fly. *Ah-Hah — A New Approach to Popular Education*. Toronto: Between
the Lines, 1983.
> This book describes an educational method which connects economic and
> political systems to an individual's personal life and utilizes a group-centered
> approach to examining how social systems work and how to change them.

Groome, Thomas. *Christian Religious Education*. San Francisco: Harper & Row,
1981.
> Drawing on the theory and practice of Paulo Freire, Tom Groome
> develops a methodology well suited for the critical thinking, shared
> discussion, theological reflection, and personal and communal action
> needed in justice education.

Justice and Peace Education Council. *Dimensions of Justice and Peace in
Religious Education*. Washington, D.C.: NCEA, 1989.
> The authors present a description of justice and peace education, the basic
> concepts of peace and justice, the seven skills and competencies needed
> by children and youth, and suggestions for infusing justice and peace into
> specific content areas of religious education.

O'Hare, Padraic, editor. *Education for Peace and Justice*. San Francisco: Harper
and Row, 1983.
> A collection of essays which present foundational issues, educational
> issues, and related ministerial issues in educating for peace and justice.

Warren, Michael. *Faith, Culture, and the Worshipping Community*. New York:
Paulist, 1989.
> This book is a collection of essays on the relationship of faith and culture/
> society, and the development of a critical (and counter-cultural)
> consciousness.

Warren, Michael. *Youth, Gospel, Liberation*. San Francisco: Harper & Row, 1987.
> This book presents a series of essays that encourages youth ministry to
> reconceptualize itself in light of a vision of youth in church, society, and
> culture.

B. EDUCATIONAL & CURRICULUM MATERIALS: PUBLISHERS & ORGANIZATIONS

Benziger Publishing Company, 17337 Ventura Blvd., Encino, CA 91316
Peace through Justice. Sr. Louise Marie Prochaska, S.N.D. 1983
Student Text for high school youth: 296 pages.
Teacher Manual: 8.5 X 11, 192 pages including articles for enrichment and
student handouts.

> This text seeks to awaken students to the social dimension of Christian faith
> and begins to empower them to respond to the critical issues of the day. The
> first section of each chapter draws on the student's experience to situation
> justice issues in the context of their lives. The second section guides the
> students through social analysis and theological reflection on the issue. The
> third section of each chapter directs the students toward action. The text
> addresses human dignity, hunger, peace, lifestyle, science, and technology.

Bread for the World, 802 Rhode Island Ave., N.E., Washington, D.C. 20018
(202) 269-0200

> BFW Institute publishes and distributes study guides, books, worship services,
Scripture studies, and background papers that are designed to increase public
understanding of the causes of hunger and to stimulate active citizen involvement
in longer-term solutions to hunger. Educational resources of particular usefulness
for educational programs for youth and young adults are listed below. Write for
their complete catalog of materials.

Third World Debt: The Human Cost. BFW. ($8.00)
> This resource packet provides background information on international
> debt, components for a three-session study course and potential follow-up
> activities.

Video: *Heart of the Matter.* Produced by the British Broadcasting System. ($10
rental)
> Using the Dominican Republic as a case study, this 35-minute video
> examines the causes and impact of debt on Third World countries and low
> income people.

Hunger in a Land of Plenty. BFW. ($2.00)
> Educational program on hunger with charts and illustrations.

Land and Hunger: A Biblical Worldview. BFW. ($2.00) (Leader Guide: $1.00)
> A six session study course which includes short simulation exercises to
> help participants experience the relationship between land and hunger.

A Hungry World. BFW. ($2.00) (with Leader Guide)
> Educational program on hunger: facts, causes, solutions, biblical perspectives.

Biblical Basics on Justice. BFW ($.05)

Lazarus — A Musical on Hunger and Poverty. BFW.
> Based on Luke 16: 19-31, the 75-minute musical draws on a variety of
> musical styles to hold the age-old problem of hunger and poverty to the
> timeless prism of biblical faith.

Background Papers ($0.25 each)
U.S. Hunger: The Problem Grows.
Women and Children: Hungry in America.
Hungry for Work.
Working for Our Own Needs. (Africa)
Haiti: A People's Struggle for Hope.
Poverty and the World Pocketbook: The Debt of Poor, Developing Countries.
Conflict and Poverty in Central America.
Hunger and Apartheid in Southern Africa.

BROWN-ROA Publishers. 2460 Kerper Blvd, P.O. Box 539, Dubuque, IA 52001 (800) 338-5578

Achieving Social Justice. Ronald J. Wilkins and Veronica Grover, S.H.C.J.
Student Text for Grades 10-12: 294 pages; $9.75.
Teacher Manual: 535 pages; $25.95.

This text is intended to provide a basis for discussion of the problems and a faith vision to motivate students in seeking solutions. It encourages students to bring to social structures and organizations the Christian view of justice. Reproducible tests and supplementary activities are contained in the teacher's manual.

The Leaven Movement. Loretta Carey, R.D.C. and Kathleen Kanet, R.S.H.M.
Price: $6.25 per booklet.

Leaven is a 12-session, consciousness-raising program for small groups. Each session is approximately two hours long. Each participant has a self-explanatory booklet which introduces the issue, concept, and skills; provides common background; and has numerous fill-in spaces for personal observations, reflections, and social analysis. Topics: *Human Rights, Poverty and Affluence, Racism, War and Peace, Sexism, Global Limits, Change in a Democratic Society, Conflict Management, Structural Analysis, U.S. Culture, Leaven Alive, Leaven Changes.*

People Living for Justice. Canadian Christian Movement for Peace.
Price: $29.95 per book.

Each unit has ready-to-teach lesson plans which include introductory information, topic background, goals, activities, resources, and evaluation guidelines. There are between 30 and 40 reproducible activities for each unity. Titles in the series include:

> *Political and Social Rights and Human Dignity*
> *Economic Rights and Human Development*
> *Militarism and Hope*
> *Work and Co-Creation*
> *Women and Human Wholeness*

Rich World, Poor World. Canadian Christian Movement for Peace. 1987.
Price: $29.95

This self-contained resource for junior high youth with lesson plans, teacher background readings and reproducible student activity handouts covers youth internationally, poverty and wealth, basic human rights, hunger, values and culture, and from powerlessness to action.

ROA Media has produced a number of social justice videos on topics such as Central America, nuclear war, the Church, and the poor. Write for their complete catalog.

Catholic Relief Services, Global Education, 209 West Fayette Street, Baltimore, MD 21201-3403 (301) 625-2220

(Order materials through: CRS c/o Postal Church Service, 8401 Southern Blvd., Youngstown, OH 44512-6798.)

CRS develops and distributes printed and audio-visual educational materials on global awareness and justice issues, and suggests opportunities for action which supports international development on behalf of the poor. Write for their complete catalog of materials.

Global Realities Fact Sheet. ($1.50; $10 for a bulk order of 10 copies; $20 for 25 copies)

Information about life in the developing world, under themes of environment, quality of life, global poverty and hunger, and military spending.

The Development Kit. ($6.00)

This kit includes twelve pieces designed to help groups increase their awareness of development issues and their ability to act on behalf of the poor.

Economic Justice For All. ($5.00 for the set; $1.00 each)

A set of five colorful posters focusing on the international themes of the U.S. Bishops' Pastoral Letter on the Economy. Each poster is accompanied by a fact sheet which includes discussion questions, activities, and resource suggestions.

Foodfast. ($4.95)

This kit is a step-by-step program to involve youth in a 24-hour fast with discussion on the causes of world hunger. Includes a manual for the leader, recruiting poster, sponsor envelope, sponsor information page, button, "graduation" certificate.

Annual *World Food Day Materials.*

Annual *Operation Rice Bowl Education and Worship Materials.* (Free)

Renewing the Earth: Youth Guide for Groups. CAFOD. London, England: CAFOD, 1989. ($8.00)

This resource booklet on the environment contains activities for each of the four movements of the Pastoral Circle: Look at Your Experience, Investigate Further (social analysis), Reflect (theological reflection), and Take Suitable Action.

Beyond Familiar Borders. Quarterly Newsletter. (Free)

CRS Audiovisuals — CRS produces and/or distributes a number of global

200 ACCESS GUIDES TO YOUTH MINISTRY

awareness videos. Write for their audiovisual listing. Their most recent titles include:

> *The Mouse's Tale* — an animated cartoon from Australian Catholic Relief about a "fat" cat and a mouse (his conscience) which explores issues surrounding international food production and its relationship to hunger and famine around the world.
>
> *Voices for Development*— introduces viewers to the concepts of international development and the reasons why we should care about and become involved in supporting development efforts.
>
> *Our Children, Our Future* — explores the situation of children in our world today and efforts to assure them a better future.

CRS Audiovisual Catalog — The Global Education Office of CRS has produced a catalog of twenty-eight audiovisuals on a variety of development topics. A description of each film is provided, highlighting its main theme and its intended audience. Information on ordering is also given. ($1.00)

Center for Learning, Box 910, Villa Maria, PA 16155 (800-767-9090)

Mission: Growing in Peace and Justice.
Student Edition: $5.95; contains readings, activities, prayer, journaling.
Teacher Edition: $7.95; contains 40 or more detailed lesson plans, non-textbook based activities, and A-V.
Also available in *Mini-Units* covering the basics in 10 lessons. ($14.95)

> Promotes responsibility in peace and justice in multiple contexts. Emphasizes the community's potential to accomplish change. Topics: peace and justice, building the community, human dignity, structural transformation, nonviolence, multicultural understanding.

The Church's Social Mission.
Student Edition: $3.85; contains exercises.
Teacher Edition: $5.50; contains 40 detailed lesson plans, non-textbook based activities, and A-V.

> Contrasts Gospel values with society's norms on topics like the elderly, the poor, the handicapped.

The Faces of Haiti — Slides/Tape
Includes 80 slides, background information, and study guide. ($19.95)

> A documentary which prompts social awareness and action about Haiti, the poorest of the poor, the Fourth World.

CTIR Press (Center for Teaching International Relations),

University of Denver, Denver, CO 80908 (303) 871-2164

Teaching about Human Rights. David Shiman. 1988.
Comb-bound, with reproducible student handouts/exercise sheets for teaching grades 7-12. ($29.95)

> The activities in this book focus on political, civil, social, and economic rights and are primarily based on the framework provided by articles of

the *Universal Declaration of Human Rights.*

The New State of the World Atlas. Michael Kidron and Ronald Segal. New York: Simon and Schuster, 1987. For grades 7-12; Price: $13.95.

Activities Using the New State of the World Atlas. Heidi Hursh and Michael Prevedel. 1988.

Loose-leaf bound, with reproducible student handouts/exercise sheets for teaching grades 7-12. ($29.95)

This book contains a selection of teaching activities designed to be used with *The New State of the World Atlas.* The three sections of the book explore geopolitical and cultural characteristics of nations, justice issues, and research skills for using the *Atlas.*

Teaching about World Cultures — Focus on Developing Regions. Michelle Sanborn, Rachel Roe, and Heidi Hursch, with Robert Andersen and Pam Newman. 1986.

Perfect bound, with reproducible student handouts/exercise sheets for teaching grades 7-12. ($29.95)

This book contains thirty activities that help students examine culture, modernization and their interrelationships and complexities. The nations and/or regions addressed in the book are Africa, China, Latin America, India, Southeast Asia, and Japan — as a counterpoint.

Teaching about Ethnic Heritage. George Otero and Gary Smith. Revised by Edith King. 1984.

Perfect bound, with reproducible student handouts/exercise sheets for teaching grades K-12. ($21.95)

Twenty-one activities help students assess the role of ethnicity in their lives. The book is designed to aid students in linking their ethnicity, identity, and heritage.

Global Primer — Skills for a Changing World. H. Thomas Collins and Fred R. Czarra. 1986.

Comb-bound, with reproducible student handouts/exercise sheets for teaching grades K-8. ($29.95)

This book offers a wide variety of high-interest, skills-oriented global studies learning activities. Each activity identifies the specific social studies, math, science and/or language art skills to be developed with its use. The book is divided into four major areas: world basics, world awareness, world communications, and map and global skills.

Global Issues — Activities and Resources for the High School Teacher. Kenneth Switzer, Paul Mulloy and Karen Smith. 1987.

Perfect-bound, with reproducible student handouts/exercise sheets for teaching grades 9-12. ($24.95)

This book teaches about contemporary global concerns with background material and activities on global awareness, economic development, human rights, the environment, technology and international conflict.

Exploring the Third World — Development in Africa, Asia and Latin America. American Forum. 1987

A *Curriculum Package* for grades 7-12, includes a Teacher's Guide, a full color wall map, a wall chart, and 10 Student Booklets. ($35; additional packages of 10 Student Booklets are $16).

An examination of the linkages between U.S. communities and the Third World provides the basis for student investigations into the problems of the less developed nations of the world.

World Citizen Curriculum — Teaching Activities for a Global Age. Kirk Bergstrom. 1987.

Loose-leaf bound, with reproducible student handouts/exercise sheets for teaching grades 9-12.

($39.95; Student Handbook: $7.95)

This book teaches students information and skills to help make them more aware of—and more responsible citizens of—their communities, their nation, and the world. The book's activities address topics such as global interdependence, cultural diversity, human rights, and communications.

Other CTIR Titles:

Teaching about the Consumer and the Global Marketplace. Bruce Koranski, editor. 1985.

Perfect-bound, with reproducible student handouts/exercise sheets for teaching grades 4-12. ($29.95)

Teaching about Global Awareness using the Media. Steven L. Lamy, Robert B. Myers, Debbie Von Vihl and Katherine Weeks. 1985.

Comb-bound, with reproducible student handouts/exercise sheets for teaching grades 6-12. ($21.95)

Teaching Global Awareness with Simulations and Games. Steven L. Lamy, Robert B. Myers, Debbie Von Vihl and Katherine Weeks. 1986.

Perfect-bound, with reproducible student handouts/exercise sheets for teaching grades 7-12. ($29.95)

Teaching about Conflict, Nuclear War and the Future. John Zola and Reny Sieck. 1984.

Perfect-bound, with reproducible student handouts/exercise sheets for teaching grades 7-12. ($24.95)

Teaching about Peace and Nuclear War — A Balanced Approach. John Zola and Jaye Zola. 1986.

A Teacher's Handbook teaching grades 7-12. ($10.95)

Teaching about the Future. John D. Haas with Jacquelyn Johnson, Robert LaRue, Barbara Miller, and Ron Schukar. 1987.

Perfect-bound, with reproducible student handouts/exercise sheets for teaching grades 7-12. ($24.95)

Church World Service, P.O. Box 968, 28606 Phillips Street, Elkhardt, IN 46515 (219) 264-3102 (Or contact your regional CWS/CROP office)

Church World Service offers a wide variety of printed materials in addition to their films, videos, slides, and simulation games, which are available from the

CWS/CROP office in your region or at the national office. There is no rental charge for audio-visuals except mailing the material back to the respective office. CWS/CROP also organizes events for youth and young adults (a FAST, Walk or Marathon) to provide young people with action possibilities to complement global education programming. Write for their complete catalog. (For update information on the work of CWS, call the CWS hotline 800-223-1310, in NY 800-535-2713.)

World Food Day Curriculum. Office of Global Education. ($.35 each; one sample of each, no charge)

One hour sessions on world hunger for grades: K-3, 4-7, and 8-12.

Poster-Related Curricula. Office of Global Education. ($.50 each; $3.00 per set)

Six 50-minute curricula based on posters which explore the connections between hunger and: *Children, Refugees, Water, Global Security, Militarism,* and *Women.*

Fact Sheets. Office of Global Education. (Free)

Beginning briefing sheets on facts and resources for: *Security at Risk, Children at Risk, Environment at Risk, Hunger, Myths and Realities, Rural Crisis, Women at Risk, Water.*

Global Education Reprint Series. ($0.25 each; one free sample of each)

Youth and World Hunger. Patrick Bruns.

Towards Genuine Solidarity with the Poor: One American's View. Richard Dickinson.

World Hunger: Asking the Right Questions. Susan George.

Selling Human Misery. Larry Hollon.

A Radical Challenge to Inherited Education Patterns. William B. Kennedy.

Development Education in the United States. Jayne Millar-Wood.

Americans in the Global Learning Process. Stephen H. Rhinesmith.

Act Locally: Think Globally. Nico van Oudenhoven.

Columban Mission Education/Awareness Resources, St. Columbans, NE 68056 (402) 291-1920.

Columban Mission Education/Awareness Resources is a service of the Columban Fathers to the home Church. Columban audio visual resources can stimulate young people to a more active involvement in those issues which affect the Church's mission between the first and third worlds. **All resources are offered on a free loan basis.**

Social Volcano — A Compact Justice & Peace Program.

Two 16-minute video programs with complete lesson plans, background information, Scripture search guide, discussion guides, and additional resource materials.

Focusing on the southern Phillipino sugar cane workers, this program presents a social analysis of the current Third World situation, a theological reflection on the situation, and two basic responses to social evil: the charity response of temporary and adequate assistance and the justice response of tackling the underlying cases of social evil.

The Barrio Video Series: *Charo of the Barrio, Bread for the Barrio*, and *Messages from the Barrio*. 1990.

Each of the three units contains a video program and a leader's manual, which includes two themes and lesson plans, Scripture background, activity/worksheets for duplication, background information, suggested resources and prayer services.

Charo of the Barrio (22 minutes). Charo, a young Peruvian girl growing up in a poor dusty barrio of Lima, tells her story. It is the challenging story of the struggle of the young people of Peru. Faced with poverty and rejection, they somehow find hope and faith. It is the story of young people everywhere...

Bread for the Barrio (16 minutes). Sr. Monica Lachcik organizes a small group of poor women to alleviate starvation in a Lima, Peru barrio. This film shows what one person's faith and vision can accomplish. It challenges us to bond together to change unjust structures that cause hunger anywhere in the world.

Messages from the Barrio (21 minutes). Do the poor of Peru have anything to share with us? What does option for the poor mean? These messages from the barrio will challenge some of our assumptions and ideas. Columban missionaries, living with the poor in Lima, Peru, witness a faith that does justice.

* Recommended for a deeper learning experience.

Columban Mission Education Program for Elementary Schools.

A comprehensive 5-lesson program for grades 1-8 for religion and social studies. Includes manual, lesson plans, audio-visuals, worksheets, liturgies, and activities. *Teaching Global Awareness Kit* is a 15-minute introductory video for teachers.

Columban Mission Magazine. $1 for each teacher/leader and young person per school year.

Mission Awareness Audio Visuals. Columban Films and Videotapes.

Each film/video comes with a discussion guide. Write for the complete catalog.

Friendship Press, P.O. Box 37844, Cincinnati, OH 45237

Making a World of Difference. Office of Global Education. 1989. ($15)

An excellent resource manual with an extensive collection of activities and resources to promote global awareness.

A New View of the World. Dr. Arno Peters. 1987.

A handbook for use with the Peters Project Map.

World Map: Peters Projection. Dr. Arno Peters, developed with the assistance of the U.N. Development Program. 1983. ($8.95)

This unique map seeks to provide a more accurate projection of the actual relative sizes of the earth's land masses and oceans, especially helpful in viewing the true size of the Third World.

FOOD FIRST, 145 Ninth Street, San Francisco, CA 94103
(415) 864-8555
FOOD FIRST is a nonprofit research and education center, dedicated to identifying the root causes of hunger in the United States and around the world since its founding in 1975. FOOD FIRST provides a wide array of educational tools — books, articles, slide shows, films, and curricula for elementary schools and high schools. Write for their complete catalog.

An Annotated Guide to Global Development. ($7.95)

Diet for a Small Planet: Tenth Anniversary Issue. Frances Moore Lappe. ($3.95)

Exploding the Hunger Myths: A High School Curriculum. Sonja Williams. 1987. ($15)

Food First: Beyond the Myth of Scarcity. Frances Moore Lappe and Joseph Collins. 1979. ($3.95)

The Food First Comic. 1982. ($1.00)

World Hunger: Twelve Myths. Frances Moore Lappe and Joseph Collins. 1986. ($9.95)

Strangers in Their Own Country — A Curriculum Guide on South Africa. William Bigelow. 1985. ($14.95)

Hi-Time Publishing Corp., P.O. Box 13337, Milwaukee, WI 53213-0337
(800) 558-2292

Justice and Peace and Me. Terry Cotting Mogan and Will Sousae. 1990.

Six session program for senior high youth; one 16-page pamphlet per session with teacher guide.

Student Edition: $4.30 each; $3.10 for 5 or more.

Teacher Edition: $7.85 each; $4.50 for 5 or more.

This program looks at the basic rights of each person, confronting injustice, understanding how change takes place and what young people can do, and making a commitment to work for peace and justice as part of our daily lives.

Institute for Peace and Justice, 4144 Lindell #122, St. Louis, MO 63108
(314) 533-4445.

The Institute for Peace and Justice, an independent ecumenical not-for-profit center begun in 1970, is committed to the challenge, "If you want peace, work for justice." The center provides resources and services in education for social justice and peacemaking with a special emphasis on family programming.

Helping Kids Care — Harmony Building Activities for Home, Church, and School. Camy Condon and James McGinnis. Institute for Peace and Justice and Meyer Stone Books, 1989. ($8.95)

This book provides dozens of ideas to help children, ages 8-12, venture forth "to meet the different" (enemies, other races, the disabled, the old) and return with friends.

Helping Families Care. Jim McGinnis. Institute for Peace and Justice and Meyer Stone Books, 1989. ($9.95)

This book focuses on the family that crosses the generations and on how it can work toward the goals of caring and compassion. It includes ideas for games, exercises, activities, and stories to help make these goals realities.

Journey into Compassion — A Spirituality for the Long Haul. James McGinnis. Institute for Peace and Justice and Meyer-Stone Books, 1989. ($9.95)

This book develops a spirituality to be lived in the midst of the world, connecting the inner health of one's soul with the well-being of the world.

Partners in Peacemaking — Family Workshop Models Guidebook for Leaders. Jim McGinnis, editor. 1984.

This books offers a variety of fully designed program models for the whole family (workshops, retreats, camps) and for youth (retreat, camp).

Parenting for Peace and Justice — Ten Years Later. Jim and Kathleen McGinnis. Maryknoll: Orbis, 1990.

Revised and updated for the 90s, this book offers viable solutions to the perennial problem: how to act for justice without sacrificing our children, how to build family community without isolating ourselves from the world.

Building Shalom Families: Christian Parenting for Peace and Justice. Jim and Kathleen McGinnis. 1986.

Complete video package containing: two 120-minute VHS videotapes, 32-page guidebook, *Parenting for Peace and Justice* book, and worksheets and action brochures. ($149.95)

A comprehensive parenting program that assists participants in dealing with important issues confronting today's families. By using creative visuals, music, presentations, prayerful reflections, and practical "how-to" sessions, the video enables the participants to experience the McGinnises and their message.

Starting Out Right — Nurturing Young Children as Peacemakers. Kathleen McGinnis and Barbara Oehlberg. 1989. ($9.95)

The key to teaching young children to be peacemakers is to understand children's abilities and their worldview. This book is filled with stories and examples of do-able plans and ideas for building peacemaking behavior in children, what works, what doesn't work—and why.

Educating for Peace and Justice. James and Kathleen McGinnis and other contributors. 1985.

Three volume set of activities and resources on global, national, and religious dimensions of peace and justice. Each unit of all three volumes contains development of basic concepts, teaching strategies for all age levels, action strategies, student readings and worksheets, bibliography, and directions for teaching the unit. ($14.95 per volume)

Volume 1: National Dimensions (12 units). Topics: Nonviolences, Poverty, Sexism, Racism, Disabled People, Older People, Multicultural Education, Advertising/Stewardship.

Volume 2: Global Dimensions (8 units). Topics: World Hunger, Global Poverty and Development, Global Interdependence, U.S. Foreign Policy, Military, War and Alternatives.

Volume 3: Religious Dimensions (6 units). Topics: Peacemakers, Peace & Justice, Prophets, Gospel-Culture Contrasts, Peace & War, Service Programs.

Bread and Justice. James McGinnis. New York: Paulist, 1979.
Text ($4.95) and Teacher's Book ($6.95).

This book examines the causes of hunger and poverty, describes the kind of global changes that must take place to eradicate these ills, and offers ways in which the concerned citizen can work toward this goal. It examines what the Gospel and the Christian religious tradition tell us about justice among people.

YOUTHPEACE — a quarterly newsletter for youth workers with articles, resource updates, and practical ideas. (Subscription: $10 per year)

Maryknoll Mission Education, Maryknoll, NY 10545.

Maryknoll Educational Resources is an extension of the Maryknoll Mission Vision. Their purpose is to help the people of the United States and especially young people develop a greater awareness of their poorer brothers and sisters in the farthest corners of the world.

Focus on Central America. (*Maryknoll World Awareness Curriculum Series*) Sr. Jane Keegan. ($12 for the set)

A supplementary curriculum with comprehensive lesson plans, activity sheets, maps and fact sheets, and historical overviews contained in four different units with a separate *Related Readings* book. Designed for grades 7-12 and young adults. *Focus on Central America* can be taught as a course in itself or a supplement to courses in religion, social studies, humanities, art, current events.

Unit 1: *The Story of the People of Central America* — focuses on El Salvador, Guatemala, Honduras, and Nicaragua.

Unit 2: *A Global Vision* — explores global interdependence and a geographical and historical look at Central America.

Unit 3: *Central America and Our Christian Responsibility* — presents the option for the poor, basic Christian communities as a model for change, faith and worship, and heroes and martyrs.

Unit 4: *Creative Expression: Religion and Culture* — examines the religious and cultural expressions of the Central American people and compares them to faith and cultural expressions of U.S. students.

Focus on China. (*Maryknoll World Awareness Curriculum Series*)
($15 for the book)

A comprehensive study of values and religion in China. The 13 lessons for junior and senior high school students are all in one booklet. This booklet includes up-to-date history, discussion questions, multi-level assignments, vocabulary worksheets, basic, easy-to-read primary source material, role-playing activities, value clarification, and two one-act plays.

Focus on the Philippines. (*Maryknoll World Awareness Curriculum Series*) Sr. Jane Keegan. ($20 for the set)

21 comprehensive lesson plans contained in four different units with a separate *Related Readings* book. Designed for grades 7-12 and young adults. *Focus on the Philippines* can be taught as a course in itself or a supplement to courses in religion, social studies, humanities, art, current events.

Unit 1: *Faith in Action* — invites students to examine the role of the Church.

Unit 2: *People Power* — lets the students meet inspiring people working to build a more just society.

Unit 3: *Geography and History* — engages the students in exploring a vital and complex nation of 7,000 islands.

Unit 4: *Current Realities: A Social Analysis* — helps the students correlate issues in the Philippines with issues in their own lives.

Maryknoll World Awareness Posters.

(Maryknoll Missioners, Att: Mission Education Posters, Maryknoll, NY 10545) Each poster focuses on one country and includes a basic lesson plan. (Prices: 1-9 posters = $2.00 each; 10-19 = $1.50; 20+ = $1.00)

Africa: Egypt, Kenya, Sudan, Tanzania

Asia: Bangladesh, Hong Kong, Nepal, Philippines, South Korea

South America: Bolivia, Brazil, Chile, Peru, Venezuela

Central America: El Salvador, Guatemala

Additional Posters: Christ of the Americas, Modern American Martyrs

Maryknoll Magazine.

$1 per person per year; bulk order discounts available. A monthly teacher's guide is also provided. *Maryknoll Magazine* and *Revista Maryknoll*, a Spanish/English version, are available in low-cost bulk orders to school and parish groups (October-June issues). Send for a bulk order form to: Maryknoll Fathers and Brothers, Fulfillment/Mail Processing Department, Maryknoll, NY 10545.

Maryknoll World Video and Film Library

Outside NY: (800) 227-8523; NY Phone: (914) 941-7591; (extensions 308 or 577)

Maryknoll has an extensive global awareness library of films and videos for purchase or rental. Among their classic titles are *Gods of Metal* and the *Business of Hunger*. Write for their complete catalog. Some of the newest videos include:

Central American Close-Up — the stories of four Central American young people: Jeremias of Guatemala and Flor of El Salvador (Tape 1); and Carlos of Honduras and Balty of Nicaragua (Tape 2).

Kenyan Youth: Preparing for the Future — three stories of determination, hard work, and dreams of a bright future from the youth of Kenya.

Bento — the story of a young African-Brazilian who is determined to make life better for himself and his neighbors in a poor neighborhood of Sao Paulo.

Consuming Hunger — three videos on the role the media played in making the U.S. aware of the famine in Ethiopia and in shaping our

response to it. Includes: Part I - *Getting the Story*; Part II - *Shaping the Image*; Part III - *Selling the Feeling*.
Starving for Sugar and *Philippine Diary* — two videos that examine the Philippine past and sound a call for a new sense of social responsibility.
The *Common Table* Video Series are half-hour shows that cover a wide range of topics from around the world. Each presentation is directed toward a better understanding of issues or concern to all of us.

Pax Christi USA, 348 East Tenth Street, Erie, PA 16503 (814) 453-4955

Pax Christi is the international Catholic peace movement. The USA organization develops resource materials for Pax Christi groups, as well as peace education programming. Write for their complete catalog.
Reflection Guide on the Challenge of Peace. ($3.50)
Easy Reading Version of the Challenge of Peace. ($1.00)
Study Guide on the Challenge of Peace. ($1.00) (Leader's Guide, $2.00)
Q & A Booklet. ($.40)
Way of Peace: A Guide to Nonviolence. Gerard Vanderhaar and Mary Lou Kownacki, O.S.B., editors. ($5.00)
    An introduction to nonviolence for social change and personal life. Prepared for use in the classroom, by study groups, and for personal reflection.
A Race to Nowhere — An Arms Race Primer for Catholics. Mary Lou Kownacki, O.S.B., editor. ($4.00)
    This book faces 26 questions that call for answers if the arms race is to be brought under control.
A New Moment: An Invitation to Nonviolence. ($3.50)
    Twelve brief study sessions on nonviolence for groups and individuals.
Following the Nonviolent Jesus. Mary Evelyn Jegen, S.N.D.. ($5.00)
    A workbook organized around the fourth part of *The Challenge of Peace* with special sections geared to youth, parents, educators, parishes, military personnel, artists, defense workers, scientists, and public officials.
Peacemaker Pamphlet Series. ($1.25 each; set of 8 for $8.00)
    Jean Donovan: The Call to Discipleship. John Dear, S.J..
    Martin Luther King, Jr.: The Dream of a Just Community. J. Milburn Thompson, Ph.D.
    Gandhi the Peacemaker. Eknath Easwaran.
    Dorothy Day and the Permanent Revolution. Eileen Egan.
    Thomas Merton's Struggle with Peacemaking. Jim Forest.
    Imagine. Mary Lou Kownacki, O.S.B..
    John Timothy Leary: A Different Sort of Hero. PC Center on Conscience and War.
    Franz Jaegerstaetter: Martyr for Conscience. Gordon Zahn.

St. Mary's Press, Terrace Heights, Winona, MN 55987-0560 (800) 533-8095
The Christian Call to Justice and Peace. Joseph Stoutzenberger. 1987.
Student Text for high school youth: 288 pages; $7.96 each for twenty or more.
Teacher Manual: spiral bound, 252 pages plus handout masters; $17.95.
> This text explores the historical and scriptural call to faith and justice. It
> then personalizes the message by examining six areas of concern —
> poverty, hunger, sexism, racial prejudice, ageism, and ecology. The final
> section links faith and justice with peace. Each issue is approached using
> a methodology of experience—analysis—theological reflection—action.
> The teaching manual provides major concepts, answers to questions,
> goals, and teaching techniques for each chapter. Suggested activities
> related to major themes help to flesh out the contents of the text. Forty-
> seven handouts are included to help students focus on justice and peace
> issues.

Giving and Growing: A Student's Guide for Service Projects. Frances Hunt
O'Connell. 1990.
Student's Guide: (8.5 X 11), 56 pages; $3.50.
Leader's Manual: (8.5 X 11), 32 pages, $3.95.
> The book provides information and self-directed exercises to assist
> students who are doing service projects in school or parish settings. There
> are five units that correspond to the stages in a project, as well as an
> appendix that contains forms such as permissions, records, supervision
> reports, and evaluations. The leader's manual contains background
> information, directions, prayer services, and trouble-shooting hints, as
> well as activities that raise awareness of the spiritual aspects of service
> experiences.

Seeking Justice (The Discovering Program). Lynn Neu. 1990.
Student Booklet for junior high students: (8.5 X 11), 24 pages; $2.50.
Teacher Guide: (8.5 X 11), 50 pages; $6.00.
> This book seeks to help junior high youth recognize Jesus as the model
> for justice, see the Church as a powerful resource and a personal support
> in achieving justice, and recognize their own ability to be effective
> peacemakers.

The Video Project, (Films and Videos for a Safe & Sustainable World)
5332 College Ave., Suite 101, Oakland, CA 94618 (415) 655-9050
> The Video Project is a non-profit organization that provides quality, affordable
> educational video and film programs on the issues and ideas critical to our future
> on the planet. They currently have over 120 documentary programs. They publish
> a general catalog of all their titles and a special "Preserving the Environment"
> catalog. Write from both catalogs.

III. SERVICE & SOCIAL CHANGE RESOURCES

Section III is a listing of service and social change resources specially selected to assist teachers/leaders in organizing and conducting service and action programming with younger and older adolescents. The resources listed below include guides to organizing service/action programming with sample program models, idea books for engaging youth and young adults in service/action, listings of national and global service/action placements, and materials for youth themselves.

Bobo, Kimberley. *Lives Matter - A Handbook for Christian Organizing.* Kansas City: Sheed and Ward, 1986.

A how-to manual for Christians who want to increase their effectiveness in work against hunger.

Bodner, Joan. *Taking Charge of Our Lives — Living Responsibly in the World.* San Francisco: Harper & Row, 1981.

This handbook shows what steps people of any age, background, and financial circumstances can take to explore personal and political changes, and to move — in large ways and small — toward making those changes happen.

Buell, Becky and Karl Hamerschlag. *Alternatives to the Peace Corps.* 1988. (Available from Oxfam America or Food First Books)

Campolo, Anthony. *Ideas for Social Action.* LaJolla: Youth Specialties, 1983.

This book offers over 200 practical and specific ways that Christian young people can become involved in social action and service to others.

Connections — A Directory of Lay Volunteer Service Opportunities. Washington, D.C.: St. Vincent Pallotti Center for Apostolic Development, Inc. Published annually. (715 Monroe St. NE, Washington, DC 20017-1755) Free

Coover, Virginia, Ellen Deacon, Charles Esser, and Christopher Moore. *Resource Manual for a Living Revolution.* Santa Cruz: New Society, 1985.

This is a handbook of skills and tools for those working for fundamental social change from a holistic nonviolent perspective.

Dass, Ram and Paul Gorman. *How Can I Help? — Stories and Reflections on Service.* New York: Alfred A. Knopf, 1985.

This practical helper's companion, provides support and inspiration in our efforts to help meet each other's needs through sound advice and personal accounts of service and social action.

Earth Works Group. *50 Simple Things You Can Do to Save the Earth.* Berkeley: Earthworks, 1989.

Earth Works Group. *50 Simple Things Kids Can Do to Save the Earth.* Berkeley: Earthworks, 1989.

If you want to take an active role in saving our planet, but don't know where to begin start with these books. They are practical, entertaining, and informative guide to fifty concrete, do-able things people can do to help protect the earth.

Fagan, Harry. *Empowerment.* New York: Paulist, 1979.

This is a practical guide for helping parishes and neighborhood groups to organize themselves into effective social action agents.

Hollender, Jeffrey. *How to Make the World a Better Place — A Guide to Doing Good*. New York: Quill/William Morrow, 1990.
This is an essential guide for addressing many of the social problems facing our world. It presents over 120 specific actions people can take which will make a difference. Each issue is presented with specific suggestions for action, phone numbers and addresses of organizations to work with, background statistics on each issue, quotable information, and bibliographies.

How to Lobby for Just Legislation. Washington, D.C.: NETWORK, 1987. (806 Rhode Island Ave, NE, Washington, DC 20018; 202-526-4070)

Hunger Action Handbook: What You Can Do and How to Do It. Leslie Withers and Tom Peterson, editors. *Seeds* Magazine, 1988. (Seeds, 222 East Lake Drive, Decatur, GA 30030)

Invest Yourself — The Catalog of Volunteer Opportunities. New York: Commission on Voluntary Service and Action. Published annually. (P.O. Box 117, New York, NY 10009)

Kohler, Mary Conway. *Young People Learning to Care — Making a Difference through Youth Participation*. San Francisco: Winston-Seabury, 1983.
Using examples from across the country, this book shows how the principles of youth participation have been applied to over 30,000 programs nationwide to help young people learn to care.

Let the Spirit Blow — The Response 1990. Washington, D.C.: International Liaison of Lay Volunteers in Mission. Published annually. (4121 Harewood Road NE, Washington, DC 20017; 1-800-543-5046)
This annual directory offers a detailed description of lay volunteer programs and service agencies in the U.S. and other countries.

MacEachern, Diane. *Save our Planet — 750 Everyday Ways You Can Help Clean Up the Earth*. New York: Dell, 1990.
This book provides a brief glimpse into some of the great environmental dilemmas the world faces and then suggests practical ideas corresponding to where we lead our lives: home, school, office, community.

O'Connell, Frances Hunt. *Giving and Growing: A Student's Guide for Service Projects*. Winona: St. Mary's, 1990. (Student's Guide and Leader's Manual)
[For description see St. Mary's Press listing above.]

Parish Action Handbook: Legislative Advocacy. Washington, D.C.: NETWORK, 1987. (806 Rhode Island Ave, NE, Washington, DC 20018; 202-526-4070)
NETWORK, a national Catholic social justice lobby, has developed this booklet for people who want to lobby for just legislation.

Shaw, John C. *The Workcamp Experience: Involving Youth in Outreach to the Needy*. Loveland, CO: Group, 1987.
This is a step-by-step guide for planning, organizing and completing a workcamp project, including budgeting and fund-raising tips, guidelines and worksheets for organizing a workcamp, and 33 quick service project ideas to use all year.

Simon, Arthur. *Christian Faith and Public Policy — No Grounds for Divorce.*
Grand Rapids: Eerdmans, 1987.
This book points out the inseparability of Christian faith and social
concern and suggests ways for Christians to become involved in public
policy issues. A good primer on helping people become involved in social
or structural change for justice.

IV. RESOURCE GUIDES

Examining Faith and Justice in the U.S. Economy: An Annotated Bibliography.
McGregor S.J., Mark and Mark Plausin, O.S.F.S. Washington, D.C.: Center of
Concern. ($8.00)

First Steps to Peace — A Resource Guide. Prepared by the Joel Brooke Memorial
Committee of the Fund for Peace. New York: The Fund for Peace. (The Fund
for Peace, Suite 207 M, 345 East 46th St., New York, NY 10017)

Third World Resource Directories. Compiled and edited by Thomas P. Fenton and
Mary H. Heffron, Third World Resources Project, The Data Center, Oakland,
California. [Also available through Orbis Books.]
These *Directories* will direct you to the sources and materials for
background, for in-depth coverage, for information traditionally hard-to-
obtain. Each directory gives you concise, yet complete, descriptions of
organizations and their activities. They also include thumbnail sketches of
books, pamphlets, articles, directories, and catalogues on every facet of
the topic. Also included are listings of audio-visual resources.
*Third World Resource Directory — A Guide to Organization and
Publications.* ($12.95)
Human Rights — A Directory of Resources. ($9.95)
Africa — A Directory of Resources. ($9.95)
Asia and the Pacific — A Directory of Resources. ($9.95)
Food, Hunger, Agribusiness — A Directory of Resources. ($9.95)
Latin America and Caribbean — A Directory of Resources. ($9.95)
Middle East — A Directory of Resources. ($9.95)
Women in the Third World — A Directory of Resources. ($9.95)
Transnational Corporations — A Directory of Resources. ($9.95)

V. ORGANIZATIONAL RESOURCES

*In addition to the organizations listed in Section II: Educational &
Curriculum Resources, the following organizations publish periodicals,
resources, and/or sponsor action programming useful to those involved in
ministry with youth.*

American Friends Service Committee, 1501 Cherry Street, Philadelphia,
PA 19102
AFSC focuses on issues of peace and social justice, operating programs in many
third world countries. Applicants for volunteer service should have development
experience and and volunteer skills.

Basic Needs International, P.O. Box 36, Wayne, PA 19087
Basic Needs is an organization designed to enlist citizens of rich nations in the struggle against poverty. BNI serves as a source for development education resources.

CARE, 660 First Avenue, New York, NY 10016
CARE focuses on feeding programs for school and pre-school children. It is also active in other basic needs projects - housing, nutrition, health care, water supply. It operates programs in 37 countries, in the poorest sections of the world. It offers career opoportunities for service-oriented persons.

Global Education Associates, 475 Riverside Drive, New York, NY 10115 (212) 870-3290.
BREAKTHROUGH is a quarterly magazine that links the worldwide GEA network and features articles, reviews, and reports by GEA associates and others. (Subscription: $25 per year, entitles you to become a GEA member; $5 per back issue)

Habitat for Humanity, Habitat & Church Streets, Americus, GA 31709
Habitat is an ecumenical Christian housing ministry that builds low-cost homes in 24 countries. Houses are sold to occupants at modest cost with no-interest mortgages. Local committees choose who gets the houses. Habitat also provides advice to 330 independent, affiliated projects in the US, Canada and South Africa.

Heifer Project International, P.O. Box 808, 825 West Third Street, Little Rock, AR 72203
Heifer project supplies rural families in poor countries with livestock and training. The aim is to aid them in food specific projects, for one to three months.

International Catholic Child Bureau, ICO Center, 323 East 47th Street, New York, NY 10017 (212) 355-3992.
Children Worldwide is published three times a year and focuses on justice issues related to children/youth and the work of ICCB worldwide. (Subscription: $17 per year)

Mennonite Central Committee, Akron, PA 17501
MCC places service-oriented volunteers in a variety of countries for work in agricultural development, nutrition, education, medical services and other welfare projects.

NETWORK (National Catholic Social Justice Lobby), 806 Rhode Island Avenue NE, Washington, DC 20018 (202) 526-4070.
NETWORK lobbies on issues with a potential to effect structural and systemic change. NETWORK issues are selected at the beginning of each congress and

include: Housing, Arms Control, Welfare Reform, Disarmament, Budget Policy, Full Employment, Economic Equality for Women, Central America, International Debt Crisis, South Africa.

NETWORK Connection— a bimonthly publication that provides issue analysis, reflection pieces, news from the grassroots, legislative updates and calls to action, and information on resources.

Action Alerts as well as *Phone Alerts* on bills that need immediate lobbying response.

Information Packets for NETWORK selected issues.

Annual Voting Record of senators and representatives.

Sojourners Magazine & Resource Center, Box 29272, Washington, DC 20017

The Sojourners Community of Washington, DC is a long-time community of prayer, reflection, and social action which produces the nationally-acclaimed, *Sojourners* Magazine, and a variety of educational resources, as well as sponsoring conferences and engaging in social activism.

Sojourners Magazine — an excellent voice for the poor and voiceless, and for the Church's role in the work of peace and social justice. Provides both social analysis and theological reflection on issues, as well as an alternative source of information about the world. Each issue has a major theme. (New subscriptions are $19.97 per year for ten issues at the special savings rate.)

Crucible of Fire — The Church Confronts Apartheid. Jim Wallis and Joyce Hollyday, editors. Maryknoll: Orbis, 1989. ($9.95)

America's Original Sin — A Study Guide on White Racism. Washington, D.C.: Sojourners Resource Center. ($4.95; discounts for orders of 10 or more)

This seven-session resource is intended to make visible the realities of white racism that are often hidden by examining the roots and current manifestations of racism from historical, theological, and personal perspectives.

The Stanley Foundation, 216 Sycamore Street, Suit 500, Muscatine, IA 52761.

Teachable Moments is a four-page newsletter, published 18 times per school year, containing an essay, practical strategies, and new resource materials for teaching peace and justice. Back issues are available in sets of 20 issues for $10.

Subscriptions: $6.97 per year; $12.97 for two years. Send subscriptions to: Stanley Foundation, Payment Processing Center, P.O. Box 2091, Cedar Rapids, IA 52406-9882.

World Hunger Year (WHY), 261 West 35th Street #1402, New York, NY 10001 (212) 629-8850.

Hungerline — WHY's media resource service provides extensive source materials and contacts to journalists reporting on hunger-related issues. *Hungerline Reports*, the service's monthly newsletter, provides hunger-related stories, statistics, and analysis to print and broadcast journalists. *Food Monitor* — WHY's internationally acclaimed quarterly magazine features articles by leading experts on global and domestic hunger, homelessness and jobs, health and nutrition, foreign aid and trade, and development and the debt crisis. *Food Monitor* is available at a yearly subscription rate of $18, or a limited income rate of $10.

ACCESS GUIDES TO YOUTH MINISTRY

SPIRITUALITY
Edited by Sharon Reed
What is a spiritually challenging vision for youth? The contributors
to this Access Guide provide a theological base to help readers
answer this question. Thomas Hart, Joan Chittister, Thomas
Groome, and Kathleen Fischer, among others, offer foundational
insights into adolescent spiritual life. Practical strategies regarding
spirituality and education, justice, prayer, liturgy and spiritual
direction are presented in the second part of this volume.
    Paperback   210-2 $14.95

RETREATS
Edited by Reynolds R. Ekstrom
A complete resource for learning how to develop youth retreats:
the nature and purposes of youth retreats, principles, guidelines,
models and strategies for implementing your own retreat.
Everything from planning to follow-up.The best theory and practice for
    •Confirmation coordinators
    •Retreat ministers
    •DREs, campus ministers
    •Search, TEC, COR teams
    Paperback   152-1 $14.95

EVANGELIZATION
Edited by John Roberto and Reynolds R. Ekstrom
The why and how-to of evangelizing youth by America's foremost
experts in the field. Contributors: Mark Bouchard, Joanne
Cahoon, Thomas Groome, James Dunning, Maryann Hakowski,
Jeff Johnson, MA, Rev. Don Kimball, Lynn Mahoney, Jon Sobrino,
SJ, Robert Webbe, John Roberto, Reynolds Ekstrom.
    Paperback   140-8 $14.95

LITURGY & WORSHIP
Edited by John Roberto
An introduction to liturgical theory with emphasis on the social
and developmental needs of young people. Part Two carries theory into practice with ideas for successful worship experiences
with youth. Guides for liturgies and reconciliation provide a process for preparing youth worship.
    Paperback   141-6 $14.95

ACCESS GUIDES TO YOUTH MINISTRY

LEADERSHIP
Edited by John Roberto
Offers a contemporary understanding of Christian leadership based on scripture, theology, social theory. Practical essays help readers develop personal skills: getting organized, team work, managing volunteers. A practical handbook for the leader of a comprehensive youth ministry. For campus ministry, youth ministry, young adult ministry, DREs, junior and senior high schools.
   Paperback   150-5 $14.95

MEDIA & CULTURE
Edited by Reynolds R. Ekstrom
This volume will help you broaden your media horizon regarding: television awareness, consumerism and American youth, television's mythic world, the Gospel of Jesus and the gospel of culture, methods for using rock media in your programs, and more....
   Paperback   219-6 $14.95

EARLY ADOLESCENT MINISTRY
Edited by John Roberto
A gold mine of theory and practice for educators, youth ministers, and all adults working with younger adolescents.
   Paperback   207-2 $14.95

CALL TOLL FREE
1-800-342-5850
IN NY 914- 576-1024

THE WORLD OF
DON BOSCO
MULTIMEDIA